PENGUIN BOOKS

COOPER'S CREEK

Alan Moorehead was born in Melbourne in 1910. Educated at Scotch College, Melbourne, and Melbourne University, he served as foreign correspondent of the *Daily Express* from 1936 to 1939, one of his first assignments being the Spanish Civil War. During the Second World War he was a war correspondent in the Middle and Far East and in much of Europe and was awarded the O.B.E. His other books include *African Trilogy* (1944), *Montgomery* (1946), *Gallipoli* (1956), which won the *Sunday Times* 1956 Book Prize and the Duff Cooper Memorial Award, *The Russian Revolution* (1958), *The Blue Nile* (1962) and *The Fatal Impact* (1966). *No Room in the Ark* (1959), *The White Nile* (1960) and *Darwin and the Beagle* (1969) are also published in Penguins. He was awarded the C.B.E. in 1968. He was married to Lucy Milner, a former Women's Page editor of the *Daily Express*, and they had two sons and a daughter.

Alan Moorehead died in September 1983.

ALAN MOOREHEAD

Cooper's Creek

PENGUIN BOOKS

Penguin Books Ltd, Harmondsworth, Middlesex, England
Viking Penguin Inc., 40 West 23rd Street, New York, New York 10010, U.S.A.
Penguin Books Australia Ltd, Ringwood, Victoria, Australia
Penguin Books Canada Limited, 2801 John Street, Markham, Ontario, Canada L3R 1B4
Penguin Books (N.Z.) Ltd, 182–190 Wairau Road, Auckland 10, New Zealand

First published by Hamish Hamilton 1963
Published with amended Note by Nelson Publishers 1985
Published in Penguin Books 1988

Made and printed in Great Britain by
Richard Clay (The Chaucer Press) Ltd
. Bungay, Suffolk
Typeset in Baskerville

Contents

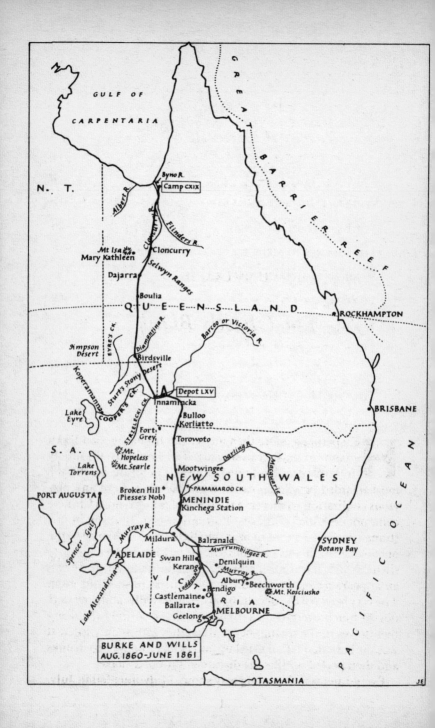

GULF OF
CARPENTARIA

N.T.

Byno R.
Camp CXIX

Mt Isa
Mary Kathleen   Cloncurry
Dajarra   Selwyn Ranges

Boulia

Q U E E N S L A N D   • ROCKHAMPTON

Barcoo or Victoria R.

Simpson
Desert   Birdsville
Kopperamanna   Sturt's Stony
Lake   Desert
Eyre   Innamincka   Depot LXV
                     • Bulloo
S.A.   Fort   Korliatto
              Grey   • Torowoto
        Mt.
        Hopeless   Darling R.
        Mt. Searle
                     • Mootwingee   N E W S O U T H W A L E S   BRISBANE
        Lake
        Torrens   ☩ PAMAMAROO CK.
PORT AUGUSTA   Broken Hill   MENINDIE
                     (Piesse's Nob)   Kinchega Station

                                             SYDNEY
                     Murray R.   Balranald   Botany Bay
              Mildura   Murrumbidgee R.
ADELAIDE   Swan Hill   • Denilquin
              Kerang   Murray R.
                            • Albury   • Beechworth
V I C T   Castlemaine   Bendigo   Mt. Kosciusko
              Ballarat   MELBOURNE
        Lake Alexandrina   Geelong

BURKE AND WILLS
AUG. 1860–JUNE 1861

TASMANIA

CHAPTER ONE

The Ghastly Blank

Here perhaps, more than anywhere, humanity had had a chance to make a fresh start. The land was absolutely untouched and unknown, and except for the blacks, the most retarded people on earth, there was no sign of any previous civilization whatever: not a scrap of pottery, not a Chinese coin, not even the vestige of a Portuguese fort. Nothing in this strange country seemed to bear the slightest resemblance to the outside world: it was so primitive, so lacking in greenness, so silent, so old. It was not a measurable man-made antiquity, but an appearance of exhaustion and weariness in the land itself. The very leaves of the trees hung down dejectedly, and they were not so much evergreen as ever-grey, never entirely renewing themselves in the spring, never altogether falling in winter. It was the bark that fell; it dried up and cracked on the tree trunks and then peeled off like the discarded skin of a snake.

Everything was the wrong way about. Midwinter fell in July,

and in January summer was at its height; in the bush there were
giant birds that never flew, and queer, antediluvian animals
that hopped instead of walked or sat munching mutely in the
trees. Even the constellations in the sky were upside down and
seemed to belong to another system of the sun. As for the naked
aborigines, they were caught in a timeless apathy in which
nothing ever changed or progressed; they built no villages, they
planted no crops, and except for a few flea-bitten dogs possessed
no domestic animals of any kind. They hunted, they slept, just
occasionally they decked themselves out for a tribal ceremony,
but all the rest was a listless dreaming.

A kind of trance was in the air, a sense of awakening infin-
itely delayed. In the midsummer heat the land scarcely
breathed, but the alien white man, walking through the grey
and silent trees, would have the feeling that someone or something was waiting and listening. The smaller birds did not fly
away as they did in Europe. The kookaburra approached,
uttered its raucous guffaw, then cocked its head, waiting for a
response. The kangaroo stood poised and watching. The earth
itself had this same air of expectancy, as though it were willing
the rain to fall, as though it were waiting for fertilization so that
it could come to life again.

And in fact an awakening did occur in the south-eastern
corner of the continent when the first white settlers arrived in
1788. Somehow European crops were made to grow in land that
had never been tilled before, and imported cattle, horses and
sheep managed to survive in a country where the farmer had no
precedents to guide him. Every man was a Robinson Crusoe.
A flood could and did wipe out a year's labour in a single day,
and when a drought began there was no knowing when it
would ever end. Everything was new and had to be begun from
the beginning.

But it was a healthy country. Along the coast at least there
was a sparkle in the air, a sense of vigour, of light and space,
that the colonists had never known in Europe. On the whole
it was a mild climate by the sea—they had about as much rain
as England and the sun had no more than a Mediterranean
warmth—and by 1860 places like Sydney, Melbourne and
Adelaide were flourishing settlements.

Melbourne, the capital of Victoria, was by some way the most important of these places; and this had happened with bewildering suddenness. Barely ten years earlier Victoria had been a remote pastoral backwater, an appendage of the older settlement of New South Wales, a place only known vaguely as the Port Phillip district. Most of the little colony's affairs were managed from Sydney. No made roads or railways led off to the other Australian colonies, no telegraph existed, and twelve thousand miles of empty ocean divided the settlers from Europe. Apart from Melbourne and Geelong there was not another town worth the name, and it is doubtful if the population of the whole region, which was about the size of England, exceeded 80,000.

But then in 1850 Queen Victoria had agreed that a new colony should be created south of the Murray River and that it should bear her name; and in the following year gold was found near Ballarat. Gold could create a mass frenzy anywhere—it had just done so in California—but in this little frontier community where the struggle for existence had been so hard people lost their wits. Bank clerks and civil servants left their jobs overnight to go off to the diggings, and not even the offer of double wages could hold them back. Ships putting into Port Melbourne were abandoned by their crews, and in the town itself women were left to carry on the shops and businesses. 'Cottages,' La Trobe, the Lieutenant-Governor, wrote, 'are deserted, houses to let, business is at a standstill, and even schools are closed. In some suburbs not a man is left...' Prices shot up to impossible heights; an immigrant was obliged to pay £2 or more to get his luggage ashore, and as much again for a corner of a hotel room to sleep in.

And the gold was actually there, at first near Ballarat, then in Castlemaine and Bendigo and in a dozen other new 'strikes' along the inland rivers. Prospectors with nothing but a pick and shovel, a bag of flour and a little tea, spread out through the north-east, penetrating into hills and valleys that had never been explored, and it was enough for the word to go out that someone had 'struck it lucky on the Ovens River' for a new rush to begin. The gold, quite often, was lying there on the surface of the ground waiting to be picked up; they found nuggets in the roots of trees, in upturned grass, in the sands of shallow rivers. The Welcome Stranger nugget, weighing 2,284 ounces and worth £9,534, was covered by only two inches of soil.

By 1853 a thousand ships were arriving in Melbourne every year, and money had begun to lose all value in a welter of speculation. Land in the city went for £200 a foot—five times the cost of land in London—and men made money only to spend it again as quickly as possible. After months of grinding work at the diggings it was a wonderful thing for a man to light his cigar with a £5 note, to play skittles with bottles of French wine, or even in some cases to shoe his horse with golden horseshoes.

There had always been a shortage of women in Australia; at one stage of the early convict days a few hundred workhouse girls known as 'Green Linnets'[1] had been brought out from England to provide wives for the settlers. Now prostitutes swarmed in the backstreet hovels of Melbourne, and it was the delight of the newly rich miner to cock a snook at the respectable bourgeoisie by going through a mock-marriage with one of the girls, dressing her up in the best brocades, and parading her in a carriage along Collins Street.

At first there had been prohibition on the goldfields, but now it was abandoned as a farce; illicit grog shops flourished everywhere, and when the miner had money he drank himself into a stupor. Then too, with the difficulty of recruiting police and so many government departments understaffed, the outburst of crime became a sinister and a menacing thing, and it was not merely the derring-do escapades of the bushrangers waylaying the gold coaches on their way down to the coast: it was the thieving, knifing and murder in the Melbourne streets.

To the old guard of settlers—the wool-growing squatters who had first taken up the land—all this seemed very like the mob taking over, a return in a small but depressing way to the lawless and egalitarian ideas of the French Revolution. It was, Dean Macartney wrote, 'a time when the bonds of society were loosened, when most people had gone mad, and the rest paralysed by fear.'

A Mr. D. Puseley, an itinerant author of strong respectability, speaks with horror of the Melbourne he found when he first arrived, and his experiences seem to be fairly typical. The city was, he says, 'a modern Babel—a little hell on earth—a city of

[1] So-called after a man named Green who shipped them out.

rioters, gamblers and drunkards ... In 1852–53 speculation, crime, excitement and disorder in Victoria had probably attained their greatest height; the yield in gold and the price of land had touched their highest points up to that period; robbers and murderers commanded extensive trades which they prosecuted with impunity, and mostly without detection; land jobbers, many of whom were magistrates and the millionaires of the colony, made their thousands per diem, and were too much engaged on their profitable traffic to attend to the arrest or punishment of law-breakers; merchants and shopkeepers had too many additions to make on the profit side of their ledgers either to think of, or to care about anything else; swindlers and gamblers were reaping an abundant harvest...'

It is, of course, all too easy to make much of these lurid episodes, and to forget that beneath the excitement a more normal natural life was gradually growing up in the colony; farms were being quietly cultivated, houses were being built and tradesmen who were strong enough to resist the gold fever were getting on with their business. In any case the lawlessness of the gold rush soon subsided, and the boom burst. It was not that the gold failed: it was simply that nearly all the surface alluvial was exhausted and now gold had to be mined by machinery and in deep shafts. The individual prospector was replaced by the mining company employing hundreds or even thousands of workers at a fixed wage. Wool, and later wheat, were important industries, and many of the new immigrants were craftsmen with families who found they could make a living without going as far as the goldfields. All this tended to stabilize prices.

By the late fifties a railway to Ballarat was being constructed, and the more settled parts of the colony were being connected by a system of horse-drawn coaches organized by a young American called Cobb. Cobb's coaches were soon to become familiar all over Australia, and his twenty-two-horse Leviathan on the goldfields run was a mammoth contraption capable of carrying nearly 100 passengers. Soon, too, Melbourne was linked to both Adelaide and Sydney by telegraph, and fast clippers were making the voyage round the Cape from England in a little over two months; the new canal at Suez would soon make the journey even shorter. Now rapidly the old isolation was melting away.

By 1860 Melbourne had a settled air. The city had been sensibly laid out on the banks of the Yarra River, with wide, straight streets lit by gaslight, and already there was a university, a public library, a Parliament House, a chain of trading banks, and public gardens filled with imported trees. At the Royal Theatre, which seated 4,000, one paid twelve guineas for a box when Catherine Hayes, the reigning prima donna, was singing, and there were half a dozen other theatres presenting Shakespeare, Sheridan and vaudeville—a great change from the days when the theatre was merely an annexe to the pub and no respectable woman could go there. The Cremorne Gardens (a model of those in London) provided another theatre, waxworks, a dance-hall, a menagerie and such entertainments as brass bands, balloon ascents and displays of fireworks. Horseracing had a mass following, and the Melbourne Cup was about to be run for the first time. When an important game of cricket was being played at the Melbourne Cricket Ground Parliament suspended its sittings until the evening.

There was a craze for dancing the quadrille, the polka and the waltz, and thousands of guests attended the balls in the newly-built Exhibition Building. These were the well-to-do people who came in their own carriages, the women in crinolines, the men wearing top-hats and mutton-chop whiskers. By day, we are told—and it is confirmed by many charming prints and water-colours—the central streets were filled with a constant passage of private gigs, carriages and horse-drawn omnibuses, and there was a railway to St. Kilda where one could put up at a good hotel and visit the sea-bathing establishments (one for men and another for women). In the fashionable suburbs many large square Victorian mansions and pleasant villas had been built with their gardens running down to boathouses and gazebos on the river.

Life for the rich then was a good deal more expansive than it is now. A normal household would expect to have its three Irish maids, a cook, a coachman and a gardener; silver, furniture and hangings were all brought from abroad (to add to the kangaroo mats on the floor and the ornamental fans made of lyre-bird tails), and Australian refinements were added to the lavish Victorian cuisine: black swan roasted and served with a port-wine sauce was a favourite dish. Picnics known as 'bushing-parties' were very popular, and on a hot summer afternoon people would set off in boats up the Yarra to see the wallabies and the birds, to drink champagne and then sing glees as they drifted downstream in the evening.

The squatters in the bush were hardly less well off. Their homesteads were comfortable places with wide verandas, mosquito nets in the bedrooms and even bathrooms with hot water. There was an abundance of food for all comers, and a man's normal breakfast was a pound of steak, perhaps with an egg on top. When Anthony Trollope came out to visit his sheep-farming son in the seventies he fixed the social status of the squatters thus:

'A hundred thousand sheep and upwards require a professional man-cook and a butler to look after them; forty thousand sheep cannot be shorn without a piano; twenty thousand is the lowest number that renders napkins at dinner imperative. Ten thousand require absolute plenty, plenty in meat, tea in plenty, brandy and water, colonial dishes in plenty, but do not expect champagne, sherry or made dishes...'

Among the rich and the middle classes who were now arriving in increasing numbers the standard of literacy was very high, probably higher than it was in England. Something like one-third of Britain's book exports were sent to Australia, and every incoming mail brought large quantities of English newspapers and periodicals. By now too the colony had its own publications: the *Age*, the *Argus*, the *Herald* and the Melbourne *Punch*.

It was true that the more squalid aspects of life were painfully apparent. There were at least 100 brothels and 500 prostitutes in Melbourne, and drunkenness was as prevalent as the common cold. Beggars had begun to appear on the streets, and most working men were still a long way off the achievement of the eight-hour day. For a man to lose his job was a disastrous thing. But this was not poverty as it was known in Britain, where there were still a million paupers. Food, especially meat, was cheap, and in this mild climate there was no great struggle to keep warm through the winter months. Moreover, the change from poverty to security or even wealth could be very rapid, and the immigrant had much better prospects than he could ever have

hoped for at home. Even the Chinese immigrants drifting down
from the goldfields found that they could make a living by
cultivating vegetable gardens, by opening laundries and by
catching and salting fish on St. Kilda beach.

And so by 1860 the Victorians felt that they had good reason
to be confident. In ten years they had risen from being the
newest and smallest colony on the mainland to a wealth and
importance that far eclipsed all the others. In wool they supplied one-sixth of Britain's imports, and in gold one-third of the
world's production; indeed, it had been so great a flood of gold
that all the world's economy was affected, and Marx and
Engels, who had predicted a disastrous slump in Europe, found
their programme seriously delayed.

The state's population had increased to half a million—
about half the white population of the whole continent—and
Melbourne with its 140,000 inhabitants was a much more
substantial place than the older settlement of Sydney.
Moreover, in these tumultuous ten years a new kind of man had
emerged. Apart from the minorities—34,000 Chinese, 10,000
Germans and 2,500 Americans—the Victorians were over-
whelmingly of English, Irish and Scottish extraction, and
although they were still intensely influenced by British customs
and traditions their new life had altered them both physically
and mentally. They no longer thought of themselves as English, Irish or Scots, but simply as Australians. Class distinctions
were breaking down, and a self-reliant, slightly truculent attitude was beginning to appear.

This new man was a materialist, a speculator, a mocker of
authority and very often a sentimentalist. He had a certain
volonté, an instinct to 'give it a go', to take a risk, but despite—
or perhaps because of—his professed contempt for tradition he
was deeply conscious of being a provincial, and he tried to con-
ceal this inner feeling of cultural inferiority by an outward
show of aggression. The harshness of existence in a new country, with its sudden drastic setbacks and failures, convinced him
that life was an implacable struggle: he felt himself very much
in competition both with the land and with his contemporaries. It was every man for himself. Consequently, when he did
find a mate, a 'cobber', a man he could trust, he romanticized
the attachment and trusted him absolutely. Victoria had never

been a penal colony like New South Wales and Tasmania; nevertheless, some of these attitudes may have been a survival from the convict days when the prisoner, the under-dog, the outcast, naturally sought allies from among the other outcasts in his war against the warders and against the society that had shut him in. One of the fascinating things about Australia is this sense of claustrophobia in the midst of such an infinity of space.

There was, too, the question of what this new man was doing to the country he had seized and adopted. For the blacks he had a mixture of fear and contempt. He was not interested in their way of life or their tribal customs, he did not particularly care what became of them, he did not grant them any rights in their own country, he treated them almost as animals. By 1860 the blacks had all but been driven away from the vicinity of Melbourne and the larger towns, and not more than a few thousand of them were left in the whole state. They had little resistance against smallpox and other imported diseases.

In the same way Australian wild life was being banished and exterminated. Already in a day's outing from Melbourne it was becoming a rare thing to see a kangaroo, and of the many thousands of koala bears living along the banks of the Murray River soon not a single specimen would be left alive. Charles Darwin, returning home from the voyage of the *Beagle*, wrote of Australia: 'A few years since this country abounded in wild animals; now the Emu is banished to a long distance and the Kangaroo is become scarce; to both the English Greyhound is utterly destructive; it may be long before these animals are altogether exterminated, but their doom is fixed.'

In short, the land was wanted for agriculture and that ominous inflationary thing, development; this was the era of sheep, the imported rabbit and the mason and the miner. After countless millions of years of utter isolation the sudden fate of Australia and its aborigines was now to be used, to be exploited, to be forced to conform to an alien civilization.

There was nothing particularly new in all this: it had already happened or was about to happen in America, in Africa and in every other primitive country into which white men were penetrating all over the globe. But what was new in Australia in 1860 was that the settlers had as yet failed to take possession of or even explore the land they were so confidently governing. They perched on the extreme southern and eastern edge of it. The settlements of Sydney, Melbourne, Adelaide and Brisbane with their satellite townships were no more than tiny specks on a continent the size of the United States, two-thirds the size of Europe. For all the broughams bowling down Collins Street, the ladies in crinolines and the champagne being drunk at the balls in the Exhibition Hall, they were living in a little capsule, encompassed by a huge unknown wilderness, they were suspended, as it were, in space. If they stepped outside the capsule they were lost.

The coastline of the continent had been charted from the sea, but as yet very few adventurers had penetrated far into the interior. All that was known was that the further one advanced into that vast empty space the hotter and drier it became, and it was perhaps because of this aridity that the colonists dreamed that one day they would discover an inland sea, a 'new Mediterranean' in the centre of the continent. It was like the legendary Atlantis or the land of Prester John; the more serious geographers scouted the idea, yet it had the persistence of a mystery. After all, no one had actually been in the centre, no one could say with finality exactly what there was to be found there, and the fact that half a dozen expeditions had already set out to resolve the matter and had returned defeated seemed, irrationally, to suggest that some great prize was awaiting the first explorer who succeeded in breaking through.

There is a good deal about these early journeys that reminds one of the re-discovery of the Sahara in the nineteenth century. Here in Australia, as in Africa, the travellers speak of the dry antiseptic air, the cold nights, the incredibly high temperatures by day, the dreadful thirst, the mirages, the impression of empty land stretching away silently into infinity. Human beings are reduced to tiny atoms in these desolate wastes, cyclonic thunderstorms burst upon them out of a clear sky, and there is no shade or shelter anywhere.

And yet the explorers profess to love the desert, they find a kind of exhilaration there, a sense of freedom, of physical cleanliness, perhaps even a spiritual regeneration, and no matter how they are reduced by their hardships they return again and again. Every traveller likes to relate his misfortunes, but these men elevate their trials almost into a mystique, a cult of barrenness and asceticism. Warburton, the Australian explorer who penetrated into the flat depression around Lake Eyre to the north of Adelaide, might easily have been describing the Sahara when he wrote:

'Lake Eyre was dry—terrible in its death-like stillness and sterility. The weary wanderer who, when in want of water, should unexpectedly reach its shores, might turn away with a shudder from the scene which shut out all hope—he could hide his head in the sandhills, and meet his fate with calmness and resignation, but to set his foot on Lake Eyre would be like cutting himself off from the common lot of human beings. I had a cheerful companion, a good horse, and some tea and damper;[1] but I felt a dismal satisfaction in looking on this lake, hardly knowing whether I saw before me earth, water or sky; and I could not help thinking what might have been my feelings had my circumstances been less happy than they were.'

Griffith Taylor, the Australian geographer who quotes this passage, was struck by the similarity of the Sahara to the interior of Australia. He makes the point that just as the Sahara blocked emigration from Europe into Central Africa, so this wilderness protected Australia from penetration by the peoples of south-east Asia. He goes on to speak of the resemblance between the Murray, Australia's largest river, and the Nile, pointing out that the Murray rises in a well-watered region with many tributaries on its upper course and then gradually enters a barren area where it receives only one tributary—the Darling—in 800 miles.

The notion of an inland sea arose from the fact that the mountains so far discovered lay on the eastern seaboard and all the principal rivers, the Murray, the Darling, and the Murrumbidgee, flowed inland from these mountains towards the west; and in the west lay the tremendous unexplored tract, an area some 1,600 miles long by 800 miles wide, bounded by the 20th and 32nd degrees of latitude and the 115th and 140th degrees of longitude: an area more than half the size of Europe. This was 'the ghastly blank'.

---

[1] Bread made of flour, salt and water and baked in the ashes of a fire.

CHAPTER TWO

Sturt

A good deal was already known about the interior, of course, through the travels of the early explorers, and one man in particular had shown the way ahead. Charles Sturt is something of a giant in Australian exploration, and indeed of exploration anywhere, and it is strange that his name is not better known, since he was the most literate of travellers, the most persistent and the most adventurous. Like so many other remarkable Englishmen of the nineteenth century, Sturt was born in India and at an early age sent back to England to be educated, at first at Harrow and then in the army. By 1814, when he was nineteen, he had already served with Wellington against the French in the Peninsular War, and with the British in Canada against the Americans. After Waterloo he returned to garrison duty in France, and when his regiment was transferred to Ireland he was involved in the famine riots of 1821–22. In 1823 he was gazetted a lieutenant and two years later a captain. He was then sent out to New South Wales in charge of a convict guard.

These brief details conjure up a recognizable military figure of the early nineteenth century, a bully-boy young officer, ignorant of politics, eager only to advance his own career and ready to deal with any defier of authority, whether he might be an American rebel, an Irish peasant or an English criminal; more of a policeman you might say than a soldier. In point of face he was nothing of the kind. At the age of thirty, when he sailed for Australia, Sturt was a spare, tall man, with a sensitive and distinguished face; he had a talent for both sketching and writing, he was an enthusiastic botanist, and far from being a typical garrison officer in a penal colony, he loathed the whole idea. But a penniless professional soldier in the eighteen twenties had very little control over his comings and goings, and so, after a six months' voyage, he arrived at Sydney, where his destiny was awaiting him. Governor Darling met the quiet, intelligent young man and made him his private secretary.

Already in 1827 Sydney was an established settlement with cornfields and orchards running down to the sea, and it was not unusual to see forty or fifty sailing-ships in the harbour. But in 1828 a drought set in, and with the failure of the crops the settlers began to look towards the regions behind the coastal mountains, where they hoped they would find more fertile land. Sturt got in with a group of young men whose names were soon to become famous as explorers—Mitchell, Hume and others—all eager to find the 'new Australian Caspian Sea', and in 1828 he led his own party inland. With six convicts to carry the baggage he followed the Macquarie River to the point where, among swamps, it entered a large westward-flowing stream, which he named after his patron the Darling. A year later he set out again, turning southwards this time to the Murrumbidgee, and with a boat he had carried overland he sailed downstream until he reached a still more important river, the Murray, and this he followed to its junction with the Darling and then to its outlet at Lake Alexandrina, on the southern ocean.

This prodigious journey of over 2,000 miles illuminated the whole river system of the south, and earned for Sturt much praise in Sydney, and a grant of land. It also undermined his health, and for the time being ruined his eyesight. For the next ten years he was obliged to stick to his farm and administrative duties in Norfolk Island and New South Wales, and in 1839 he was appointed surveyor-general in Adelaide. But he did not like a sedentary life, and repeatedly offered himself for new expeditions. He was still dreaming of an inland sea. 'I have a strange idea', he wrote, 'that there may be a central sea not far from the Darling in latitude 29° and I should go prepared for a *voyage*.' He had also observed the parrots and the cockatoos flying north, and he hoped that beyond the arid land to the north of Adelaide there would be 'rich valleys and hills'.

In 1840 his friend, Edward John Eyre, left Adelaide in an attempt to reach the centre, and Sturt, still troubled by his eyes and unable to leave his desk, regretfully watched him go. Eyre soon came back with a report that he could get no further than Mount Hopeless and the salt lake country around Lake Torrens, some 400 miles to the north of Adelaide. Mount Hopeless was nothing more than a low flat-topped hill among many others, but it was typical of that dreadful country. 'We ascended Mount Hopeless,' Eyre wrote, 'and cheerless and hopeless was the prospect before us;' nothing but an endless waste of barren rock and sand. He gave the place its despondent name to mark his decision 'to waste no more time on so desolate and forbidding a region', and turned back to civilization. Sturt was not discouraged. 'Let any man,' he declared in an address to the colonists, 'lay the map of Australia before him, and regard the blank upon its surface, and then let me ask him if it would not be an honourable achievement to be the first to place foot in its centre.'

In 1844 at last the authorities let him go. He was now 49, but his eyesight had improved and he was still physically robust. The party that assembled in Adelaide that winter was exceptionally strong: 16 men, 11 horses, 30 bullocks, 200 sheep (to be eaten on the way), a boat, a couple of heavy carts and a year's provisions. The expedition's draughtsman was a wiry little Scots officer, five foot six inches high and under nine stone in weight, named John McDouall Stuart, and among those who came to see them off was a particular friend of Sturt's, Charles Cooper, a lawyer who was subsequently to become the first chief justice of South Australia. A farewell breakfast was given for the expedition by the colonists, and then Sturt, with a straw hat on his head and mounted on Duncan, his old grey horse, led the way out of town.

They marched first to the Murray River, and followed it up-stream to the confluence with the Darling. About 180 miles up the Darling they reached Lake Cawndilla near the little outpost of Menindie, and here, having built a stockade, they turned north-westwards into the unknown. It was mid-October, and although the summer was approaching there was still water about and all the party were healthy. To cheer his friends, and perhaps himself as well, Sturt wrote back to Adelaide: 'We seem on the high road to success with mountains and seas before us ... We have strange birds of beautiful plumage and new plants ... It will be a joyous day for us to launch on an unknown sea and run away towards the tropics.'

For the moment, however, the land was uncompromisingly dry and flat, and it was an event when presently they came on a line of low hills that stretched across the plain. The most prominent of these they named Piesse's Nob, since it so much resembled the conical hat worn by Louis Piesse, the storekeeper of the expedition. Highly magnetic iron ore was found lying about and in the years ahead mining engineers were going to examine that hill with interest.

The centre of Australia is a place of violent extremes. 'It is either a desert or a deluge,' one of the early geographers wrote; 'the rainfall can vary from 30 inches in one year to three inches the next. Watercourses that have lain dry for a decade can sud-denly turn into a flood, and land that is as hard and dry as concrete will overnight become carpeted with wildflowers and fresh young grass.'

Had they known it, Sturt and his men were marching into one of the most appalling summers ever recorded. The end of 1844 found them still toiling slowly northward—a Biblical-looking group with their ox-carts and their flock of sheep—and early in 1845 they reached the 29th latitude. Here they stuck on a waterhole for six months while the land dried up around them, unable either to go forward or to go back until rain fell.

The extreme temperatures of the centre are very bearable because of the dryness of the air, but even so the heat this year was unbelievable. It rose to 132 degrees in the shade and 157 degrees in the sun. It penetrated to a depth of three or four feet into the ground, it forced the screws out of wooden boxes and

horn combs split into fine laminae. The men's hair ceased to
grow and their finger nails became as brittle as glass. Sturt
found it almost impossible to write his diary; the lead dropped
out of his pencils when he picked them up, and when he used
a pen the ink dried as it touched the paper. Scurvy broke out
in the camp and one man died, but there was nothing to be
done; they were alone in the wilderness, even the birds had
deserted this inferno, and nothing moved on the cracked earth
except the lizards and the ants. The blacks whom they had
encountered on the way up had long since made off, saying that
there was no water anywhere—'the sun had taken it.'

'The sky generally speaking,' Sturt wrote, 'was without a
speck, and the dazzling brightness of the moon was one of the
most distressing things we had to endure. It was impossible
indeed to shut out its light whichever way one turned, and its
irritating effects were remarkable.'

By April it was a little cooler, and thunder clouds began to
bank up on the horizon. At last on July 12 a gentle but
persistent rain started to fall, and after a few days it developed
into a downpour. Now they had floods to contend with, cold
nights and even frost, but at least they could move, and as a
guarantee that life was returning to the parched earth, swans
and ducks and other migrating birds began to reappear. Sturt
sent some of his men back to Adelaide and with the remainder
pushed on to the north-west. At a place which he named Fort
Grey, close to the extreme north-western corner of New South
Wales, he formed another base where he dropped off more of
his men, while he himself and a young companion named John
Harris-Browne pushed on again, taking fifteen weeks' provisions with them. They reached and named the Strzelecki Creek,[1]
and then followed it northward until they entered a region
where the horses' hooves were cut by flint-like stones and left
no track. Here on every side there were 'stupendous and almost
insurmountable sand-ridges of a fiery red'. These ridges, Sturt
went on, 'like headlands projecting into the sea, abutted upon
an immense plain where, but for a line of low trees far to the
north-east, and one bright red sandhill shining in the sunlight,
not a feature broke the dead level, the gloomy purple hue ...'

[1]After the Polish explorer who discovered and climbed Mount Kosciusko, Australia's
highest mountain just north of the New South Wales–Victorian border.

He named this region the Stony Desert. Beyond it there were glimpses of the 'better country' for which he was searching, but presently he was again among sand dunes, and at the end of August, on latitude 25 and longitude 139, he gave up all hope of finding his inland sea in that direction. The ground was drying up again, great chasms had appeared, and they heard explosions as of a distant gun. These they put down to 'gaseous influences', but no doubt they were caused by masses of rock being split off the sides of distant hills by the extremes of temperature during the day and the night. On September 8 they turned back. 'Depend upon it,' Sturt wrote, 'I would not have retreated from such a position for a trifle. But you can form no idea of that region.'

They found their way back through the red sand-ridges with white clay pans lying in between and the cloudless sky over-head—a country of red, white and blue. If they had not quite reached the centre, at least they had been almost half-way across the continent, and they had gone further than any other man. Both horses and men looked like skeletons when they reached Fort Grey at the end of seven weeks. They had ridden nearly 900 miles.

It was now October 1845 and they had heard nothing from the outside world since they had left Adelaide fourteen months before, but still Sturt would not go back. Indeed, a kind of fixation seems to govern the actions of all these Australian explorers; they struggle on, not so much to get to a declared objective, but until they reach the extreme limit of their endurance, and then, and only then, will they turn for home.

After the briefest of rests Sturt set out for the north once more, taking with him this time his draughtsman McDouall Stuart and two men named Mack and Morgan. They had four riding-horses and four pack-horses, and once again they expected to be out for several months. Harris-Browne was left in charge at Fort Grey, and before setting out Sturt gave him instructions that he was only to retire from the place if his supply of water failed or his men fell ill. In that event he was to leave a message saying where he had gone, and this message was to be placed in a bottle and buried under a tree which they chose together. Harris-Browne was devoted to Sturt and hated being left behind, but Sturt was adamant; and so on October 9, with a

promise of rain in the air, the little party rode off into the scrub.
They headed east of Sturt's old track, making over thirty miles
a day, and they soon crossed the Strzelecki Creek and came
within sight of another creek which had been dry on Sturt's
previous journey. Climbing a sandhill early one morning they
saw three miles away in an immense sandy plain a thick line
of gum trees with hills in the distance, and they rode eagerly forward through park-like country until they came to the banks
of 'a magnificent channel covered with wildfowl'. They killed
three ducks for breakfast. Riding on again to the north for half
a mile they found still another creek, 'broader and finer than
the first... with splendid sheets of water.' It was a full 200 yards
from side to side and the banks rose up some eighteen feet
among groves of flooded gum trees. The blacks had been
recently burning off the grass, and now the ground was covered
with bright young shoots. The water in the stream was vivid
green. Sturt would have paused to investigate this important
discovery, but a thunderstorm burst upon them and he decided
to take advantage of the wet weather and go on again to the
north.

His hopes for an inland sea had revived, and it was a bitter
disappointment when once again they struck the Stony Desert.
'Coming suddenly on it,' Sturt recorded, 'I almost lost my
breath. If anything it looked more forbidding than before.
Herbless and treeless it filled more than half the horizon. Not
an object was visible on which to steer, yet we held on to our
course by compass like a ship at sea.' But this was futile; the
further they went the drearier the land became. Towards the end
of October they were becoming dangerously short of water and
there was no alternative but to retrace their steps.

The desert now assumed its most menacing aspect. Most of
the waterholes they had dug on the outward journey had dried
up. 'At the first waterless halt,' Sturt wrote, 'the horses would
not eat, but collected round me, my favourite grey pulling the
hat off my head to claim attention.' It was only by catching
sight of a pigeon darting down to a little muddy depression that
they managed to replenish their supplies. When they were still
92 miles from the splendid creek they had discovered on their
way north their water gave out entirely, and they continued on
all night by lamplight. Half dead with thirst, they reached the

creek and the shade of the trees on October 28.

The flies and the mosquitoes here were so bad that the men wore veils on their faces, but this mattered nothing at all: they could drink, they could bathe and they could shoot ducks to eat. When they had recovered a little, Sturt led the way upstream, thinking that now perhaps at last they were on the true path to some really broad expanse of water. There were many encouraging signs. The blacks, for instance, were very numerous, their tracks and crude shelters were everywhere, and within five miles they met no fewer than eight different tribes.

Sturt in his dealings with the blacks is something of a rarity among Australian explorers. He did not despise them or reject them. He treated them with kindness and tried to understand them, and in return he found them to be a gentle friendly people—embarrassingly friendly, in fact, since they invited the explorers to sleep with their grubby wives. They were, he said, an undernourished but merry people who sat up laughing and talking all night long. Being naked they suffered very much from the cold at night, and at this point he split his blanket so that he could give half to a shivering old man. He notes that they were adept at foretelling the weather from the position of the moon, and that in sight and smell they were keener than a dog.

The tribes they had first encountered on their way up from Menindie were rather a scrawny lot, and very primitive; on seeing a horseman for the first time they had thought that man and beast were one creature like the mythical centaur, and they had run off in astonishment when the man had dismounted. But here, on this green watercourse, they were a much more vigorous breed, the men six foot tall, and although by tribal law their front teeth had been knocked out, many of them were handsome. They netted fish and dived for mussels in the waterholes, they brought down birds with their spears, and from the seed of a plant they called nardoo they made a rough kind of flour that was baked into cakes.

Sturt questioned the tribesmen whenever he could, and now, by signs and by moving their arms in the manner of paddling a canoe, they indicated that there were indeed great stretches of water further to the east. With renewed hope the party went on and found that the watercourse continued to divide itself into many different channels and waterholes. With its grass and heavy timber the country was much more promising than anything they had previously seen. On November 1 they arrived at a lake with seagulls flying above it, and still further east they came on other great pools, indigo-blue in colour and very salt. Here in this wilderness they interrupted a strange scene: a group of seven men crying bitterly. Nothing could make them explain the occasion of their grief, they cried and cried and would not stop, and in the end Sturt was obliged to go on his way, having left them a present of his greatcoat.

A few days later, when they were 120 miles upstream from their original starting-point, they came on a crowd of some 400 blacks, more than they had ever seen before. The men were very fine, no tribal scars on their bodies, no bulging stomachs among them, and no missing teeth. They were very friendly once they got over their fear of the horses. They came forward with gifts of ducks and flour-cakes, and held up troughs of water for the horses to drink. But they also blasted Sturt's hopes for the last time: from this point on they said the stream diminished, and nothing lay further to the east but the desert. Riding out in that direction Sturt came on a swamp, and beyond this he was confronted by an endless plain.

Now finally he had had enough, and the party turned homeward. They retraced their steps down the creek to the point where they had first reached it, and then struck out for Fort Grey and the south. Sturt wrote: 'Before we finally left the neighbourhood where our hopes had been so often raised and depressed, I gave the name of Cooper's Creek to the fine watercourse we had so anxiously traced, as a proof of my respect for Mr. Cooper, the judge of South Australia.' And he added, 'I would gladly have laid this creek down as a river, but as it had no current I did not feel myself justified in doing so.'

The march to Fort Grey was worse than anything they had endured before. A fearful hot wind sprang up; the thermometer rose to 127 degrees and burst, the horses stood with their noses to the ground, 'the birds were mute; the leaves of the trees fell around like a snow-shower. I wondered the very grass did not take fire.' When finally the weaker animals began to stagger and fall Sturt and Stuart decided to go on ahead of the other two men to Fort Grey so that they could get help. On their last stage into the camp they travelled for fifteen hours without dismounting.

Sturt half thought as he rode along that Harris-Browne might have been forced through lack of water to retreat from Fort Grey, but he could not really bring himself to believe it. And so, when the two exhausted men at last reached the camp, a sickening feeling overcame them: all was silent. Stores, animals and men—everything had vanished. 'With my bitter feelings of disappointment,' Sturt says, 'I could calmly have laid my head on that desert never to raise it again.'

Getting off their horses they went to the tree which had been selected as a site for a cache, and there dug up a bottle with a message from Harris-Browne in it. He had been obliged to retreat to another waterhole sixty-seven miles away, he said, because the water at Fort Grey had become putrid and was causing his men dysentery. This was all too painfully evident; when Stuart went to the little pool he found that the slime there was green on top and red below.

Without eating or drinking, the two men laid themselves down on the ground to sleep. Next day Mack and Morgan struggled into camp, having abandoned all their supplies on the way, but Mack after a short rest went back on the best horse to recover the provisions and a kettle. Now at last they were able to make a damper and boil a little of the slime. It was the first time they had eaten or drunk for two days.

The sixty-seven-mile journey that still lay between them and the new depot was, as Sturt says, a privation 'of no ordinary character', but somehow they managed it, riding for twenty hours without a stop, and on arrival Sturt collapsed. He fell to the ground as he dismounted, and next day his muscles contracted and his skin went black. It was nearly three weeks before they could move him, and then the whole party began their final retreat to the Darling, 270 miles away. It was now approaching midsummer—their second in the wilderness—and once again an incredible heat overwhelmed them: 'The hot wind filled the air with an impalpable dust, through which the sun looked blood-red; and all vegetation seemed dead. So heated was the ground that our matches falling on it ignited . . . the silence of the grave reigned around.' They travelled by night, Sturt lying helpless in one of the carts, and on December

21 they reached their depot near Menindie. The Darling had
ceased to flow, but at least there were waterholes in the dry bed,
and in the middle of January 1846 they struggled into Adelaide.
When Sturt reached his home at midnight his wife collapsed
fainting on the floor.

Quite apart from the hardships they had endured—and one
is forced to conclude that men in Victorian times were tougher
than they are now—a good deal had been accomplished here.
The expedition had failed in its main objects, but they had
come within 150 miles of the centre and they had actually lived
there for a year or more, isolated from the rest of the world like
men on another planet, and they had valuable information to
impart. From now on any future expedition knew that it must
expect impossible conditions during the summer months, with
the great dangers of thirst and hunger, and, in the absence of
green vegetables, of scurvy. On the other hand, it was proved
that the blacks were not dangerous if properly handled; in fact
they could be very helpful.

Sturt had brought back with him over a hundred species of
plants and many geological specimens which were to lead on
to the great mining discoveries in the centre. He had taken careful note of the strange wild animals he had found, and his
description of the bird life around the waterholes has never been
improved upon. He observes how the raptors, the hawks and
the eagles, follow the migratory routes across the interior,
terrorizing the smaller birds, dropping on them like arrows
from the sky when they pause to drink and carrying them off
in their talons. He speaks of species like the crested wedge-bill
'which is heard in the heat of the day when all other birds are
silent'; and of the galahs which were also known as rose cockatoos, of black swans which tended to be on the wing when the
moon was shining bright, of the plover with 'its peculiar and
melancholy cry ringing through the silence of the desert', of
sulphur-crested cockatoos that posted a sentinel whilst feeding
on the ground, and of seagulls on Cooper's Creek, over 500
miles from the sea. There were half a dozen varieties of duck and
a 'ventriloquist dove' which, with the very slightest movement
of its throat, made a sound that appeared to come from far out
across the plain. Then there were the tawny-shouldered podar-
gus, with mouths that reached from ear to ear and eyes half

shut, that sat on the branches in a sort of conclave with their heads together; and the cracticus destructor, an ugly bird with dull feathers that could imitate any sound it heard—indeed, one of them used to come to Sturt's camp every morning to learn a tune his men used to whistle to it. There were times when the birds were their salvation: of the amadina castanotus Sturt writes: 'Never did its note fall on our ears but as the harbinger of good, for never did we hear this little bird but we were sure to find water close at hand, and many a time has it raised my drooping spirits and those of my companions ... The hawks made sad havoc amongst these harmless little birds, generally carrying off two at a time.'

And he says of the grey falcon: 'A pair, male and female, were observed by Mr. Piesse one Sunday in May, whilst the men were at prayers, hovering very high in the air, soon after which he succeeded in killing both. They came down from a great height and pitched into the trees on the banks of the creek, and on Mr. Piesse firing at and killing one the other flew away; but returning to look for its lost companion, shared its fate. Nothing could exceed the delicate beauty of these birds when first procured. Their large, full eyes, the vivid yellow of the ceres and legs, together with their slate-coloured plumage, every feather lightly marked at the end, was quite dazzling, but all soon faded from the living brightness they had at first.'

He writes equally well of the animals, of the dingoes, for instance, whose 'emaciated bodies standing between us and the moon, were the most wretched objects in the brute creation'.

For Sturt's leadership there could be nothing but praise. None of the usual jealousies or dissensions had occurred among his party, and he had lost only one man and a few horses. The expedition had cost just under £4,000, which was very little more than he had originally estimated, and on the whole his system of base camps and small reconnaissance parties had been successful. There had been the interesting business of the message buried in the bottle, and in other ways—especially in the use of bullocks, horses and sheep—he had been able to provide a useful guide for future explorers. In a general way they would know what fauna and flora they could expect to meet, the routine of the seasons and the contours of the land. Places like Menindie, Cooper's Creek and the Stony Desert were pinpointed on the map.

Sturt never managed to return to the centre. His eyes began to trouble him again, and in 1853 he returned to England and died there sixteen years later. But his discoveries had opened a vast new field for exploration. From every side men began to push into the interior. Thomas Livingstone Mitchell, the New South Wales surveyor-general, struck inland from Sydney on a series of journeys and discovered the Victoria River. Later his assistant Kennedy traced the Victoria downstream and found that it linked up with Cooper's Creek. Meanwhile Ludwig Leichhardt, a German botanist, travelled across the tropical north of the continent as far as Port Essington. In 1848 he set out once more from the east coast with the idea of crossing the continent to Perth, and was never heard of again.

Leichhardt's disappearance caused a great stir at the time— for years afterwards there were stories of a wild white man roaming in the interior—and Augustus Charles Gregory, the Queensland surveyor-general, made two separate expeditions to find him. In the course of these journeys Gregory also followed the Cooper, and he eventually succeeded in reaching Mount Hopeless in South Australia, thus linking up his own researches with those of Sturt and Eyre some twenty years earlier. Then in 1853 a resourceful character named Captain Francis Cadell got a small steamer over the bar at the mouth of the Murray and sailed upstream as far as Swan Hill and back. Later he started a ferry on the Darling with regular sailings to Menindie.

Finally there was Sturt's draughtsman, John McDouall Stuart, and he was proving himself to be the most persistent traveller of them all. After the 1844 expedition he made several journeys to the north of Adelaide, and in March 1860 he was preparing to set out again for the centre of the continent.

Yet still the basic objects eluded them all. North of Sturt's furthest, on latitude 25, it was still *terra incognita*. Was it possible for a party to cross the continent from south to north? It was not merely curiosity that was involved in this, the persistent urge for men to go where no one else had ever been before. In 1860 the settlements in the south were still divided from Britain and Europe by a two months' sea voyage, and the introduction of steam had not materially speeded up communications. What if you could build a telegraph line from Adelaide to the northern coast and there link up with the cable that already extended through India to south-east Asia? That was a compelling idea. If realized it would mean that instead of waiting four months you could communicate with London in a few hours. There was also the possibility of opening up trade with south-east Asia through a port on the north coast. Then of course there was the hunger for land itself: all of it free, unused, waiting there for the first-comers to take possession. One would have thought that Sturt's hardships were enough to disabuse anyone of such optomistic dreams as these, but here, as in the Sahara, mirages floated on the horizon and oases like Cooper's Creek were a promise that they could be real.

These, then, were the pressures and inducements that decided the colonists in Victoria to send out a new expedition in 1860.

CHAPTER THREE

The Expedition Assembles

The Philosophical Institute of Victoria was one of those small amorphous coteries of successful men that seem to spring up spontaneously in every community. It was a private institution devoted to scientific studies, it had no authority in public affairs, and yet it was a kind of club within the government; today we would call it a part of the Establishment. Sir Henry Barkly, the new governor, was a member, and so was Sir William Stawell, the chief justice. Then there were Dr. John Macadam, a university lecturer with political ambitions, Dr. Richard Eades, the Lord Mayor of Melbourne, Ferdinand von Mueller, a distinguished botanist and an explorer of some note,[1] Dr. George Neumayer, the meteorologist, and a number of others—wealthy squatters and merchants, a sprinkling of lawyers and politicians, a clergyman or two.

[1] Mueller, an unmarried Lutheran who came to Australia from Germany, was the founder of Victorian botany, and it was he who first introduced the eucalyptus to other countries. A scholarly and kindly man of extraordinary energy, he is reputed to have written 3,000 letters a year in his own hand.

By the late fifties the Institute had become an influential group; they had got a charter from the Queen which enabled them to change their name to the Royal Society, they had moved into comfortable rooms in Victoria Street, not far from Parliament House, and here in an easy and leisurely way they conducted their 'proceedings'. With so many extraordinary Australian phenomena crowding in upon them there was no shortage of subjects for discussion; papers were read on such matters as the geology of the goldfields, the tribal customs of the aborigines, the acclimatization of imported animals and plants and the movements of the heavenly bodies in the southern sky. Dr. Mueller, who had been with Gregory in Northern Australia, brought forward the question of inland exploration, and in 1857 a committee was appointed 'for the purpose of fitting out in Victoria an expedition for traversing the unknown interior of the Australian continent from east to west'. Early in the following year Sir William Stawell called a meeting to discuss the venture, and a prosperous dealer in provisions named Ambrose Kyte made an anonymous offer of £1,000 provided that another £2,000 could be raised by the public within a year.

For a while things hung fire—the colony was suffering from a business recession at the time—and only £900 was raised in eleven months. However, a new 'lithographic letter' was sent out to 'squatters, merchants and country gentlemen', and soon every mail brought in cheques, money orders and cash. A rural clergyman gave £100, Barkly subscribed £50, Captain Cadell offered the use of his steamers on the Murray and the Darling, and within the prescribed time £2,200 was raised to add to Kyte's £1,000. The Victorian Government, which had been reluctant at first, now voted £6,000, and with a total of £9,000 in hand the Society could afford to make plans on a lavish scale. An Exploration Committee was appointed to handle the venture, with Stawell as its chairman, and Macadam as its secretary, and they set about the business of finding a leader for the expedition. Gregory was the obvious choice since he had already been in the centre, but he did not want to go. He suggested in his place Major Warburton, an experienced South Australian explorer, but the Committee felt that this ought to be an entirely Victorian adventure, and so the post was advertised in the Melbourne Press. Fourteen candidates applied, and six were finally considered. One of these was a police superintendent from the Castlemaine district named Robert O'Hara Burke, and he was chosen by ten votes to five.

Upon several counts the choice of Burke was a surprising decision. He knew nothing of exploration and he had no scientific qualifications of any kind. Moreover he was Irish, and it has to be admitted (at the risk of fierce contention) that there is something about the Irish temperament that is not ideal for exploration; it is too quick, too mercurial, too imaginative, too headstrong and, paradoxically, too brave. The Irish have produced the greatest of British generals and the best of soldiers in the ranks, but Irish names are not usually to be found among the first flight of explorers, whether in Australia, Africa, Asia, at the poles or anywhere else. Exploration seems to require slow, unflurried tenacity and persistence, great patience and tact, a scientific rather than an emotional approach, a willingness to reject the flamboyant thing and to accept the middle of the road; all qualities which one tends to associate with the Scots and the English rather than the Irish (which is not to say that the Scots and the English cannot be mighty dull and wrong-headed at moments when the Irish have the vision and the courage to succeed).

Burke was very Irish. He came from a land-owning and military family of St. Clerans in County Galway, and action was in his blood. Having been educated at Woolwich Academy he joined a cavalry regiment in the Austrian service at a very early age. When this regiment was disbanded he went to the Irish Constabulary and then enlisted in the Victorian police force as an inspector. He arrived in Australia at the height of the disturbances caused by the gold rush and was a most successful officer; it was remembered that when the European miners set upon some 2,000 Chinese at the diggings on the Buckland River, Burke with a small detachment marched fifty miles nonstop to the scene, and restored order.

In 1854 he obtained leave of absence and went off to Europe to fight in the Crimean War, but he was too late, and he returned to Victoria, where he soon rose to the important post of superintendent of police in the populous gold-mining district of Castlemaine. At the time of his appointment as leader of the exploring expedition he was aged 39 and still unmarried.

That was the official side of the record. His private life was more bizarre. This is how a bank manager who knew him well describes him: 'He was a careless dare-devil sort of Irishman of very ordinary physique. He wore a long beard, over which he dribbled his saliva. When he was off duty he often wore a slouching sombrero-like hat, and as he did not wear braces his breeches hung in rolls about his heels, and he looked altogether untidy ... It was told of him as a good joke, but true nevertheless, that when he was returning from Yackandandah to Beechworth he lost his way, although the track was well-beaten and frequented, and did not arrive at his destination for many hours after he was due. He was in no sense a bushman ...'

Another contemporary wrote 'he is humane and tender-hearted as a woman, he seeks to hide it by a brusquerie wholly external ...' And another: 'He was kind and generous to a fault but let anything happen out of the common routine he was confused, then excited, till finally he would lose all control of his better judgment. Then again, when he had made up his mind to do a thing he never considered the consequences. He had thorough discipline and no one dared to presume to contradict him.'

'Burke,' says another, 'did not possess a dress suit, nor even a white shirt,' yet he was 'soldier-like', had 'much vigorous commonsense', and was a 'well-bred gentleman and quite at home amongst people of the best class'. (This may have been a reference to Burke's connections with a wealthy family in Cloncurry in Ireland.) Then there were his eccentricities. Once when he was getting fat he instructed his housekeeper not to spend more than sixpence a day on his food. He loved splashing about in a pool which he built in his backyard. There he sat naked in the open with his helmet on his head, reading a book.

Elsewhere we hear that Burke had great charm and was held in much affection by the police of the district. 'He was a wild, eccentric dare-devil ... Either he did not realise danger or his mind was so unhinged to that extent that he revelled in it.' He galloped his horse madly through swamps and forests and was so reckless 'some people thought him not quite sane'. He was an able linguist and had a habit of scrawling notes and quotations from French, German and Italian poets on the walls of the parlour at his police station. Visitors, glancing at these curiosities, were taken aback by an inscription: 'Do not read anything ön the walls.' He was a man who would always lend money to a friend: 'His salary coursed through his fingers as soon as he received it.' Sometimes he would disappear from his station for days at a time, and it was his particular delight to irritate a certain magistrate who used to come near to frenzy if anyone swung on his front-gate. Burke would ride thirty miles to swing on that gate. He was a martinet, a Bohemian (though no one suggests that he was a heavy drinker), and, rather surprisingly, he was a Protestant. Then again we hear: 'He was the worst bushman I ever met;' he was all for taking short cuts. At one time he had been greatly affected by the death of his brother in the Crimea, and would be found at home alone silently staring at his picture.

Then there was all the gossip about his connection with Julia Matthews, who was a young actress who had come out to Australia to sing in light opera. Burke first met her when she was playing on the goldfields, and she is described as a 'buxom and sprightly' girl in the fashion of the times. He is said to have attended every performance she gave in the town of Beechworth, and then to have followed her from place to place in a passion of adoration. According to one of his colleagues in the police force Burke was in despair when she rejected his offer of marriage. He bought a piano and retired to his house, where, with the help of a German teacher, he played over and over again the songs she sang.

Whether all this be true or not, Burke obviously had an engaging presence. When he came down to Melbourne to take up his appointment as leader of the expedition, he tidied himself up, took up quarters at the police station in the suburb of Richmond, and joined the Melbourne Club, which was another branch of the Establishment. One of his hostesses writes of him: 'When we first knew Mr. Burke we called him "Brian Boru"; and there was such a daring, reckless look about him, which was enhanced by a great scar across his face, caused by a sabre-cut in a duel when he was in the Austrian Service; he had, withal, a very attractive manner. Many a pleasant dance I had with him.'

These last impressions are not altogether borne out by the

only good likeness of Burke to survive—a daguerreotype taken shortly after the expedition set out. It reveals a well-groomed head with a receding hairline, a carefully brushed beard and no sign of the scar. The eyes are surprisingly mild, romantic and brooding; it is the face of a poet.

So then we have here an odd character in an odd position. It is impossible to deny that up to this point there is a certain triviality about Burke, or at all events his reputation, a lack of seriousness and distinction. The dashings about on horseback, the carelessness and the somewhat amateur bohemianism, the punctilious policeman on duty and the whimsical readings in the bath, the affair with the minor actress—it all has rather a naïve and provincial sound, not at all in tune with the lives and accomplishments of the gentlemen of the Royal Society. What we seem to have here is not another Sturt, not a steady or a commanding figure in any way, but a sort of neo-hero, a made-up explorer, a likeable man but still a man with greatness thrust upon him.

Why ever then did the Committee choose him? The charm, of course, must have helped, and no doubt he was modest. Clearly he was brave, he was willing, his police record was good, and he had just that dash of the adventurer about him that may well have had its appeal to these serious sedentary men who were sending him off into the unknown. His technical deficiencies could be made good by the appointment of scientists to the party, and here the Committee had some able men to choose from. Dr. Neumayer, the meteorologist, promised to lend a hand, at any rate during the early stages of the expedition, and Dr. Herman Beckler, a German doctor who had been trained at Munich, was appointed botanist and medical officer. He seems to have been a methodical and competent man, though perhaps, as a companion, a little dull. The post of naturalist went to Ludwig Becker, another German who was also a member of the Society. Becker—and to avoid confusion with his colleague one must note that he had no 'l' in his name—was a delightful man, a genuine amateur in the correct sense of the word. He was born at Darmstadt of a well-connected family; one brother was Chief of Staff of the army of Hesse and another was private secretary to the Prince Consort in England and the tutor of Queen Victoria's eldest sons.

Ludwig, though a shy and sensitive man, was a rolling stone; his travels had already taken him through Brazil, and at the time of his appointment he had been nine years in Australia, a part of the time on the gold diggings. Governor Denison of Tasmania has left an interesting description of him: 'He is one of those universal geniuses who can do anything; is a very good naturalist, geologist, etc. and draws and plays and sings ... He is travelling this country and pays his way by taking like-nesses—miniatures, which he does very nicely indeed. He is very odd-looking with a large red beard.' The governor's refer-ences to Becker's accomplishments were not greatly exagger-ated; he was one of the earliest authorities on the lyre bird, and his drawings, scientific notes and diaries (which have never been published) are in some ways the best records of the expedi-tion to survive. Indeed, he had only one serious drawback; he was about 52 at this time, and that was too old to go marching off into the interior of Australia.

For the important post of surveyor—the man who would chart the expedition's route—Dr. Neumayer produced a mem-ber of his own staff, a serious young Englishman named William John Wills. Now we know a great deal about Wills, mostly from his own correspondence, and from a book written about him by his father, and the thing that instantly emerges is that he was a most excellent and reliable young man. Had his circumstances been different he would most certainly have been the captain of his school, carrying off all the prizes, excelling at all the games. Here is one of Dickens' young heroes, fair-minded, compassionate, studious, eager to get on; he absorbed the Victorian virtues as to the manner born. His father, how-ever, was a country doctor living in modest circumstances in Devon, and was not quite able to launch the boy on the career he merited; he was articled as a surgeon, a career he did not particularly like, and was sent up to Guy's and Bartholomew's in London to study medicine and chemistry. Young Wills' real passion was for astronomy and meteorology, for precise calcu-lations and deductions, and indeed his sense of direction was so good that he unravelled the mystery of the maze at Hampton Court in ten minutes. When he had money to spend he bought scientific instruments. He was also a great reader of such works as Chesterfield's letters to his son, and among the poets (whom he often quoted in his letters to his parents) Pope was his favourite.

In the normal course of events this poor but very promising student would have remained in England, and no doubt in time would have been appointed to some useful scientific post, but in the early fifties his father, Dr. Wills, was seized with excitement about the Australian gold rush. William, aged 18, and a younger brother were dispatched in a sailing-ship to Melbourne to make their fortune, and within a year the father followed. At first the two boys got jobs as shepherds at £30 a year on a far-away sheep-station at Deniliquin in New South Wales, and we have a picture of them got up in straw wide-awake hats, blue shirts and duck trousers. Then, like so many other young men, they drifted down to the goldfields and joined their father at Ballarat.

At that time Ballarat looked as though it had suffered an aerial bombardment. On every side the land was scarred and torn up by the diggers, one man handling a windlass and a bucket while another worked with pick and shovel below. On the surface the earth was washed for gold in wooden trays known as cradles, and a continuous murmur of rumbling and splashing filled the air. The miners lived in tents and bark huts, but on the main street, billowing with dust in summer and deep in mud in winter, there was a line of weatherboard pubs and stores, even a makeshift theatre where the luckier miners gathered at night to drink and watch a variety show. Dr. Wills, assisted by William, put up a tent in the centre of the town and opened a medical practice.

Young William hated the turmoil of the goldfields, the drunkenness and the nightly brawling in the pubs, and escaped when he could to the bush, which he loved. In 1858 he wrote to his mother in England, 'Now the rush to the diggings is over people are beginning to live like civilised human beings'; and soon afterwards he got himself a job at Dr. Neumayer's 'Magnetic Observatory' in Melbourne. This he regarded as his great chance. He set himself up in a respectable boarding-house and thought of nothing but his work. Not for him the music-hall or the fireworks in the Cremorne Gardens. Just occasionally he would attend the opera or a ball, but most evenings he spent at home, either with his books and his instruments or engaging in improving conversations with the more literate of his fellow lodgers; there is no mention of any female attachment. He was a good-looking young man with a fair beard, and a quiet manner, and he was always neatly dressed; in short, he was respectable and he was on his way to the top.

If one detects here a slight touch of priggishness, and if there is little trace of humour in his letters, one must also remember that young Wills eagerly wanted to join the expedition, and that he was full of joy when he was offered the position of surveyor. So now at the age of 26 he found himself serving a leader who was in every possible way his opposite. To Burke's untidiness, his physical energy and his romantic flair, Wills apposed a bookish and examining mind, a love of figures rather than of visions. From the first the two men got on extremely well together, and Wills was to serve his leader, who was thirteen years older than he was, with devotion.

Burke himself interviewed some seven hundred applicants for the minor posts on the expedition, and eventually ten were chosen. Some were working men, others had qualifications of one sort or another, but it is impossible now to know on just what basis they were chosen. Charles D. Ferguson, the foreman, was an American who had come over from the Californian gold diggings, William Brahe was another German, and the others were Henry Creber, Owen Cowen, John Drakeford, Robert Fletcher, Patrick Langan, Thomas McDonough, William Patton, and John King. King and Brahe, as we shall see, were the most interesting of these 'assistants'.

The salaries were fixed at £500 per annum for Burke, £300 each for Beckler, Becker and Wills, £200 for Ferguson, and £120 for the assistants. All the members of the party were examined by a doctor and declared medically fit.

There remained now the question of who was to be the second in command. Wills was too young, and Beckler and Becker, the only other officers, were not deemed suitable; both were Germans and Becker did not speak English very well. In the end it was decided to appoint a new man to the post— George James Landells. Landells is something of an enigma in the story of the expedition. Apart from the fact that he was an Englishman who was supposed to be an expert on camels, that his family had been settled in Australia since the forties, that he had a wife, that he possessed the only dog taken on the journey, and that he was extremely greedy for money, we know very little about him. It was only through the camels that he happened to join the expedition at all. Someone had suggested to the Exploration Committee that camels were vital to the venture; they had proved most successful in the Sahara and in other arid regions so why not in the centre of Australia? Six camels that had been brought out to Melbourne as part of a vaudeville show were purchased, but another twenty-four were needed, and Landells was sent off to India to get them. The Indian Mutiny had barely subsided, and it was difficult to move about the country, but Landells handled the business very ably. He managed to find his way up to the camel-markets in Peshawar and Afghanistan, where he enlisted three sepoys, and twenty-five animals were driven down to the coast at the excellent rate of fifty miles a day. Before they embarked at Karachi Landells fell in with John King, who could speak the sepoys' language, and he offered him a job.

There is something very touching about King; he always seems to be the victim of circumstances, life pushes him from one place to the other, and he is not at all like the Irish soldiers in the Kipling stories, whom outwardly he so much resembles; he is much too mild. He was only 14 when he became a soldier—what else was there for the son of a poor Irish private to do?—and he was soon dispatched to India where he showed some promise at his books, and was made an assistant teacher at the school attached to the 70th Regiment. This did not save him from the violence of the mutiny, and at Peshawar he saw forty mutineers shot away from guns. After this he was ill with fever for eighteen months, and when Landells met him he was convalescing at Karachi on the west coast. By then he had served his seven years in the army and had purchased his discharge, and so he accepted the job.

There was much excitement in Melbourne when the party landed in June 1860. Both camels and sepoys were a great rarity, Landells himself was in oriental costume, and crowds followed the strange procession up to Parliament House, where quarters had been prepared in the stables. Most of the animals appeared to have withstood the voyage without harm, but no one could be sure about their reaction to Australian conditions; a wild pea growing on the Darling River was said to be fatal to them. Landells, however, was convinced that all would be well if a certain amount of rum was added to their rations, and indeed it was important that the camels should survive, for his bill was an extremely large one: £5,497 in all for the purchase of the animals and their transport. Nor was this all: on being offered the position of second in command of the expedition Landells instantly protested that the salary proposed was not enough; he must have £600 a year, which was £100 more than Burke, the leader, was getting. Burke had been gambling and had run up bills at the Melbourne Club he could not pay. Yet he generously rejected an additional £100 offered him by the Committee, and said that he did not mind in the least if Landells was paid more money than he was. Landells was given his £600.

By now the assembling of the equipment was well advanced. The prisoners at Pentridge Gaol were put to work making such things as boots and harness, and a new kind of cart that would float on rivers was constructed. The armoury comprised 19 Colt's revolvers, 10 double-barrelled guns, 8 rifles and 50 rockets, and among the general equipment were 95 sets of camel shoes, 4 dozen fishing lines, a huge amount of saddlery, 10 dozen looking glasses and 2 lb. of beads (for the natives), 12 tents, 20 camp beds, 80 pairs of boots, 30 cabbage-tree hats (hats with a high crown and large shady brim), 2 pairs of fieldglasses, several cases of surgical instruments, parcels of seeds provided by Dr. Mueller, a library of books by Sturt, Gregory, Mitchell and other explorers, 8 demi-johns of limejuice (to prevent scurvy), 4 gallons of brandy and 60 gallons of rum for the camels.

It was expected that the expedition would be away from a year to eighteen months, and large quantities of food were purchased: pemmican and meat biscuit, preserved vegetables, flour, ginger and dried apples. Nothing was skimped, nothing was forgotten. Prices of up to £50 were paid for horses, and there were twenty-three of them in all. In the end the total baggage amounted to twenty-one tons. It was the most elaborate and best equipped expedition ever to be set up in Australia.

The Committee meanwhile was giving much thought to the question of what route Burke was to follow. His great object was to cross the continent and discover what lay in the centre, but there was no point in going over ground where others had been before. Sturt had got up as far as latitude 25 and McDouall Stuart had already traversed the country further to the west. Leichhardt, the German explorer, had been across the far north, following an east-west route just south of the Gulf of Carpentaria. In Western Australia Gregory had made a journey southwards from the north coast as far as Mount Wilson, while his younger brother had explored the coastal region in the vicinity of Shark Bay. Sturt, Mitchell, Kennedy and Gregory had all been on Cooper's Creek. The thing to do now was to try and link up some or all of these discoveries and resolve the mystery of the centre.

Gregory, in a very sensible letter to the Committee, advised them to strike inland from Brisbane to Cooper's Creek and set up a depot there. He did not believe that the expedition should try and move in summer, and if it failed to cross the continent in the first winter it should retire to Cooper's Creek and wait for the next. Others suggested that the expedition should be taken round by sea to Port Augusta on Spencer Gulf, in South Australia, and that thence it should march northwards. Others again thought that a landing should be made on the Gulf of Carpentaria, and that Burke should then come south through the centre.

The Committee decided to reject all these proposals, mainly it seems because of the difficulty and expense of shipping the camels once more, and perhaps too because they felt that the expedition should emphasize its Victorian character by setting out overland from Melbourne itself. They were agreed, however, in a general way on a south-north crossing, and it was decided that Burke should first march directly to Cooper's Creek via Menindie, on the Darling.

The following instructions were drawn up and officially presented to him by Dr. Macadam on August 18, 1860:

'Sir,

I am directed by the Committee to convey to you instructions and views which have been adopted in connection with the duties which have devolved upon you as leader of the party now organised to explore the interior of Australia.

'The Committee having decided upon "Cooper's Creek",

of Sturt, as the basis of your operations, request that you will proceed thither, form a depot of provisions and stores, and make arrangements for keeping open a communication in your rear to the Darling, if in your opinion advisable, and thence to Melbourne, so that you may be enabled to keep the Committee informed of your movements, and receive in return the assistance in stores and advice in which you may stand in need. Should you find that a readier communication can be made by way of the South Australian police station near Mount Searle (about 90 miles to the south-west of Mount Hopeless) you will avail yourself of that means of writing to the Committee . . .

'The object of the Committee in directing you to Cooper's Creek is, that you should explore the country intervening between it and Leichhardt's track, south of the Gulf of Carpentaria, avoiding, as far as practicable, Sturt's route on the west, and Gregory's, down the Victoria (or Cooper) on the east. To this object the Committee wishes you to devote your energies in the first instance; but should you determine the impracticability of this route, you are desired to turn westward into the country recently discovered by Stuart, and connect his furthest point northward with Gregory's furthest southern exploration in 1856 (Mount Wilson).

'In proceeding from Cooper's Creek to Stuart's country, you may find the salt marshes an obstacle to the progress of the camels; if so, it is supposed you will be able to avoid these marshes by turning to the northward as far as Eyre's Creek, where there is permanent water, and then by going westward to Stuart's furthest.

'Should you fail, however, in connecting the two points of Stuart's and Gregory's furthest, or should you ascertain that this space has already been traversed, you are requested, if possible, to connect your explorations with those of the younger Gregory in the vicinity of Mount Gould, and thence you might proceed to Shark's Bay, or down the River Murchison to the settlements in Western Australia.

'This country would afford the means of recruiting the strength of your party; and you might, after a delay of five or six months, be enabled, with the knowledge of the country you shall have previously acquired, to return by a more direct route through South Australia to Melbourne...

'The Committee is fully aware of the difficulty of the country you are called on to traverse, and in giving you these instructions has placed these routes before you more as an indication of what is deemed desirable to have accomplished than as indicating any exact course for you to pursue. The Committee considers that you will find a better and safer guide in the natural features of the country through which you will have to pass.

'For all useful and practical purposes, it will be better for you, and for the object of future settlements, that you should follow the watercourses and the country yielding herbage than to pursue any route which the Committee might be able to sketch out from an imperfect map of Australia.

'The Committee entrusts you with the largest discretion as regards the forming of depots and your movements generally, but request that you will mark your routes as permanently as possible, by leaving records, sowing seeds, building cairns, and marking trees at as many points as possible consistent with your various other duties...

'You will cause full reports to be furnished by your officers on any subject of interest, and forward them to Melbourne as often as may be practicable, without retarding the progress of the expedition. The Committee has caused the enclosed set of instructions to be drawn up, having relation to each department of science, and you are requested to hand each of the gentlemen a copy of that part more particularly relating to his department.'

(There follow instructions to Beckler, Becker and Wills on the geographic, geologic, meteorological, zoological and botanical aspects of the journey.)

It is an odd document. Even if one makes allowance for the fact that no one knew what was in the centre and that no maps existed its wording is extremely loose. Having reached Cooper's Creek, Burke if he chose could go here, there or anywhere— north to the Gulf, west to the coast of Western Australia, or anywhere in between. This was juggling with thousands of miles of unexplored land as though it presented no more obstacle than the empty sea, and it placed an immense responsibility on the leader.

Burke, however, appears to have been content, and in fact he had a hand in drawing up his instructions, for he attended the Committee meetings every day. By now he was held by the Committee in high esteem, and they were eager to give him a free hand. But this was very far from being the case with everyone in the colony. The *Age* was now publishing letters protesting that the appointment of a leader without proper qualifications was absurd, and that neither the Committee nor any of the members of the expedition had had any real experience of the bush. Burke himself received a number of anonymous letters of a similar kind and was much upset. Others again were opposed to the whole enterprise on the grounds that if rich territory were discovered in the interior it would be damaging to Victoria's commercial and pastoral interests.

Then there were the usual cranks; one man wrote to the Committee suggesting that the expedition should pay out a hose as it went along so as to ensure its water supply. Another recommended the use of a 'fire-balloon' from which the country could be surveyed. A squatter warned the Committee that he would sue them if Burke's camels scared his cattle on their way north.

But by now they were all much too involved and too excited to turn back or even consider major re-adjustments. Barkly informed the government in England that the party was about to set out, and asked that 'instructions may be given to officers in Her Majesty's navy, or others, likely to approach the northern coast, within the next year or two, to look out for and assist such of the number as may succeed in crossing'. Some weeks previously an assembly camp had been set up for the expedition in Royal Park, an open stretch of bushland outside the city, and every day there was a great come and go along the dusty track leading out there from the centre. A tented camp was put up for the men and wooden huts for the camels. The last farewells had begun. Dean Macartney held a special service for the Expedition, and at a public dinner given in Burke's honour at Castlemaine the Reverend J. Storie declared, 'If there really exists within our great continent a Sahara—a desert of sands, parent of hot winds, we should like to know the fact. If great lakes on whose verdant banks thousands of cattle might feed, tempt men to build new cities, let us know the character and the promise of the land by the true report of a true man.' Modestly, Burke replied that he would do his best.

There also appears to be some evidence that Burke made a last proposal of marriage to Julia Matthews, who was then playing at the Princess Theatre in Melbourne, and that she said she would decide on his return.

So now they were all gathered at Royal Park, the Irish police-officer, the acquisitive camel-dealer, the two German scientists, the studious young surveyor, the American gold-miner, the assistants and the sepoys, the camels, the horses and the twenty-one tons of baggage. If there was an amateurish atmosphere about the scene, if indeed it bore some resemblance to a provincial circus taking the road, this was not at all apparent at the time. The fated feeling of a great adventure was in the air, and everyone connected with it was extremely agitated, hopeful and busy. The memory of the lost explorer Leichhardt was still very strong: was it possible that these men too would vanish into that mysterious space in the centre and never be heard from again? Probably no one believed that such a thing could happen: still the possibility was there, and Burke and his men were regarded with that special leave-taking emotion which surrounds young soldiers marching off to war.

On August 19, 1860, it was announced that everything was ready, and on the following day business in Melbourne was practically suspended while a huge crowd came out to Royal Park to see them off.

CHAPTER FOUR

The Journey to Menindie

There was some confusion about the start; the party was to have got away at one o'clock but did not actually leave till four, and even then six of the camels that had fallen ill and a quantity of stores and equipment had to be left behind. For a description of the scene we can do no better than follow the account given in the Melbourne *Herald* on August 21, 1860:

'At an early hour crowds of eager holiday folks, pedestrian and equestrian, were to be seen hieing along the dusty ways to the pleasant glades and umbrageous shade (a warm breeze, the first of the season, was blowing from the north-east) of the Royal Park. A busy scene was there presented. Men, horses, camels, drays, and goods were scattered here and there amongst the tents, in the sheds, and on the greensward, in picturesque confusion—everything premised a departure—the caravansery was to be deserted. Hour after hour passed in preparations for starting. By-and-by, however, the drays were loaded—though not before a burden of three hundredweight for each camel at starting was objected to, and extra vehicles had to be procured—the horses and the camels were securely packed.

'Artists, reporters and favoured visitors were all the time hurrying and scurrying hither and thither to sketch this, to take note of that, and to ask a question concerning t'other. It is needless to say that occasionally ludicrous replies were given to serious questions, and in the bustle of hurried arrangements, some very amusing contretemps occurred. One of the most laughable was the breaking loose of a cantankerous camel, and the startling and upsetting in the "scatter" of a popular limb of the law. The gentleman referred to is of large mould, and until we saw his tumbling feat yesterday, we had no idea that he was such a sprightly gymnast. His going-down and uprising were greeted with shouts of laughter, in which he good-naturedly joined. The erring camel went helter-skelter through the crowd, and was not secured until he showed to admiration how speedily can go "the ship of the desert".

'It was exactly a quarter to four o'clock when the expedition got into marching order. A lane was opened through the crowd, and in this the line was formed: Mr. Burke on his pretty little grey at the head.[1] The Exploration Committee of the Royal Society, together with a distinguished circle of visitors, amongst whom were some of our most respectable colonists and their families, took up a position in front. The Mayor of Melbourne then mounted one of the drays and said: Mr. Burke, I am fully aware that the grand assemblage, this day, while it has impeded your movements in starting, is at the same time a source of much gratification to you. It assures you of the most sincere sympathy of the citizens. (Hear, hear.) I will not detain you; but for this great crowd, and on behalf of the colony at large, I say—God speed you! (Cheers.)

'His Worship then called for "three cheers for Mr. Burke", "three cheers for Mr. Landells", and "three cheers for the party itself", which, it is needless to say, were responded to with all the energy and enthusiasm that are characteristic of popular assemblages. He then concluded with again saying, "God speed and bless you!"

'Mr. Burke (uncovered) said, in a clear, earnest voice that was heard all over the crowd: Mr. Mayor—On behalf of myself and

[1] Burke was wearing a conical black hat, a blue coat, and a red shirt.

the Expedition I beg to return to you my most sincere thanks. No expedition has ever started under such favourable circumstances as this. The people, the Government, the Committee—all have done heartily what they could do. It is now our turn; and we shall never do well until we entirely justify what you have done in showing what we can do. (Cheers.)

'The party at once got into motion. Following the leader were several pack-horses, led by some of the assistants on foot. Then came Mr. Landells on a camel, next Dr. Becker, similarly mounted, and these were succeeded by two European assistants, riding on camels—one leading the ambulance camel, and the other leading two animals loaded with provisions. Sepoys on foot led the remainder of the camels, four and five in hand, variously loaded, and the caravan was closed by one mounted sepoy.

'Altogether twenty-seven camels go with the Expedition. Two new wagons, heavily loaded, followed at a good distance. These were built expressly for the Expedition, and one of them is so constructed that at a very short notice it can be taken off the wheels, and put to all the uses of a river punt, carrying an immense load high and dry on the water. If it be necessary to swim the camels, air bags are provided to be lashed under their jowls, so as to keep their heads clear when crossing deep streams. Two or three hired wagons, and one of the new ones, were detained in the park until nearly dusk, in charge of the astronomer, Mr. W. J. Wills, and the foreman, who had to look to the careful packing of instruments, specimen cases etc. The hired wagons will proceed as far as Swan Hill only.

'Issuing from the south gate of the park, the party went down behind the manure depot, and thence on to the Sydney Road, and the whole camped late last night near the village of Essendon.'

Not surprisingly it took the party a little time to shake down, and there were a number of hitches during the next few days while they moved slowly northward. Both animals and vehicles were too heavily laden, and several of the wagons broke down. One of the sepoys, a muhammadan, discovered that his religion forbade him eating the food that had been provided, and he walked back to Melbourne. He was in tears. Everywhere the camels spread fear and amazement; flocks of white cockatoos screamed at them from the tree-tops, the blacks fled at their approach, and one day Landells killed a seven-foot carpet snake while it lay, head erect, gazing at the procession. The horses too were terrified of the camels, perhaps because of their smell, and had to be led forward in a separate column.

It was still winter and very cold at night, and although it was warm by day the rain poured down on the black soil plains to the north of Melbourne, making the going very heavy. When only two days out Ludwig Becker wrote in his diary: '... Before we reached Bolinda, near Capt. Gardner's place, at 5 p.m. it commenced raining and ere night had set in it came down in torrents. No tea, no fire; we slept in the wet.' Four days later at Mia Mia it was still raining. Burke telegraphed Macadam, the secretary of the Committee: 'The exploring party arrived here last night. We halt today, Sunday, and proceed tomorrow. The roads are very bad.' We also have one of his rare letters to the Committee, written about this time on a quarto sheet of white paper. In his large, scrawling, confident hand he wrote: 'Sir, I have the honour to report that the Expedition arrived here (Booth and Holloway's Station) last night and remain today as the weather and the roads were very bad. All well. Your obt. servant, R. O'Hara Burke, Leader.'

They were passing through settled districts all this time, un-dulating plains and hills that were very green in the rain, and occasionally they could put up at wayside hotels and station homesteads. Everywhere along the route they were greeted by settlers who had ridden in many miles from outback farms to see the procession go by. After a week they reached the Cam-paspe River and crowds came out from the Bendigo goldfields to welcome them.

And now they left the hills behind them and plunged into plains that were as flat as a cricket field. The birds in the swamps were marvellous: flocks of ibis with their scimitar beaks marching in line and stirring up the grasshoppers with their feet, the screeching grey galahs with their delicate pink breasts; grey herons, plovers, crows, black swans and magpies which were smaller and sprightlier than the European species. And always in the branches of the eucalypts, which still had a winter bareness, the laughing kookaburra. At Terrick Becker found that the plains looked like 'a calm ocean with green water', and the horizon appeared to be 'much higher than the point the spectator stands on, the whole plain looks concave. On you go, miles and miles: a single tree, a belt of timber, appear at the horizon, affected by the mirage. You reach that belt of small trees, a wallaby, a kangaroo-rat disturbs for a moment the monotony and a few steps further on you are again on a green calm ocean.' With his sensitive and accurate pencil he sketched the expedition advancing, the line of camels on the left, the line of horses on the right, and Burke, on his little grey Billy, riding in between.

The weather was now improving and Becker observed butterflies among bare gigantic boulders near Pyramid Hill, and from his bed by the campfire he listened to the bells of the hobbled horses 'in the serene and silent night'. Occasionally there would be a disturbance—the camels taking fright in the darkness and bolting—and then there would be a long delay while they tracked them down in the morning.

Wills wrote in a letter to a friend: 'Riding on camels is a much more pleasant process than I had anticipated, and for my work I find it much better than riding on horseback. The saddles, as you are aware, are double, so I sit on the back portion behind the hump, and pack my instruments in front. I can thus ride on, keeping my journal and making calculations; and need only stop the camel when I want to take any bearings carefully; but the barometers can be read and registered without halting. The animals are very quiet and easily managed, much more so than the horses.'

They crossed the Loddon River at Kerang, and on September 6 rode into Swan Hill (which was also known as Castle Donnington), their first important objective. Here they camped on the banks of the Murray, about half a mile to the south of the town. Becker sent off three snakes in a bottle by Cobb's Coach to Melbourne.

They had now been nearly three weeks on the road, and it was time to take stock. One thing was absolutely clear; they had far too many stores with them, the expedition was overloaded. It was raining again and the drays or wagons had been left far behind on the track in heavy mud. When, four days later, they struggled into Swan Hill Burke decided to dump some of the stores, and put them up to public auction among the local settlers. From Melbourne meanwhile he had letters saying that the Committee was becoming seriously concerned at the growing expense of the expedition; the leader was urged to be as economical as possible. Could he not save money by dispensing with the hired drays on the next stage of his journey? At the same time the Committee urged him to make haste lest he should be forestalled by some rival expedition.

From now on Burke was to be under this constant jogging to get on, and it is worth taking particular notice of the fact, for it goes a long way towards explaining his actions. The expedition had attracted a great deal of attention. The Australian papers were full of discussions of its progress and of its chances of getting ahead of Stuart, who was known to be assembling yet another expedition at Adelaide, with a promise of a reward of several thousand pounds if he succeeded in crossing the continent. Stuart favoured horses, and Melbourne *Punch* came out with a poem and a cartoon entitled 'The Great Australian Exploration Race'. It depicted Burke mounted high above the desert on a camel and gazing apprehensively at the determined little figure of Stuart trotting on a pony at his side. The poem declared:

> *A race! A race! so great a one*
> *The world ne'er saw before;*
> *A race! A race! across this land*
> *From south to northern shore.*
>
> *The horseman hails from Adelaide*
> *The camel rider's ours—*
> *Now let the steed maintain his speed*
> *Against the camel's powers.*

Macadam wrote: 'My dearest Burke, Every success; all well—one especially—you know who![1] Everyone wishes you well. The honour of Victoria is in your hands. We know and feel assured that you will vindicate the confidence reposed in you. May God bless and preserve you. Yours ever, J.M.'

Stawell, the chairman of the Committee, went further; he wrote:

[1] Probably a reference to Julia Matthews.

'My dear Burke,

I have just returned from Beechworth Circuit Court and heard of Stuart's expedition ... As he is now to start with an increased number—12 in all and 36 horses—it will to a certain extent be a race between you and him—now I know how exciting this must be to you or to anyone with a spark of spirit and now will come the time of trial for your coolness and caution. Hitherto I think you have done as well as you could have done since you left us. We all made the expedition too large—for that you were no more to blame than we were, but you have corrected the mistake as prudently I think as was possible. Stuart's party after all his experience will be about the same in number as yours—but you are much better equipped and the 60 mile plain of which he speaks as presenting him so much difficulty will not stop you very long.

'I do not offer you any suggestion about your route; you will determine that yourself, so soon as you receive the last accounts of Stuart. Depend on this that so long as you act as you have hitherto done the Committee to a man will support you and under any circumstances you know you have one you can rely on. I trust you were not annoyed at the newspaper paragraphs and letters. I know when you are by yourself such matters—unexplained—produce a different impression than if they were merely read in Melbourne—but you know how to appreciate them.[1]

'The Committee were rather alarmed at finding the expense greater than they anticipated...

'Adieu my dear Burke,

                    Your sincere friend,

                              William F. Stawell.'

Now in point of fact Burke never received either of these letters, but he was very well aware of the feeling in Melbourne, and it can hardly have been less than irritating now, at Swan Hill, to be urged to push on and at the same time cut the expense. Moreover, while the idea of a race was well enough, it hardly created the right atmosphere for a serious scientific expedition. By September 11, however, they were ready to go on again; the party attended a farewell banquet given by the settlers of Swan Hill, and in the afternoon crossed the Murray

[1] A reference to Burke's critics who had been attacking him in the Melbourne Press.

and camped on the New South Wales side. The route now lay due north to Balranald on the Murrumbidgee, and still they progressed from homestead to homestead on the flat plain; Becker speaks of a young lady in a black riding-gown named Ann Jane Jones who led them into 'M'Kenzie's place'. On September 15 they rode into Balranald, which was then an outpost of a couple of dozen sheds of bark, timber, calico and even paper. A 'wretched punt' ferried them across the Murrumbidgee.

The troubles of the little group had now become acute. The wagons were still miles behind, the expense of hiring them was growing greater every day, and the male camels were fighting over the females and breaking loose; worse still, John Drakeford, the cook, got drunk and some of the other men were giving trouble. Burke decided to take drastic action. He dumped another consignment of stores: 15½ cwt. of sugar, 8 demijohns of lime-juice, 2 rifles and several revolvers, and three tents with their poles. Some of the troublesome men were dismissed, and Ferguson, the American foreman, was asked to accept a reduction of salary. When he refused and resigned Burke let him go.[1]

Some, but not all, of these dealings were wise. The strength of the party was not seriously reduced; Burke had been able to pick up an extra man named Charles Gray in Swan Hill, and he had also been joined by William Hodgkinson, a young journalist attached to the Melbourne *Age* and a very able bushman. On the other hand, he was getting the reputation of being rather highhanded and liable to lose his temper when opposed; and in this country where scurvy was so prevalent one would have thought that other stores, rather than sugar and lime-juice, should have been left behind. Shortly after this the Committee in Melbourne received an anonymous letter from a settler saying that the quarrelling and money-grubbing in the expedition were disgraceful. They should look to the example of Dr. Livingstone in Africa. It was absurd to send so many valuable stores up-country and then auction them.

Burke meanwhile was forcing the pace. After only one day at Balranald they struck out for Menindie on the Darling, 160 miles away. It was dry, flat country where the horses pulling the

---

[1] Ferguson sued the Committee for wrongful dismissal when he got back to Melbourne, and obtained a judgement for £183 6s. 8d.

drays could make scarcely one and a half miles an hour through the sand, and still great storms, rising to hurricane force, burst upon them. The nights were very cold, and there was hoar frost on the ground in the morning. 'The scenery,' says Becker, 'was marked by great silence: scarcely a bird was seen or a note heard from them.' Up to this point he had found time to make drawings of the passing landscape and the blacks' encampments, of birds, insects and lizards, and he had kept up his diary and natural history reports, which were a vital part of the purpose of the expedition. Now all this was changed. Burke gave orders to Becker and Beckler that they must abandon their scientific observations and take their share of the manual work as ordinary assistants. All the camels and horses, he said, were needed to carry stores, and any clothing or instruments that exceeded the weight of 30 lb. per man must be left behind at one of the stations for the time being.

Becker, being older than the others, felt very much the strain of the heavy work of loading and unloading the 400–lb. packs of the camels—a job which took several hours every day—and when one of the horses stepped on his foot he became lame. Often he was still up at midnight working on his notes by lamplight. 'You should have seen old B——'s face,' Burke wrote in a letter to Melbourne, 'upon my announcing that all the officers would have to act as working men, and that we should only carry 30 lb. of baggage for each man. Loading camels and then marching them 20 miles is no joke. The first two days of it nearly choked poor B——, and I think he will not be able to stand it much longer.' It was a callous letter, but it is only fair to remember that Burke was under some strain, and perhaps was forced to be ruthless in order to get his unwieldy party over the ground. After all, this was a military operation of a kind, many hazards still lay before them, and a physically weak man could be a danger to them all.

Towards the end of September they reached the Darling River at a point somewhat upstream from its junction with the Murray, and they found it rising and 'café-au-lait' in colour. The bed of the river was thickly wooded with many varieties of eucalyptus, mulga, box, black oak, native pine and a very pretty acacia which, at this season of the year, was just coming into flower with a lemon-coloured blossom. In these drier latitudes new insects and reptiles were beginning to appear; there was a caterpillar which made a nest like that of the weaver birds—a ball of writhing grubs suspended from the branches—and it demolished entirely the foliage from the trees. If one touched these nests a painful irritation was set up and it lasted for days. There was also a little black scaly lizard with a stumpy tail that looked equally harmless and was equally poisonous. Its face had the mild expression of a kitten, and it lay dull and motionless in the dust; but a bite from its great triangular bird-like mouth left a suppurating sore. The goanna, which was a lizard resembling a monitor, grew up to four feet or more in length, and went scuttling up the bare branches of the trees; and everywhere they met emus, pacing away like enormous chickens on their horny toes, and great dark kangaroos. Now too on the river bank they were back with the birds again: pelicans circling round an up-draught to gain height, brilliantly coloured parrots and cockatoos, and the small olive-green butcher bird uttering its bugle call. Becker and the surgeon sketched, made notes and collected specimens whenever they could.

Burke in the meantime was engaged in a blood row with Landells over the camels. For some time he had been critical of the way they were being handled—they were constantly straying—and he did not believe that their famous rum ration was really necessary to prevent them from contracting scurvy. Landells, on the other hand, was very solicitous about his animals, which he regarded as his own personal charge, and he objected to Burke's interference. He went about the camp declaring that Burke was unfit for the leadership, that he was mad—so mad that it was dangerous to stay in the same tent with him—that if he remained in charge the expedition would go to the devil. 'I have,' Landells wrote later to the Committee, 'on several occasions entertained grave doubts about his sanity. His temper was quite ungovernable. He usually carried loaded fire-arms and often I was fearful that he would use them dangerously while in a passion.'

Some of the members of the party, notably Dr. Beckler, the surgeon, were inclined to take Landells' side in the affair, but young Wills, the surveyor, was not. Up to this point Wills had been an important but very self-effacing member of the party.

He had refused to be photographed at the departure from Melbourne, he had gone quietly and persistently about his work, charting the route, making his reports in a neat, scholarly hand, taking his share of the heavy manual work and instantly obeying his orders. He wrote to Dr. Neumayer (who had accompanied the expedition for some distance and had now left it) a very sober account of the dispute, saying that a most unhappy atmosphere had developed and that, while he was still friendly with Landells, there was no doubt that Landells was intriguing against the leader.

'It came out,' Wills wrote, 'that Mr. L. had been playing a fine game, trying to set us all together by the ears. To Mr. Burke he has been abusing and finding fault with all of us: so much so that Mr. B. tells me Landells positively hates me. We have apparently been the best of friends. To me, he has been abusing Mr. Burke, and has always spoken as if he hated the Doctor and Mr. Becker; whereas with them he has been all milk and honey. There is scarcely a man in the party whom he has not urged Mr. Burke to dismiss.'

Later on it was going to be suggested that Landells was a coward, that he deliberately inflamed the quarrel with Burke because he did not intend to continue with the expedition once it left the settled districts. There seems to be no truth in this at all. He was a complainer—what the Australians call a 'no-hoper'—a man who always thought he was being put upon, and he had a strong vein of hysteria in his character, but there is no reason to doubt his courage. He had done very well in getting the camels to Australia in the first place, and we have Ludwig Becker's word that he had worked extremely hard in bringing them thus far from Melbourne.

The truth seems to be that the expedition was falling into two camps: those like Wills who were fired by Burke's vigorous way of handling things, and those who thought him altogether too slapdash and impulsive. The first group were mostly younger men and, because they liked Burke's style, they were perfectly ready to forgive him an occasional outburst of temper, it made him seem more human. But Landells and the older men were not so ready to indulge him. They did not like being treated as schoolboys or police recruits, to be encouraged one minute and abused the next, and Burke's Irish quixotry was to them merely a sign of arrogance and instability. Beckler, the surgeon, a man of teutonic thoroughness, was, we know, seriously alarmed at what might happen under such an erratic leader once they were entirely removed from civilization; but like Ludwig Becker, who was a mild and biddable fellow, he would probably never have forced an open breach of his own accord. The fact that they were both German, and in a minority, may also have had something to do with the matter. But Landells was an Englishman who considered himself every bit as good as Burke; he was not exactly a subtle character—his contemporaries describe him as a heavily built man with rather a lowering, sullen manner—and when Burke ordered him about he answered back.

A series of violent quarrels seems to have ensued, and Landells, having written out his resignation, was barely persuaded by Burke to rescind it. It was clearly a situation which could not continue, and matters came to a head when they reached Kinchega, an outlying sheep station on the Darling, some six miles from Menindie. Here by some means not altogether clear, either by purchase from Landells or by theft, the sheep shearers on the station broached the camels' rum. There followed a wild debauch in which some of the expedition's assistants probably took part, and Burke, when he heard of it, declared that he had had enough: the remainder of the rum was to be abandoned and not one drop of alcohol was to be carried further by any member of the party. Landells, at the end of another towering scene about the swimming of the camels across the Darling, resigned and departed for Melbourne. Dr. Beckler also resigned, saying that he could not endure the manner in which Burke had addressed his second in command, but he agreed to remain with the expedition until a replacement could be sent up from Melbourne. So now, harassed by dissension in his camp, by shortage of money and shortage of time, and with his wagons still a long way in his rear and the summer coming on, Burke set up his camp in Menindie.

Menindie (or Menindee as it is now spelt) is a native word that means 'many waters', and it had been visited years before by the explorer Mitchell, who had named it Laidley's Lakes. Sturt, as we have seen, had made a depot there in 1845. It was an obvious point of departure into the centre. The Darling here breaks up into half a dozen swamps and lakes which give ample water for drinking throughout the year, and the stream is navigable all the way down to the Murray; in fact, one of Captain Cadell's paddle-boats arrived with stores the day Burke marched into the settlement. Northwards the land is flat and parched, but here on the lakes large trees grow to an age of many hundreds of years, and there is usually fodder for sheep and cattle. It is not quite like an oasis—the surrounding country is a great deal more fertile than a desert—yet there is a sense here of respite from the overwhelming sun, a feeling of refuge from the aridity and harshness that lies beyond, and it is a frontier of a kind. Seagulls and many other waterfowl fly over the water and there is a crystalline quality in the dry air; temperatures of 90 degrees in the shade mean nothing at all. At sun-set a blue light rests on the lakes and against the bright orange colour of the banks you will sometimes see the monolithic silhouette of a kangaroo and the shapes of pelicans settling down on a sandbank for the night. Tempests can rage here and frightful dust-storms, but normally there is a monumental stillness in the sky.

At the time of Burke's arrival in October 1860, Menindie was still an outpost and no other settlements lay beyond towards the centre. It consisted of a little handful of shacks, a shanty pub run by a man named Thomas Paine, one of Captain Cadell's stores, an outhouse or two, and a landing-stage for the river steamers. A few tribesmen hung about the settlement and could be employed as guides and labourers. It was very much a pioneers' centre, a jumping-off place for the interior. There was a constant come and go of settlers pushing out in search of new grazing lands, new lakes and rivers, and the local gossip was mainly concerned with who was 'out', and how far they had gone, and what they had found, and when they were expected back again. Every new arrival and his equipment were closely inspected and commented upon; every man who returned to the settlement was questioned about his experiences, his dealings with the blacks, the route he had taken and the condition of the waterholes. Thus it was an obvious place for Burke to re-group, and make a permanent camp while he was waiting for his wagons to come up.

His arrival caused a great stir in Menindie; nothing quite like this had been seen before, such a mass of equipment, such an imposing train of animals, carts, tents, baggage and men. To the veterans on the station there was, no doubt, a slightly 'new chum' air about the expedition, an impression of eager amateurishness, but they were very ready to do business with these important strangers who had come up 'from town'.

Burke was not long in making his appointments. First, for the vacant position of second in command, he chose young Wills who was every day showing his ability. Next King, the soldier from India, was given charge of the camels and the three sepoys. Brahe, the German, was installed as foreman; he was an educated man who had had experience on both sheep stations and on the goldfields, and recently Wills had been giving him instruction in the use of surveying instruments. In addition an entirely new recruit for the party was found, a man who was destined to alter all their lives. This was William Wright, whom they had fallen in with at Kinchega. Until recently Wright had been manager of the station there, but a change of ownership had taken place and he had been dismissed from his post. Wright was not a very prepossessing man—he was an illiterate who could barely write his own name—but Burke seems to have got on well with him from the first; he was a practised bushman and he had already been out over the country to the north. He was enlisted on a temporary basis, mainly in the capacity of a guide.

The party was now composed of:

Officers:	Burke, leader;
	Wills, the surveyor, second in command;
	Dr. Beckler, the surgeon, due for replacement;
	Ludwig Becker;
	William Wright;
	Brahe, the new foreman.
Assistants:	Hodgkinson;
	Gray;
	McDonough;
	Patton;
	King, now in charge of camels;
	Three Indian sepoys.

A total of fourteen in all, and later on three men, Charles Stone,

William Purcell and John Smith, who were station hands at Menindie, were added.

For the first few days at Menindie they were kept busy sorting out their equipment and stores. A more suitable camp was then found about seven miles up the Darling on a spit of land where the Pamamaroo Creek came in, and preparations were made for removing there.

Burke's position was very difficult. The season was now well advanced and the local settlers warned him against exposing himself to the extreme summer temperatures in the centre. Cooper's Creek, his next objective, was more than 400 miles away to the north, and a great deal of the intervening ground was unexplored and possibly waterless. On the other hand, he had his orders to press on, and it was not in his own nature to sit idly on the Darling for the next three or four months waiting for rain to fall. Wright was willing to act as guide for the first part of the way, and thought that they would get through to the permanent water at Cooper's Creek, provided they had no trouble from the blacks. So now Burke made his decision to split the expedition into two groups: a small, lightly-laden party would push on while the remainder set up the depot at Menindie and rested some of the animals that had fallen ill. This rear party would then follow on in his wake with the heavy stores.

For the advance column Burke chose eight men: himself, Wills, Brahe, King, Gray, McDonough, Patton and a sepoy, Dost Mahomet (he was not actually an Indian but a Pathan from Kashmir), and they were to take the best sixteen camels and fifteen horses. Wright was to lead them for the first few days. Becker was invited to join the advance party, but was told that there would be no time for scientific research and that he would have to walk the whole way. Since he was still lame this was manifestly impossible, and he was left behind with Dr. Beckler, who was to take charge of the Menindie group until his replacement arrived. There were obvious objections to this general plan: Burke was proposing to advance without a doctor or any scientist other than his surveyor, and with only a fraction of his stores. But he was confident that they would all eventually catch up with him on Cooper's Creek before he set off on the next stage to the north. He wrote to his sister in Ireland: 'I am *confident* of success, but know that failure is possible; and I feel that failure would, to me, be ruin; but I am determined to succeed, and count on completing my work within a year at farthest.'

It had been an appalling start: five men had already left the expedition with bitterness, and a sixth was about to go. Instead of this weary month of dragging unwanted stores up from Melbourne how much better it would have been to have followed Gregory's advice or to have come up on the shorter route from Port Augusta. Yet perhaps the worst of the expedition's administrative troubles were over, and it was a good thing that the weaker men and the useless stores had been discarded before the real adventure began. All the members of the advance party were healthy and seemed eager to go on; King, in the absence of Landells, was handling the camels very well. Then, too, there was a certain feeling of exhilaration in putting civilization and all its petty difficulties behind them. On October 19 they marched out of Menindie to the north.

CHAPTER FIVE

Menindie to Cooper's Creek

Wright led them off along a route that was somewhat to the east of Sturt's track of fifteen years before, and by making twenty miles a day they hoped to accomplish the 400-mile journey to Cooper's Creek in under a month. It was a pity they had left the scientists behind because they were now breaking fresh ground, and with every mile they were coming on plants, insects, birds and natural phenomena that had never been observed, or at any rate classified, before. For anyone whose eye was customarily filled with green in nature it was, perhaps, a desolate country, but now the spring had begun and wild flowers were starting to cover the red earth; wild hops of a brilliant magenta colour, the yellow and white marshmallow, Sturt's wild pea (which proved to be quite harmless to the camels), an everlasting daisy, its petals as dry as paper, the salt bush and the blue bush.

For mile after mile the plain stretched away in front of them, and even a small object on the horizon—a low line of purple hills, a clump of gums round a waterhole—became a great goal to be reached because it was new, because it was something on which to fix the mind in so much uneventful space. By night

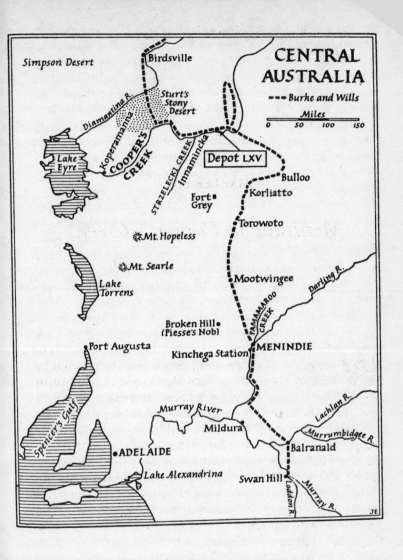

CENTRAL
AUSTRALIA

- - - Burke and Wills

Miles

0   50   100   150

Simpson Desert

Birdsville

Sturt's
Stony
Desert

Diamantina R.

Koperamana

COOPER'S
CREEK

Lake
Eyre

STRZELECKI CREEK

Innamincka

Depot LXV

Bulloo

Korliatto

Fort
Grey

Torowoto

Mt. Hopeless

Mt. Searle

Lake
Torrens

Mootwingee

Darling R.

PAMAMAROO CREEK

Broken Hill
(Piesse's Nob)

Port Augusta

Kinchega Station   MENINDIE

Spencer's Gulf

Murray River

Lachlan R.

Mildura

Murrumbidgee R.

ADELAIDE

Balranald

Lake Alexandrina

Swan Hill

Loddon R.

Murray R.

JE

nlight flooded down, and in this clear air the stars
to multiply and become twice their natural size; once
w seconds a meteor blazed over their heads trailing a tail
lliant light, and then suddenly went out. Being so numer-
ou a party there was no real reason for them to be afraid of the
blacks who appeared from time to time; they merely stood and
gazed open-mouthed at the camels and then ran off jabbering
into the distance. No amount of calling and friendly gestures
could bring them nearer than the distance of a spear's throw.
Nevertheless each night Burke hobbled his animals and set a
guard on the camp.

Presently they arrived at a point where the plain broke up
into jagged hills and gullies, and the storm-water, coursing
along gutters in the natural rock, had gathered in deep silent
pools. This was Mootwingee, a native word meaning 'green
grass'. Even today it is an extraordinary place, for there is much
evidence here of the existence of an inland sea in prehistoric
times; marine fossils are found, and the conglomerate rock,
which looks like a currant pudding, is filled with pebbles that
appear to have been formed by the action of rough waves. The
weight of oldness in these rocks, possibly some 500 million
years, is very great. Strange trees and plants dot the landscape
and straggle up the ravines: the beefwood with its dark corru-
gated bark and its blood-red timber, the leopard tree coated with
a spotted parchment, the flowering acacia, grass with the scent
of lemons, native pines and snow-white gums that do not grow
like other trees but twist and turn in grotesque shapes. Except
for the screeching of the white and pink cockatoos there is great
silence and immobility in the landscape. The big red kangaroo
and the emu vanish without a sound; it is a place of snakes and
lizards, the carpet snake and the little gecko with its padded
toes, and of small creatures like the hedgehog and a grey mouse
that hops. A dragonfly of pure scarlet hovers above the green
slime of the pools, and in the sand the ant-lion makes his hole
and waits for the black ant to slither down the slope into his
jaws. In the pale blue sky the wedge-tailed eagle spreads his six-
foot wings and cruises in endless circles, watching the ground
below.

For the blacks this was a sacred place. They came here for
their circumcision rites and other tribal ceremonies, and in the

overhanging caves they made drawings and rock carvings. They stencilled the outlines of their delicate hands and the soles of their feet by placing them on the rockface and by blowing a spray of red ochre over them from their mouths. They drew a carpet snake twenty-eight feet long and chipped out the outlines of kangaroos, emus, boomerangs, the diminutive figures of men, patterns of flowers, and knobbed elongated objects which may have been lizards or phallic symbols. They piled up ceremonial mounds of rocks and hollowed out flat stones on which to grind the nardoo seed. And from sharp pebbles they made axe-heads and the 'bull-roarer', which is a notched stone that is whirled around at the end of a string and gives forth a roaring noise. It must have echoed sepulchrally in these silent ravines. Ludwig Becker would have delighted in all this, but Burke and his party appear to have gone by Mootwingee almost with a shudder. Wills in his field-book speaks of 'gloomy gullies', and despite the abundant water they did not camp.

Then again they were out on the boundless plain, working their way from creek to creek. At every camping-place they cut a prominent 'B' and the number of the camp in Roman numerals into a tree, so that eventually the rear party could follow on their route. When they had covered 200 miles without mishap Burke called a halt at a place they called Torowoto Swamp, and here it was arranged that Wright should turn back. Burke wrote a letter to the Committee for him to take with him, and in it he reported that they had been travelling through 'fine sheep-grazing country', that both horses and camels had improved in condition and that all the party were well.

He then goes on: 'Mr. Wright returns from here to Menindie. I informed him that I should consider him third officer of the expedition, subject to the approval of the Committee, from the day of our departure from Menindie, and hope that they will confirm the appointment. In the meantime I have instructed him to follow me up with the remainder of the camels to Cooper's Creek, to take steps to procure a quantity of salt meat; and I have written to the doctor (Beckler) to inform him that I have accepted his resignation, as although I was anxious to await the decision of the Committee, the circumstances will not admit of delay, and he has positively refused to leave the settled districts. I am willing to admit that he did his best until his fears for the safety of the party overcame him, but those fears, I think, clearly show how unfit he is for his post. If Mr. Wright is allowed to follow out the instructions I have given him I am confident that the result will be satisfactory; and if the Committee think proper to make inquiries with regard to him, they will find that he is well qualified for the post, and that he bears the very highest character.

'I shall proceed on from here to Cooper's Creek. I may, or may not, be able to send back from there until we are followed up, perhaps it would not be prudent to divide the party; the natives here have told Mr. Wright that we shall meet with opposition on our way there. Perhaps I might find it advisable to have a depot at Cooper's Creek, and to go on with a small party to examine the country beyond it. Under any circumstances, it is desirable that we should be soon followed up. I consider myself very fortunate in having Mr. Wills as my second in command. He is a capital officer, zealous and untiring in the performance of his duties, and I trust that he will remain my second as long as I am in charge of the expedition.

'The men all conduct themselves admirably, and they are most anxious to go on, but the Committee may rely upon it that I shall go on speedily and carefully, and that I shall endeavour not to lose a chance, or to run any unnecessary risk.

'I have, etc. R. O'Hara Burke, Leader.'

In a private letter to an uncle in Ireland Burke was much more explicit about Landells and Beckler. 'My second in command and doctor,' he wrote, 'resigned at Menindie from sheer cowardice when they saw that I was determined to go on, as they wanted to pass the summer on the Darling. They will of course assign other reasons.' He went on to say that he was very proud of the new well-grassed country he had discovered and was eager to go on. 'However,' he ends, 'rely upon it that I shall take care of them [his men] and myself and not run any unnecessary risks. Goodbye. My best love to Hessie [his sister], Lady Cloncurry and all. Your aft. nephew, R. O'Hara Burke.'

Before Wright left, Burke lined up his men and asked if any of them wished to take this opportunity of returning to Menindie. None wished to do so.

On October 29 Wright set off for the south, and Burke turned north into the unknown once more. As they penetrated deeper

into the centre it was still cold in the early mornings but very
hot by day, and they were so beset by flies and dust they wore
goggles and veils. Beyond Torowoto Swamp the land became
steadily drier and the rocky ground made the going difficult.
But they were getting a rhythm into their march, and there was
still water to be found; whenever they reached a rise Wills
climbed to the top and was sure to see a creek lined with mulga
and box trees cutting the plain ahead. Even if the creek was dry
there would be waterholes with polygonum reeds growing
about it, and the camels thrived on the salt bushes and the
native grasses. If they were yearning for their rum there was no
sign of it.

Burke himself did not keep a field-book, but Wills wrote
elaborate notes which he read over to his leader every night.
Thus we learn in some detail how they came within sight of
Sturt's old track above Torowoto and then continued on over
the Queensland border—that border which had been marked
on the map but never traversed—to Bulloo. Whenever they did
not pick up a native name for some feature in the landscape they
honoured one of their own party; and so we have Brahe's Creek,
Wright's Creek, Mount King and so on—names, incidentally,
which have long since been replaced and forgotten. Most of the
way they saw very little of the natives, and except for wild dogs
and occasional emus and kangaroos very few animals. But
where there was water there was life. At Bulloo they found an
encampment of some sixty blacks, and there were fish in the
swamp and vast flocks of birds. Like Robinson Crusoe they
now came upon unexplained tracks in the sand: wheel marks
that had apparently been made by a dray, and later on the hoof
prints of a solitary horse. They thought that these might have
been the traces of some settler pushing out alone into the
unknown in search of grazing grounds, but they found no other
sign.[1]

For a while they cast about through a series of low ridges that
looked like flat-topped hills in the distance, and all the
surrounding ground was covered with sharp dark brown stones
that were terrible to walk on. These ridges, and the constant
search for water, took them on a circuitous course, but at last,
on November 11, twenty-three days out from Menindie, they

[1]See page 136.

struck Cooper's Creek on latitude 27.49 and longitude 142.20.
It was every bit as fine as Sturt had described it fifteen years
before: deep waterholes of a mile or more in length and wooded
with eucalyptus, polygonum grass and the dark red mulga with
its paper-like bark curling off the trunk and its leaves or spines
like those of a casuarina tree. Everywhere, Wills noted, there
were logs and bushes caught high up in the forks of the trees,
indicating that there had recently been violent and destructive
floods.

A plague of rats descended upon them as soon as they made
camp; nothing was safe unless it was suspended from the
branches of trees, and they kept moving downstream in search
of a better place. At the same time Burke kept casting north of
the creek for a route along which he could make his march towards the Gulf of Carpentaria. He himself first went out with
Brahe and returned on the second day without finding water.
Next Wills set out with McDonough and three camels, and they
reached a point ninety miles north of the Cooper before they
turned back defeated; indeed, they very nearly died of thirst.
Their camels strayed in the night and could not be found, and
it was only by their making a forced march of forty-eight hours
on foot that they managed to rejoin the others. Two more forays
to the north were equally fruitless, and Burke decided that his
only chance now was to go down the creek until he got on to
Sturt's old track and then strike up towards the Gulf. But first
he had to set up a depot. Some miles downstream from the point
where they had originally reached the Cooper they found a site
on the northern bank of a fine stretch of water, and a camp was
marked out beside a large coolibah tree. It was in many ways
a beautiful place, with the water curving round, fairly thick
trees to give them shade and an outlook across the creek to the
green polygonum reeds and the belt of eucalypts on the other
side. Birds of every kind teemed in thousands, and there were
fish as well as mussels to be had from the creek. This place they
called Depot LXV and the large coolibah tree was marked
accordingly.

It was now very hot—up to 109 degrees in the shade—but this
heat, Wills wrote, was no worse than anything they had endured in Melbourne because of the dryness of the air. He made
light of their experiences in a letter to his sister in England:

'The journey hitherto has been but a picnic party.' And this despite the fact that 'for water such as *you* would not even taste, one smacks one's lips as if it were a glass of sherry or champagne'. Wills' physical toughness at this stage was astonishing; in his various reconnaissances from Cooper's Creek he must have covered nearly 500 miles, many of them on foot.

It was now mid-December, but Burke was not greatly worried at the failure of Wright to appear; for the moment they had plenty of provisions. He decided that there was no real necessity to wait for Wright's arrival, since he was bound to turn up within a few days—no real reason why he should not push on with the vital part of the adventure that still lay before them, the dash to the Gulf of Carpentaria. The party would have to be split up again: four men—Brahe, Patton, McDonough and the Indian, Dost Mahomet—would remain behind at Depot LXV to build a stockade and to receive Wright on his arrival. The remainder—himself, Wills, Gray and King—would go on with six of the best camels and one horse and try to break through to the Gulf by way of Sturt's route along Eyre's Creek.

On December 13 Burke wrote to the Committee reporting his movements up to date, and saying that he had now established a permanent depot at Camp LXV. 'The feed upon this creek is good,' he wrote, 'and the horses and camels have greatly improved in condition; but the flies, mosquitoes and rats which abound here render it a very disagreeable summer residence.

'From Camp 63 we made very frequent excursions, in order to endeavour, in accordance with instructions, to find a practicable route northward between Gregory's and Sturt's tracks, but without success ... I am satisfied that a practicable route cannot be established in that direction, except during the rainy season, or by sinking wells, as the natives have evidently abandoned that part of the country for want of water, which is shown by their having sunk for water in all directions in the beds of the creeks...

'I have therefore left instructions for the officers in charge of the party, which I expect will shortly arrive, to endeavour during my absence to find a better and shorter route between the depot [Camp LXV] and Wright's Creek [near Torowoto], or between the depot and the Darling. I proceed on tomorrow with the party as per margin [he wrote the names of his party

on the side], to Eyre's Creek. And from thence I shall endeavour
to explore the country to the north of it in the direction of
Carpentaria, and it is my intention to return here within the
next three months at latest.

'I shall leave the party which remain here under the charge
of Mr. Brahe, in whom I have every confidence. The feed is very
good. There is no danger to be apprehended from the natives
if they are properly managed, and there is, therefore, nothing
to prevent the party remaining here until our return, or until
the provisions run short.

'I did not intend to start so soon, but we have had some severe
thunderstorms lately, with every appearance of a heavy fall of
rain to the north; and as I have given the other route a fair trial,
I do not wish to lose so favourable an opportunity.

'We are all in good health, and the conduct of the men has
been admirable. Mr. Wills co-operates cordially with me. He is
a most zealous and efficient officer. I have promoted Mr. Brahe
to the rank of officer. The position he is now placed in rendered
it absolutely necessary that I should do so. He is well qualified
for the post, and I hope the Committee will confirm the appointment.

'I have given instructions to Mr. Brahe to forward this letter
by the first opportunity.

'I have, etc. R. O'Hara Burke, Leader.'

There appears to have been some discussion between Burke
and Brahe as to what should be done if the party did *not* get back
within three months. But Burke was very confident; he thought
they might even make the whole journey within a month. He
had no intention either of finding a ship on the Gulf to take
him back to civilization or of returning on a new route to the
east coast through the settled districts of Queensland; he would
return to Cooper's Creek. In any case, Burke said, if Wright
arrived within the next few days Brahe was to follow on with
a small party and deliver any dispatches Wright had brought,
but after a few days it would be too late and Brahe was to stay
where he was. No written instructions were given to Brahe; it
was simply understood between them that he was to expect
Burke back at a maximum of three months, and that if, by some
mischance, Burke did not return within that time, he was to
hang on as long as his provisions lasted and then take his party

back to the Darling.

Two horses were now killed and the meat was jerked—that is to say, it was cut into strips and dried—and a division of the provisions was made. Burke's share was 3cwt. of flour, 50lb. of oatmeal, 100lb. of the dried horseflesh, 100lb. of bacon and salt pork, 30 or 40lb. of biscuit, 50lb. of rice, 50lb. of sugar, 12lb. of tea, 5lb. of salt, and a few tins of preserved vegetables and butter; quite sufficient, it was judged, to keep four men alive for twelve weeks. They also carried guns and ammunition and hoped to shoot game along the way. There was no liquor, and they had no tents.

On the night before their departure Burke handed over to Brahe a number of sealed papers with instructions that if he should die or not return they should be burnt. There is some evidence that these letters contained references to Julia Matthews, that having left a will in her favour Burke had now thought better of it, but nothing really certain is known. Apart from his salary he had very little to leave; indeed, he had debts amounting to £18 5s. 3d. at the Melbourne Club.

Wills also left a number of private papers and letters behind, and to Brahe he gave an aneroid barometer and four thermometers so that he could keep meteorological records at Cooper's Creek.

On Sunday, December 16, the camels were packed in the early dawn, and at 6.40 a.m. Burke lined up the men who were to stay behind. It seems to have been an emotional farewell; all of them wanted to go with him, and Patton was in tears. 'Patton,' Burke said, 'you must not fret; I shall be back in a short time. If I am not back in a few months you may go away to the Darling.'

With this they were off. Brahe rode with them a distance of twenty-two miles to their first camp further down the creek and then returned to the depot. Just before he left Brahe said to King, 'Goodbye, King, I do not expect to see you for at least four months.'

Now finally they were on their own. They were doing what Gregory had expressly advised them not to do: travelling in mid-summer. They had no line of communication with their rear and no maps for their forward journey. If any of them fell ill there was no doctor to attend to them. Apart from Wills, there was no trained man to take note of their discoveries, of the rocks, the plants, the wild life or the natives. In short, it was an expedition no longer: it was an endurance test, a race.

But they were all in good spirits, all of them had been toughened by the journey from the Darling, and the animals were rested after a month's good feeding on the Cooper. Burke himself had certainly not lost heart.

CHAPTER SIX

To the Gulf

They were now getting to know one another very well. The social distinctions remained: Burke and Wills were officers and gentlemen and gave orders, Gray and King were men and did what they were told. But they were now committed together, all of them were encompassed by the same risks, the same hardships and the same hope; and this feeling of a shared adventure counted for much more than the differences between officers and men, between Irish and English and between the young and the older. Any weakness in one man weakened them all, and each little triumph—a day's march completed, a lost camel brought back, a waterhole discovered—was a shared accomplishment. Moreover, they were now building up that intimate network of habits, the knowing of one another's abilities and failings and oddities, and the acceptance of these things, that develops among any group of men who are isolated on a long journey and entirely dependent upon one another. One man was best with a rifle, another at cooking, a third with his physical strength, and all these matters were established

without pride or jealousy and were fitted into a pattern. Everything depended of course upon their liking and respecting one
another, and this they evidently did. Burke was accepted as the
unquestioned leader, and even when they doubted his judgement they thought his leadership was more important than any
error he might commit. Wills was their navigator and techni-
cian. None of them would ever have dreamed of contesting his
calculations, and he was so thorough and painstaking they
never at any time got lost. King was only 22, and by some way
the most junior of the party. He had entirely recovered from his
illness in India, and now he was a strong, rather serious-minded
boy, eager to be thought well of; and he was particularly
devoted to Burke.

Gray, who was originally a sailor, was in his forties and a year
or two older than Burke. But there was something about him—
a lack of presumption, a take-it-easy sort of fatalism, an aura
of good nature—that made everyone call him Charley. Probably he wasn't very bright. Long afterwards Thomas Dick, the
publican who had employed Gray at Swan Hill, came forward
with a public statement about him. Before Gray joined the
expedition he had employed him, Dick said, for fifteen months
'as a general servant, at another time as a cook, at another as
an ostler, and another as a puntsman for the punt across the
River Murray. In fact, when I was short-handed, or any of the
servants got the worse for drink, I generally made a point of
sacking them at once. Gray was the only man I had to fall back
upon in every respect.'

'Was he a sober man?' Dick was asked.

'A sober man. He has been repeatedly the worse for drink
when he got his wages once a month, as I settled with him once
a month. He might take a spree for an afternoon or something
like that, but as a general tippler I wish to state he was not.'

'Was he a stout hearty man?'

'A stout hearty man and a better bushman was not to be
found.'

And so, given these circumstances, which were not at all easy,
they were an integrated and resourceful group; for the purposes
of this long walk—1,500 miles to the Gulf and back to Cooper's
Creek—they knew what they were doing. Only at times of crisis
were the animals ridden; all were needed to carry water and

stores. As a rule Burke and Wills walked ahead, keeping direction by turns with a pocket compass, while Gray followed on behind leading Billy, the horse, and King the six camels. It was never easy walking. Anyone who has been in the centre of Australia will bear witness to those sharp, ankle-twisting stones, the clay as hard as concrete and full of cracks, the peculiar stickiness of the mud in the swamps. After the first few steps the sweat starts out and one has to keep one hand free and swing it across one's face to deal with the pestilential, never-ending flies. One sees and hears and smells far more, of course, when one is on foot, but the mechanical monotony of this tremendous walk is something not easily to be understood by a twentieth-century mind; hour after hour, mile after mile and always the same plain ahead; never to arrive at anywhere really significant; always to get up in the morning with the prospect of doing the same thing all over again. The world narrows in these conditions; one's boots have the disembodied fascination of a clockwork pendulum, weariness is subdued by the dull compulsion of the rhythm, and ground is not ground but simply distance to be put behind one. In this apathy of movement, this concentration merely upon keeping going, this coma of walking, any intrusion is resented, and any call upon the mind is an effort.

And so the imagination that held these men on to their objective and the skill with which they overcame a thousand intrusions is something to be very much admired. They could not simply move ahead on a previously mapped-out course. They had to alter their direction when swamps and ridges blocked the way, they had to watch the flight of birds that might lead them to a waterhole, they had to know the right moment when it was time to call it a day. The sand-storms in the centre are frightful. It is not so much that the fine red dust makes a gritty coating over one's clothes and seems to bite into one's very skin: often one cannot see more than a few yards ahead. A hellish grey leaden light filters down; grass, leaves, every green thing and every flower are blasted, and the tumbleweed slithers past in the semi-darkness, tumbling over and over, scattering its seed, the lone thing doing any good for itself in this reversal of nature. Such storms can blow for days at a time; having blown the dust down from the north, the wind shifts round to the south and blows it straight back again, and all birds and animals go to ground. These were the days when the little party would have to pause and wait.

But for the most part they kept going, usually getting up at dawn and walking on for an hour or two before stopping for breakfast, and then on again. Sometimes, when the daytime heat was too fierce, they marched at night under the glow of the stars or the bright moon. They camped usually where there was feed for the camels. The daily rations were portioned out: each man had 1 lb. of damper, ¾ lb. of dried horsemeat, ¼ lb. of salt pork, ⅛ lb. of boiled rice, tea, sugar, but no fruit or vegetables. For vitamins they boiled portulaca, a succulent plant they found growing wild. The country yielded very little else; they could not spare the time for prolonged fishing or shooting and in any case most of the game was not palatable. Kangaroo meat is extremely tough, the emu is altogether uneatable, and the indigenous parrots were not much better.[1]

If our knowledge of the progress of the party depended upon Burke we would be little wiser; he was no diarist. His tattered notebook has survived with its clasp and its pocket in the side for a pencil, but the handwriting is often illegible and a number of pages have been torn out. Yet it is an interesting document. Apropos of nothing known to us, he starts off: 'Think well before giving an answer, and never speak except from strong convictions.' Then we get a short scrappy list of dates and camping places, and there follows:

'20*th* (*December* 1860).—Made a creek where we found a great many natives; they presented us with fish, and offered their women. Camp 70.

21*st*.—Made another creek: Camp 71. Splendid water; fine feed for the camels; would be a very good place for a station. Since we have left Cooper's Creek we have travelled over a very fine sheep-grazing country, well-watered, and in every respect well suited for occupation.

22*nd December* 1860.—Camp 72. Encamped on the borders of the desert.

23*rd*.—Travelled day and night, and encamped in the night in the bed of a creek, as we supposed we were near water.

[1] The recipe for cooking the beautiful galah is said to be as follows: you boil it with an old boot and when the boot is tender you throw the galah away and eat the boot.

24*th*.—Encamped on the morning of this day on the banks of Gray's Creek, called after him because he was detached on horseback from the party, and found it good water. The third day without it. Now for a retrospective glance. We started from Cooper's Creek, Camp 66, with the intention of going through to Eyre's Creek without water. Loaded with 800 pints of water, four riding camels carried 130 pints each, horse 150, two pack camels 50 each, and five pints each man.

25*th* (*Christmas Day*).—Started at 4 a.m. from Gray's Creek and arrived at a creek which appears to be quite as large as Cooper's Creek. At two pm Golah Sing (one of the camels) gave some very decided hints about stopping by lying down under the trees. Splendid prospect.

26*th December; 27th December; 29th December.*—Followed up the creek until it took a turn to the south-east which I thought rather too much to put up with, therefore left it on the morning of the 30th December; 12.30 on the road. Started at seven o'clock; travelled 11 hours.

31*st*.—Started 2.20; 16½ hours on the road. Travelled 13½ hours.

1*st January* (1861).—Water.

2*nd January*.—From King's Creek; 11 hours on the road. Started at seven; travelled nine and a half hours. Desert.

3*rd January*.— Five started. Travelled 12 hours, no minutes.

4*th*.—Twelve hours on the road.

5*th*.—Water at Wills' or King's Creek. It is impossible to say the time we were up, for we had to load the camels, to pack and feed them, to watch them and the horse, and to look for water; but I am satisfied that the frame of man never was more severely taxed.

13*th January*, 1861.—As I find it impossible to keep a regular diary, I shall jot down my ideas when I have an opportunity, and put the date. Upon two occasions, at Cooper's Creek and at King's Creek, on New Year's Day, whenever the natives tried to bully or bounce us, and were repulsed, although the leaders appeared to be in earnest, the followers and particularly the young ones, laughed heartily, and seemed to be amused at their leader's repulse. The old fellow at King's Creek, who stuck his spear into the ground, and threw dust in the air, when I fired off my pistol, ran off in the most undignified manner. Names for places: Thackeray, Barry, Bindon, Lyons, Forbes, Archer, Bennet, Colles, O. S. Nicholson, Wood, Wrixon, Cope, Turner, Scratchley, Ligar, Griffith, Green, Roe, Hamilton, Colles.

18*th January.*—Still on the ranges; the camels sweating profusely from fear.

20*th January.*—I determined today to go straight at the ranges, and so far the experiment has succeeded well. The poor camels sweating and groaning, but we gave them a hot bath in Turner's Creek, which seemed to relieve them very much. At last through—the camels bleeding, sweating and groaning.'

Here the diary breaks off, several pages are torn out, and there is no further entry until the end of March.

From Wills we get a much fuller account; indeed, it is remarkable that, day after day, in these hard conditions and no doubt when he was very tired, he was able to make these entries of 400 or 500 words in his neat, careful handwriting, with never a fault of spelling or grammar; and this in addition to his regular meteorological and astronomical observations which he recorded in pencil in a separate leather notebook.

We learn then from Wills that on leaving Depot LXV they travelled down Cooper's Creek for several days until they got on to Sturt's old track at Innamincka. The Cooper's Creek tribesmen were immensely diverted by these fantastic visitors. 'A large tribe of blacks,' Wills wrote, 'came pestering us to go to their camp and have a dance, which we declined. They were very troublesome, and nothing but the threat to shoot will keep them away; they are, however, easily frightened, and, although fine-looking men, decidedly not of a warlike disposition. They show the greatest inclination to take whatever they can, but will run no unnecessary risk in doing so. They seldom carry any weapons, except a shield and a large kind of boomerang, which I believe they use for killing rats etc.; sometimes, but very seldom, they have a large spear; reed spears seem to be quite unknown to them. They are undoubtedly a finer and better-looking race of men than the blacks on the Murray and the Darling, and more peaceful; but in other respects I believe they did not compare favourably with them, for, from the little we have seen of them, they appear to be mean-spirited and contemptible in every respect.'

Wills was to take a more generous view later on. Even now,

although the white men were not willing to play with these childlike people, to dance with them and to make love to their women (women, like everything else, were sometimes shared in this communal world), they were very ready to accept gifts of fish from them and in return they offered beads and boxes of matches. Wills tested the muddy water in the fish-ponds and found it to be 97.4 degrees. 'As may be imagined,' he says, 'this water tasted disagreeably warm, but we soon cooled some in water-bags, and thinking that it would be interesting to know what we call cool, I placed the thermometer in a panikin containing some that appeared delightfully cool, almost cold, in fact. Its temperature was, to our astonishment, 78 deg.'

They now left Cooper's Creek and turned north-west, still finding abundant water; they were heading, in fact, into the region now known as the Channel country, where in a good year the Cooper, the Diamantina and other creeks will flood the land for many miles around. Loose ridges of sand covered with porcupine grass began to multiply before them, and the camels had to step carefully to avoid the places that had been honeycombed by rats. Then on December 22 they struck Sturt's Stony Desert. Wills looked on it with a surveyor's, not a painter's, eye. He wasted no words on the extraordinary colours of the red, white and blue landscape but says instead: 'I was rather disappointed, but not altogether surprised, to find the [desert] nothing more or less than stony rises that we had before met with, only on a larger scale, and not quite as undulating ... in fact, I do not know whether it arose from our exaggerated anticipation of horrors or not, but we thought it far from bad travelling ground, and as to pasture, it is only the actually stony ground that is bare, and many a sheep run is, in fact, worse grazing than that.'

They were lucky, of course; had they been a little further to the west they would have been in Simpson's desert, which is a true desert and not to be lightly entered even now. The rainfall there is barely four inches a year.

They paused for a day on December 24 in a delightful oasis, and by Boxing Day they were through Sturt's desert; but instead of continuing to the north-west as Sturt did they hit the Diamantina and followed it upstream to the point where there is now a settlement named Birdsville. Now Birdsville is an arid place where it is not easy to imagine that any bird would ever sing, but there was good water in the Diamantina that year, and even when it turned east, and they abandoned it, they found other creeks. Presently they were across the Tropic of Capricorn, which was further north than Sturt had ever been.

Early in January they were working up Eyre's Creek and right on their course. It was still extremely dry country, but there were advantages in being away from timber and out in the open for they were free of mosquitoes and ants, sometimes even of flies, and the air was marvellously pure. The blacks had now entirely disappeared. The horizon here, in the glimmering heat of midsummer, is a delusion, and every claypan reflects the sheen of water that does not exist. But they never had to carry water for more than three days, and the nights at least were cool. On January 7 they had to endure a tremendous gale of wind, but it was soon over and the next day there were very definite signs that they were entering more fertile country. They saw the plains turkey, which is an excellent bird to eat, make its slow lumbering flight into the air. Now they were again among trees, which meant the mosquitoes had to be kept at bay by lighting large fires, and the cicadas shrilled loudly in the branches all night long.

A little of the excitement of exploration—the joy of coming upon things that have never been seen before—almost, but not quite, enters Wills' staid, straightforward prose. 'As we proceeded,' he wrote, 'the country improved at every step. Flocks of pigeons rose and flew off to the eastward, and fresh plants met our view on every rise; everything green and luxuriant. The horse licked his lips, and tried all he could to break his nose-string to get at the feed.'

Then again (on January 9): 'Traversed six miles of undulating plains, covered with vegetation richer than ever; several ducks rose from the little creeks as we passed, and flocks of pigeons were flying in all directions.'

And again (January 11): 'Started at five am and in the excitement of exploring such fine well-watered country forgot all about the eclipse of the sun, until the reduced temperature and peculiarly gloomy appearance of the sky drew our attention to the matter; it was then too late to remedy the deficiency, so we made a good day's journey, the moderation of the midday heat, which was only about 86 degrees, greatly assisting us. The country traversed has the most verdant and cheerful aspect, abundance of feed and water everywhere.'

A large range of hills rose up before them, an immense event after nearly a month on the flat plains, and as they approached them they crossed streams with water 'as pure as crystal'. Ant-hills appeared, and now once more there were blacks about; a lubra—a native woman—with her piccaninny was dreadfully frightened when King came over a rise with the camels. On gaining the hills they found them to be about 1,000 feet high and of 'very rugged quartz'; pieces of iron ore were scattered everywhere. On January 19 they were still struggling through this rough country (the Selwyn Range) which, as Burke noticed, so alarmed the camels, and the next day they were through. And now finally, in the vicinity of the present town of Cloncurry, they were entering the tropics. They had travelled almost 500 miles.

There is something very strange about the Australian tropics. The humid heat is there, the tremendous downpours of rain, the flowers and the myriad insects, yet this is still Australia, the prevailing tree is still the eucalyptus, and the colours are muted. It is not at all like the lush green jungle country in the Indo-nesian islands, just a few hundred miles away to the north. The landscape persists in its sense of extreme antiquity, its stillness and its isolation. There are, it is true, mangrove swamps and a few palms and flowering shrubs along the Gulf, but this is predominantly a country of dry spinifex grass, of thin scrub rather than jungle, of black soil plains and of tens of thousands of huge anthills that sometimes give the land the appearance of a graveyard. The eucalypts, however, are not precisely like the trees in the centre and the south; many of them grow a darker bark, a thicker, greener foliage, and the smell of euca-lyptus oil given off by a leaf crushed in the hand is not quite the same. Along the rivers there are paperbark trees with a whitish, yellowish bark that peels like paper, and patches of tropical, orange-coloured grass. Nothing here cools down at night as it does in the desert. The daily breeze off the Gulf dies away in the evening, and the lovely snow-white bole of the ghost-gum is still warm to touch long after sundown.

Burke had expected to find buffaloes, wild pigs and other

tropical animals near the coast, but instead they continued to encounter emus, kangaroos and the same native dogs they had seen a thousand miles away to the south. The land they traversed was very flat, and they saw the brolga, the large heron-like bird which is the most beautiful living object in Australia. Sometimes forty or fifty of them will rise over these grassy plains into the pale blue sky, and they create the effect of a Japanese screen. In the black soil swamps the jabiro stalks about with its black and white wings, its long orange legs and its glaring eye; and the galahs, perching in thousands on the dead trees, make them appear as though they had broken into pink blossom.

They had struck the wet season; day after day the warm rain poured down, and the camels hated it. They floundered about in the boggy ground, moaning and groaning, and Billy the horse grew very weak. Something like 170 miles still divided them from the sea, and they followed the Cloncurry River downstream to the point where it joined the Flinders River (not the Albert River, as Wills thought; this was one of the rare mistakes he made on the journey). Wills told the others that they were now in country that had already been traversed by Gregory and Leichhardt, but this scarcely made it familiar ground; it was as hostile and almost as unknown as it had ever been. The moon had risen, and by its light they marched by night to avoid the enervating heat of the day. By the end of January they had reached the Flinders River, and were moving slowly down the Byno, which was one of its outlets to the sea. The mud was frightful.

'Started at half-past seven am,' Wills wrote on January 30. 'After several unsuccessful attempts at getting Golah [the camel] out of the bed of the creek it was determined to try bringing him down until we could find a place for him to get out at; but after going on in this way for two or three miles, it was found necessary to leave him behind, as it was almost impossible to get him through some of the waterholes, and King [had become separated] from the party, which was a matter for very serious consideration, when we found blacks hiding in the box trees close to us.'

When they were still some thirty miles from the sea Burke decided that it was impossible to take the remaining camels any further over the boggy ground. A camp—No. CXIX—was made beside the Byno, and King and Gray were instructed to remain there while Burke and Wills went on with the horse Billy. On Sunday, February 10, they started out after breakfast with three days' rations. Although he was only carrying a saddle and 25 lb. of provisions on his back, Billy got bogged within a few hundred yards of the camp—'so deeply,' Wills says, 'as to be unable to stir, and we only succeeded in extricating him by undermining him on the creek side, and then lunging him into the water.'

Five miles further on he was bogged again, and again they got him out and struggled on over soft clay that was ankle-deep and sometimes knee-deep in water. By chance then they came on a native path that was well-trodden and hard, and this led them into a forest where a tribe of blacks had recently been digging yams around their campfires. These yams, Wills says, were 'so numerous that they [the blacks] could afford to leave lots of them about, probably having only selected the very best. We were not so particular, but ate many of those they had rejected, and found them very good.'

Half a mile further on they came on a black lying by his campfire with his lubra and a piccaninny. 'We stopped,' Wills said, 'for a short time to take out some of the pistols that were on the horse, and that they might see us before we were so near as to frighten them. Just after we stopped the black got up to stretch his limbs, and after a few seconds looked in our direction. It was very amusing to see the way in which he stared, standing for some time as if he thought he must be dreaming, and then, having signalled to the others, they dropped on their haunches, and shuffled off in the quietest manner possible.' There was a fine hut close by—large enough for a dozen blacks to 'comfortably coil in it together', and the surrounding scene was idyllic: an extensive marsh on the edge of the forest and hundreds of wild geese, plover and pelicans feeding there. They crossed this marsh and came to a channel of water. 'Here,' Wills continued, 'we passed three blacks, who, as is universally their custom, pointed out to us, unasked, the best part down [the channel]. This assisted us greatly, for the ground we were taking was very boggy. We moved slowly down, about three miles, and then camped for the night.' Tasting the water in the channel, they found it brackish and undrinkable. An eight-inch tide flowed in from the sea. They had reached their goal.

They considered making an attempt to get to the actual shore next day by crossing to the west bank of the channel, but it was impossible; mangrove swamps blocked the way, the rain streamed down, the horse was 'completely baked', and their provisions were running out. It seems sad, even across this distance of time, that Burke and Wills did not have their Cortez-vision of that leaden sea that washes along the Gulf of Carpentaria; after so many hardships it would have been for them a splendid thing, and it was more than galling to be thwarted at the last minute. 'It would have been well,' Burke wrote, a little wistfully and very honestly, 'to say that we reached the sea, but we could not obtain a view of the open ocean, although we made every endeavour to do so.' Yet it was enough; they had crossed the continent, they had done what they had set out to do. They turned back next morning at daybreak and rejoined Gray and King in Camp CXIX.

The one thought now in all their minds was how to reach the depot on Cooper's Creek before their rations ran out.

CHAPTER SEVEN

The Rearguard

On Cooper's Creek, meanwhile, the depot was well established. After he had seen off Burke's party on December 16, Brahe had ridden straight back to Depot LXV and had got his men to work cutting timber for a stockade. He pressed on with this work, since the blacks had now begun to gather round the camp, and they were constantly pilfering things. They were not really aggressive—they were like boys robbing an orchard—but on December 26 they got away with six camel bags which had been washed and laid out on the bank of the creek to dry. Sometimes they stalked the camp by night, and the guard on duty had to keep a close lookout when there was no moon. One night Brahe saw a group of them coming stealthily along the creek under the cover of the bank, and they were being directed by another man who was hiding behind the trunk of a large tree. Brahe waited until they were within twenty yards of him, and then he shouted out and fired a shot over their heads. They stood terrified for a moment and then bolted into the night.

Then again early in the New Year a large party came right

into the camp by daylight. Brahe grabbed one of the men and shoved him so hard that he fell down. In the afternoon the whole tribe returned, some of the men armed with spears and boomerangs and with their faces and bodies painted—a sign of war. Brahe walked out to meet them, and while they watched he drew a large circle round the camp. He then indicated by signs that if any man crossed the line he would fire. Out of bravado some of the men did cross the line and Brahe shot off his gun into the trees. At this the whole tribe ran off, and although they did not return he could still see from their camp-fires that they had not gone far off.

So long as Brahe and his men had their fire-arms the depot was safe enough; still, no one could be absolutely sure; other explorers and settlers had been killed in the bush before this, and McDouall Stuart had been strongly attacked in his last journey to the centre. It was a question of constant watchful-ness, of handling childish minds that were disposed to be friendly and yet, through fear or misunderstanding, could give way to a sudden convulsive rage. The tribesmen seemed to like the camels and never molested them, but one day they sur-rounded the horses while they were grazing and appeared to be about to drive them off. Once again Brahe went out with his gun and there was a wild stampede of both animals and men when he pulled the trigger. It was not until after nightfall that they managed to round up the horses and bring them back.

After this the blacks became less troublesome, or rather they seemed to accept the fact of these strangers living among them, and occasionally they would come up to the camp with gifts of fish and nardoo cakes. Brahe thought it wiser to refuse these gifts, but he offered the blacks some of his beads and cast-off clothes and they seemed delighted.

By the New Year the depot was entrenched. The stockade was a solid palisade of saplings driven deep into the ground and covering an area of twenty feet by eighteen. In it Burke's tent was erected and the fire-arms and ammunition were stored. The other tents were set up outside the stockade, close to the cooking fires and the place where the twelve horses and six camels were tied up at night. The provisions were hung in sacks from all the surrounding trees to keep them safe from the rats, and some-times they killed as many as forty rats a day.

Brahe was not altogether satisfied about the site of the camp; the blacks indicated to him that in the wet weather all this land might be under water, but there was no sign of rain as yet, the nights were often intolerably hot and sultry, and the level of the water in the creek was dropping slightly every day.

Apart from Brahe's account we do not know much about the other members of the little party at this time—Patton, Mc-Donough and the Pathan, Dost Mahomet—except that Dost Mahomet had a mortal fear of the blacks; but they appear to have got along very well together. They worked hard at first building the stockade, and then settled into a routine of daily jobs. Each morning one man went out with the camels and another with the horses, while two men stayed in camp. They never cared to take the animals to grazing grounds that were more than six or seven miles away for fear of the blacks, but there was still good feed close by. Inside the camp the days went by in a regular routine of cooking, washing, mending the equipment, taking observations with the instruments Wills had left behind, shooting rats and ducks, and fishing in the creek. The flies were appalling but they managed to deal with the mosquitoes by lighting fires. Burke had left them with provisions for six months, and until the constant shooting scared them off they had plenty of duck to eat. They had rice and sugar for breakfast, and then at noon their main meal of the day—damper, tea, and, while it lasted, salt pork or beef. In the evening they had tea and biscuits. In short, they had all they wanted to eat, and because of the heat none of them was ever very hungry.

It must have been a life of extraordinary dullness; one suspects that they sat around for hour after hour drinking tea and simply gazing at the campfire; without books, without work, without amusement of any kind, what else was there for them to do? Yet it was not exactly a garrison life, their circumstances were too outlandish for that; the element of danger was always there, the sense of being suspended in the unmapped bush out of space and time. Despite its drabness and its heavy stillness and silence the bush had its moments of spectacle as well. In central Australia fantastic dawns and sunsets break across the sky: colours of such leaping brilliance that all the earth, every bush and tree and the dry ground itself, is illuminated for a few minutes in shades of scarlet, orange, pink and gold. It is doubtful if any of these men were keen students of wild life, but they can hardly have failed to be impressed by the continuous movement along the creek, for the waterholes of the Cooper must be one of the great bird sanctuaries of the world. The pool at the site of Depot LXV, about a quarter of a mile long and a hundred yards across, is a particularly good place; one sits on the bank during the hour before dusk like a spectator in a theatre. As the full fierce blaze of the sun begins to soften at last, the white cockatoos, the corellas, come in by the thousand, screeching hideously, and they settle on one tree after another, never quite able to make up their minds.

On the ground the timid little coots that have been hiding in the reeds all day emerge into the open and come nervously down to the water to drink. The slightest disturbance is enough to make them scuttle back into cover again, and with their black feathers and red beaks they look like frightened chickens as they run. Now everywhere the trees are alive with parrots and cockatoos—the mulgas skimming by in green flocks, the parrot-cockatoos in grey, the Major Mitchells in pink—and it is not possible for the eye to follow all the arrivals and departures, the plovers, the eagles, crows, the harlequin colours of the blue-bonnets, the little waxbills, the ring-necks and the herons. Sometimes there are black swans on the pool, and the pelicans, with their curious undulating flight—a series of upward flaps and a down-glide—descend in line, each bird braking himself for his landing on the water by putting out his webbed feet before him. As the light fades the colour of the pool turns to gold, and this is the moment when the galahs, two by two, come in to drink from the bank, anxiously jerking up their heads to look around between each sip, and the bright pink of their breast feathers is reflected in the gold. With darkness silence and stillness return, but then some idiot corella falls off the rotten twig on which it has perched and the whole white flock wheels screeching into the air again. One can expect this to happen half a dozen times but in the end all is quiet.

These evenings are the reward for the hot day, and it is possible on Cooper's Creek for the traveller to have a sense of great contentment, at any rate for an hour or two. But then an inertia supervenes, and in the case of these men no doubt a dead weight of waiting. Day after day the same thing: never a visitor, never a word from the outside world. In these conditions men lose their volition, the judgement falters, the mind becomes obsessed with imagined grievances and doubts, and there is a powerful inducement to dream and to do nothing.

They were not really so well off as the Carpentaria party, who, despite all their discomforts, had the daily stimulus of movement, the necessity of getting somewhere, and the prospect of seeing over the other side of the next hill. After a while Brahe and his men did not bother to fish or to shoot ducks any more; what was the use? It was easier just to go on with the rations they had. This was dangerous, since they needed fresh food, but the creeping paralysis of a static routine made it each day more difficult to do anything out of the ordinary. Did he keep a diary, Brahe was asked later. No, he said, he did not, what was the point? Nothing happened.

So they sat round their depot, and the myriad insects that crept and crawled and flew about them in the light of the campfire—the horrendous six-inch centipedes with their great nippers, the scorpions, the soft moths, the stick insects, the beetles with huge veined transparent wings and the teeming ants—were, for them, a long way from being an interesting manifestation of nature in a new country; they were simply poisonous bugs that had been sent, like the flies and the rats, to plague them in this dreary wilderness. Cooper's Creek, as Burke had said, was not really a desirable summer residence. And so they waited, because there was nothing else for them to do.

As February drifted into March, Brahe was not greatly disturbed about the failure of Burke to return; after all, he could not reasonably expect him before the three-month period was up, and that would be in the middle of March. But the failure of Wright to appear was absolutely baffling. He had turned back from Torowoto at the end of October with the explicit understanding that he would bring the bulk stores up to the Cooper as soon as possible. But now more than four months had gone by, time enough to have made several journeys to the Cooper, and not so much as a message had arrived from him. What could be happening at Menindie? Why did he not come?

For months the temperature at the depot had remained at a

steady 112 degrees in the shade, but on March 24 it suddenly
dropped. Now Brahe and his party had thunder and lightning
ranging around, the wind blew hard and the nights were very
cold. The blacks were still about—they got away with a pack-
saddle one night, and it was torn to pieces when Patton
retrieved it from a mile down the creek—but the depot's supplies of food were still holding out. The trouble was that they had
no dried fruit or vegetables, and early in April Patton began to
complain that his gums were sore and that he was not feeling
very well. He was the blacksmith of the party, and as the horses
needed shoeing he set about the work at once in case his illness
gained on him. On April 4 the job was done and Patton
collapsed. His legs and arms were swollen and his mouth was
now so sore he could not eat. They put him to bed in one of the
tents and there he lay. About this time too both Brahe and
McDonough began to observe the same symptoms in themselves. They had no idea of what the affliction was—no one
appears to have warned them of scurvy—and only the Pathan,
Dost Mahomet, was entirely well.

It was now nearly four months since Burke and his party had
gone away—a month longer than they had predicted—and
Brahe rode out to the hills around the creek to search the
horizon: to the south-east for Wright, to the north for Burke.
Absolutely nothing broke the stillness of the plain. Brahe kept
revolving the problem round and round in his mind: what were
they to do? Were they to go on like this forever, never to have
news from anywhere, never to have an end of this waiting in
a vacuum? Burke's last words were recalled again and again; he
could be considered 'perished', he had said, if he was not back
in three months. No, he did not expect to be picked up by a boat
on the Gulf, nor would he make for the settled districts of
Queensland if he had any chance of getting back to Cooper's
Creek. And yet was it not possible that he *had* been picked up,
that he *had* gone to Queensland? Then why no news, why nothing from Menindie? Was it possible that the little party on the
Cooper had been altogether forgotten? Were the others, being
all safe and sound, simply expecting him to come back to
civilization now that the three months had run out? How much
longer could he *afford* to stay, with Patton unable to leave
his bed and getting feebler every day, and he himself and

McDonough also failing in health? Their ankles now became swollen every time they got on a horse. Suppose Burke were dead or stuck fast in the centre, was it not his duty to go back now and get help? After all, the Cooper's Creek party were the only ones who knew anything definite about Burke's plans; they were his last link with the outside world. Yet Burke had specifically said that they were to hang on at Cooper's Creek so long as the rations lasted; and the rations were lasting. They were sick to death of them but there was enough. And the weather was cooler, they had actually had some rain. Should he set a date then, Brahe wondered, should they wait, say, until May?

Each day these questions posed themselves and there was never any answer.

CHAPTER EIGHT

The Return from the Gulf

As soon as they rejoined Gray and King at Camp CXIX on the Gulf of Carpentaria on February 12, Burke and Wills took stock of their situation. They had been fifty-seven days on the outward journey from Cooper's Creek, and in that time they had eaten more than two-thirds of their three months' supply of rations. There remained now only 83 lb. of flour, 3 lb. of pork, 25 lb. of dried meat, 12 lb. of biscuit, 12 lb. of rice—say one month's provisions in all, or just half of what they required.

This could be supplemented, of course, by portulaca, which was now flowering in the wet season, by such birds as they could shoot—mainly ducks, hawks and crows—and by fish; but their experiences in coming up to the Gulf had shown that they could not expect much from this source. On the other hand, they still had five camels and the horse Billy, and there was a reasonable prospect of recapturing Golah, the camel they had left behind. Some at least of these animals could be killed and eaten.

They had roughly 700 miles to go in order to reach the depot on Cooper's Creek, and on the outward journey they had managed between twelve and fifteen miles a day. There seemed to be no reason why they should not repeat this performance; the animals' loads were lighter, they knew the way, and except for Gray, who was complaining of headaches, they were all reasonably fit. The animals, it was true, were in need of rest and would have benefited from three or four weeks' feeding around Camp CXIX, but the shortage of rations made any such delay impossible. Even as it was they would have to live on a greatly reduced diet, and Burke fixed on a basic daily scale of twelve sticks of dried meat and ¼ lb. of flour for each man.

Before they left Camp CXIX they cut the initial B on a circle of fifteen trees, and buried a parcel of books together with a letter saying who they were and what they had done. Then, on February 13, after only one day of rest, they set out. It was still raining.

We know a good deal less about this return journey than we do of the outward one. Burke took no notes at all, and Wills no longer kept any exact record of their line of march or of their progress. In his field-books he mostly contented himself with noting down dates and the names of camps, and one can measure his increasing weariness by the way in which the entries grow more and more scrappy and laconic. They were probably all much more tired than they realized, and the constant rain had turned the ground into a quagmire. It rained and rained and they had no tents; they slept in the wet. When they had had a week of it, Wills made a typical entry in his diary: 'Between four and five o'clock a heavy thunderstorm broke over us, having given very little warning of its approach. There had been lightning and thunder towards S.E. and S. ever since noon yesterday. The rain was incessant and very heavy for an hour and a half, which made the ground so boggy that the animals could scarcely walk over it. We nevertheless started at 10 minutes to seven am, and after floundering along for half an hour, halted for breakfast. We then moved on again, but soon found that the travelling was too heavy for the camels, so we camped for the remainder of the day. In the afternoon the sky cleared a little, and the sun soon dried the ground, considering. Shot a pheasant, and much disappointed at finding him all feathers and claws.'

And then on the following day: 'A fearful thunderstorm in the evening about eight pm, E.S.E., moving gradually round to the S. The flashes of lightning were so vivid and incessant as to keep up a continual light for short intervals, overpowering even the moonlight.'

As the four men crawled over the enormous landscape like wet insects they began to long for the dry fresh heat of the desert. It was still hot here in the north, but it was the dull enervating heat of the tropics, and now King as well as Gray began to suffer from headaches and pains in his legs and back. Wills, who was the most vigorous of them all, wrote in his diary: 'The evening [February 23rd] was most oppressively hot and sultry, so much so that the slightest exertion made one feel as if he were in a state of suffocation. The dampness in the atmosphere prevented any evaporation, and gave one a helpless feeling of lassitude that I have never before experienced to such an extent. All the party complained of the same symptoms, and the horses [*sic*] showed distinctly the effect of the evening trip, short as it was.'

Even by travelling at night like this they were making nothing like twelve miles a day, and at the beginning of March they were still trudging up the Cloncurry River more or less on their old route. But now they found Golah. 'He looks thin,' Wills wrote, 'and miserable, seems to have fretted a great deal, probably at finding himself left behind, and he has been walking up and down the tracks till he has made a regular pathway. Could find no sign of his having been far off it, although there is splendid feed to which he could have gone. He began to eat as soon as he saw the other camels.'

It was too late however. Somehow the heart had gone out of the beast, and they had to abandon him four days later when he absolutely refused to come on, even when his pack and saddle were taken off. Meanwhile there was the incident of the snake: 'In crossing a creek by moonlight,' Wills wrote, 'Charley rode over a large snake. He did not touch him, and we thought it was a log until he struck it with the stirrup-iron. We then saw that it was an immense snake, larger than any I have ever before seen in a wild state.' It had a black head, a pattern of brown and yellow stripes on its back, and measured eight feet four inches in length. It did not appear to have poisonous fangs, and inspired, perhaps, by their having seen the blacks eat snakes, but mainly by their own hunger, they cooked this monster. The next night they started out at 2 a.m., but Burke almost immediately complained of severe dysentery. He felt giddy, and when he got on to his horse he was unable to keep his seat. They were forced then to give up all further progress for the night, and for the next two days Burke dragged himself miserably along.

By the end of the first week of March they had covered barely a hundred miles, but at last there was a first whiff of the dry desert air. Only Gray failed to respond to it. 'Mr. Burke,' Wills' diary says, 'almost recovered, but Charley is again very unwell, and unfit to do anything. He caught cold last night through carelessness in covering himself.'

They did not entirely believe in Gray's complaints, they thought he was 'gammoning'—trying to get out of his fair share of the work. After all, he was under no more strain than the others, and Burke was absolutely impartial about the rations; at each meal he carefully doled out the food on to four numbered plates which he covered with a towel. The others were then obliged to stand with their backs turned and to call a number, and were each served with the plate of that number. Food now entirely dominated their lives, and so the incident that occurred on March 25 was for them all a shocking and outrageous thing.

Wills describes it thus: 'After breakfast took some altitudes, and was about to go back to last camp for some things that had been left, when I found Gray behind a tree, eating skilligolee (or gruel). He explained that he was suffering from dysentery, and had taken the flour without leave. Sent him to report himself to Mr. Burke and went on. Having got King to tell Mr. Burke for him, was called up and received a good thrashing. There is no knowing to what extent he has been robbing us. Many things have been found to run unaccountably short.'

King's version of the affair does not quite agree as to 'the good thrashing'; he states that Gray merely received 'six or seven slaps on the ear', and he goes on to say that, apart from this, he had never known Burke strike a man before. One must recall, of course, that King was devoted to Burke, and that Wills was a disciplined and self-controlled young man; from now on in his notes he refers to Charley as Gray, and clearly he believed that Gray deserved nothing less than a good thrashing. Be all this as it may, Burke was in a towering rage—one understands it very well—and henceforth Gray, who had been in charge of the stores, was put on to other duties.

By now, March 25, they had been forty days on the return journey and were only about half-way back. But they were through the Selwyn Ranges, and in the more bracing air of the centre they made better time. No day went past without their struggling on to another camp, even though the rain continued to fall. Wills' diary becomes a string of *ad hoc* place names: Fig Tree Camp, Sandstone Cave, Scratchley's Creek, Humid Camp, Muddy Camp, Mosquito Camp, Three Hour Camp, Native Dog Camp and Saltbush Camp. There is also more than one 'Feasting Camp'. We do not know exactly when or in what circumstances each of the animals was killed, but a 'Feasting Camp' no doubt was a place where the starving men gorged themselves and then cut up as much meat as they could carry. On March 30 we have an entry: 'Boocha's Rest. [Boocha was one of the camels.] Employed all day in cutting up, jerking and eating Boocha. The day turned out as favourable for us as we could have wished, and a considerable portion of the meat was completely jerked before sunset.'

Then eleven days later, on April 10, we have: 'Remained at Camp LII R. all day to cut up and jerk the meat of the horse Billy, who was so reduced and knocked up for want of food, that there appeared little chance of his reaching the other side of the desert; and as we were running short of food of every description ourselves, we thought it best to secure his flesh at once. We found it healthy and tender, but without the slightest trace of fat in any portion of the body.'

Now there is a great deal of meat on a horse, let alone a camel, and in the end only two camels of the original six remained. One would have thought that there was enough meat here to keep four men going for a very long time, and one can only conclude that they were all now growing very weak, and quite unable to carry more than a light pack. And in fact they were beginning to discard every article that was not absolutely essential. On March 20 they had already jettisoned 60 lb. of equipment, hanging it from the branches of a tree so that it could be found if they ever came back; and they began to take turns at riding the two remaining camels. Cyclonic storms either blowing with rain or red dust continued to hold them back, and once they 'halted fifteen minutes to send back for Gray, who gammoned he could not walk'. And now, on April 10, they faced Sturt's Stony Desert again. Wills says very little of the passage except that they managed to find water on the way—the spring was now well advanced—and they appear to have got through in several days. On April 15, two months out from the Gulf, they were moving slowly down towards Cooper's Creek in driving rain, and they had to pause for a while when Landa, one of the camels, became knocked up and would not go on. Gray by now could no longer ride by himself and had to be strapped to the saddle.

He was not really gammoning. On April 17 we get the simple entry in Wills' diary: 'This morning about sunrise, Gray died. He had not spoken a word distinctly since his first attack, which was just as we were about to start.' According to King, they found him dead in his bedroll when they went to call him in the morning. They buried him as he was, in his flannel trousers, his short-sleeved shirt and his wideawake hat, and they were so feeble it took them all day to dig a grave three feet deep. When it was done they abandoned the last of their equipment. Wills already had lost nearly all his instruments—some had been broken when a camel had rolled on them, others had been buried—but he still clutched his field-books, the only written record of what they had achieved; and now to mark Charley's grave they placed a rifle above it on a tree and some unwanted camel-pads, intending to come back for them later. They were seventy miles from the depot, and on April 18 they set out again, carrying with them a little dried meat, a couple of spades, the remaining fire-arms and a few camel-pads for bedding. Burke in particular had been generous in giving away his spare shirts to the blacks, and they were all badly in need of new clothes and boots. They were so cold when they laid down to sleep they had to keep a fire going throughout the night.

Friday, April 19, was a bad day; the Cooper's Creek blacks had again caught sight of these incredible bearded white men who dragged themselves along on their aimless journeys as though bewitched by some fetish, and they would not leave them alone. Wills wrote: 'Camped again without water on the sandy bed of the creek, having been followed by a lot of natives who were desirous of our company; but as we preferred camping alone, we were compelled to move on until rather late, in order to get away from them. The night was very cold. A strong breeze was blowing from the south, which made the fire so irregular that, as on the previous two nights, it was impossible to keep up a fair temperature.'

On Saturday, April 20, they trudged on again, Burke riding one camel and Wills and King taking turns with the other, and that night, their sixty-sixth night since leaving the Gulf, they camped within thirty miles of the depot. They made a division of their remaining provisions and ate them all except for the last pound and a half of dried meat. On April 21—it was another Sunday, all the great events on this journey seemed to be occurring on Sunday—they made a superhuman effort. Rising early, they set out to cover in one day the entire thirty miles that divided them from the depot. They paused only to allow King to take pot-shots at hawks and crows, and at nightfall they were still going. In other circumstances they would have long since collapsed, but now they were driven on by dreams of food and rest and companionship, and beyond this they hardly knew what they were doing any more. The moon came up and by its light Burke rode on ahead through the silent scrub. 'I think I see their tents ahead,' he kept saying, 'I think I see them.' As he neared the site of the depot he raised his voice in the long-drawn-out bushman's cry: *Coo-ee, Coo-ee,* and he shouted out the names of the men they had left there, Brahe, McDonough, Patton. And then again *Coo-ee.*

There was no answer from the silent bush, no movement anywhere in the moonlight.

It was just 7.30 p.m. when they came into the camp and saw the wooden stockade, the ashes of burnt-out fires, bits of discarded equipment scattered about, and fresh traces of horse and cattle dung, but no sign of men or animals anywhere. They stood for a moment in a confused daze, and Burke said: 'I suppose they have shifted to some other part of the creek.'

It was hardly likely and they all knew it. No equipment would have been left behind had Brahe merely set up a depot in another place. Then Wills caught sight of a fresh blaze on the coolibah tree and they read the words that had been cut into the wood with a knife:

DIG

3 FT. N.W.

APR. 21 1861

'If they had shifted to another part of the creek,' Wills said, 'they would not have left that.'

Burke collapsed on the ground in despair, and Wills and King paced out the distance from the tree to a spot where the earth had been freshly turned over. Digging down two feet they came on a camel box containing rations, and there was a bottle with a message written in pencil inside it. King smashed the bottle and handed the message to Burke. By the bright light of the moon he read aloud:

'Depot, Cooper's Creek, 21 April 1861,

The depot party of the V.E.E.[1] leaves this camp today to return to the Darling. I intend to go S.E. from Camp LX, to get into our old track near Bulloo. Two of my companions and myself are quite well; the third—Patton—has been unable to walk for the last eighteen days, as his leg has been severely hurt when thrown by one of the horses. No person has been up here from the Darling.

We have six camels and twelve horses in good working condition.

William Brahe.'

The date of the message was perhaps the most agonizing thing: Brahe and his men had left the depot that same morning. After four months they had missed them by a matter of nine or ten hours, or even less. Even now they were probably encamped no more than twenty miles away. If they had gone a week earlier the situation would have been just the same, but to have been too late by one day—the day that they lost by burying Gray—this was too bitter. Why at least could Brahe's party not have heard King's rifle as he shot at the hawks and crows further down the creek that morning? Why couldn't the blacks have told them that there were white men approaching the camp? And where was Wright? Why hadn't he come up? Why wasn't he here now?

[1]Victorian Exploring Expedition.

In the last hundred years the scene that night on Cooper's Creek has become something of a legend in Australian history, and it made a strong appeal to the illustrative artists of the day. Even as late as 1907 John Longstaff painted an enormous canvas showing the three haggard men grouped around the fatal tree, Burke in his tattered shirt and trousers staring dully into the distance, Wills slumped on one of the camel packs, with bowed head and his hands on his knees, and King lying prone on the ground. The spade is flung down beside the opened cache, and in the background the two camels have sunk to their knees in utter exhaustion. The silent and unresponsive bush envelops them all. As a study of helpless despair it could hardly be improved upon.

And probably it was like that. Such brief descriptions as have been left behind by the three men make it clear that at first they simply could not bring themselves to believe that Brahe had gone, and that after all this enormous struggle to reach the camp, and the visions they had had of rest and safety, they were now alone.

When they had recovered a little their first instinct, of course, was to consider their chances of being able to follow Brahe while there was still time. Burke put it to Wills and King: were they able to march on through the night? They both answered no, and Burke then said that he also was too exhausted to go on. Then what to do? To eat certainly, and then to rest. And then? Wills and King were all for travelling on in Brahe's wake; after all, something might happen to delay him, and they would then catch him up. Burke was emphatically against this. It would be madness, he thought; in his message Brahe specifically said that his six camels and twelve horses were in good condition. How could they possibly catch them with their own two exhausted camels? There was no water for long stretches on the way to Menindie, and Menindie was over 400 miles away. A much better plan would be to go down Cooper's Creek to Mount Hopeless, where they knew there was a police-station, only 150 miles away, and from there the journey to Adelaide would be through settled districts. Gregory had done the journey from the Cooper to Mount Hopeless in a week; the Committee in Melbourne had recommended that route as a line of communication. In the end both Wills and King were persuaded.

They now broached the rations that Brahe had left behind. They were so weak that King had to crawl on his hands and knees to fill a billy from the creek, but they all felt better after the meal and stretched themselves out on the ground to sleep.

Next day they hung listlessly about the camp gathering their strength, and debating their predicament over and over again. Why had Brahe gone? Why on that very day? Admittedly they had been away longer than they had thought, but he still had provisions—he could have eaten the horses. Why had Wright never come up? Why had they been abandoned? In his bitterness Burke declared that Brahe and his men would be punished; their salaries would go to Wills and King. He would arrange it when they got back.

An inventory of rations in the cache revealed that they had a month's supply, just about enough to get them to Mount Hopeless if all went well. They had left clothes behind at the depot, and now that they needed them so badly it was one more charge against Brahe that he had had the idiocy to take them away with him.

In the circumstances, the letter that Burke now wrote was exceptionally restrained:

'Depot No. 2, Cooper's Creek, Camp no. LXV.

The return party from Carpentaria, consisting of myself, Mr. Wills and King (Gray dead), arrived here last night and found that the depot party had only started on the same day. We proceed on tomorrow slowly down the creek towards Adelaide, by Mount Hopeless, and shall endeavour to follow Gregory's tracks, but we are very weak. The two camels are done up, and we shall not be able to travel farther than four or five miles a day. Gray died on the road from exhaustion and fatigue. We have all suffered much from hunger. The provisions left here will, I think, restore our strength. We have discovered a practicable route to Carpentaria, the chief portion of which lies on the 140th meridian of east longitude. There is some good country between this and the stony desert. From there to the tropic [Capricorn] the country is dry and stony. Between the tropic and Carpentaria a considerable portion is rangy, but it is well watered and richly grassed.

We reached the shores of Carpentaria on the 11th February 1861. Greatly disappointed at finding the party here gone.

R. O'Hara Burke, Leader.

22 April 1861.

P.S.—The camels cannot travel, and we cannot walk, or we should follow the other party. We shall move very slowly down the creek.'

Wills in his diary was more outspoken:

'Sunday 21st April 1861.—Arrived at the depot this evening, just in time to find it deserted. A note left in the plant by Brahe communicates the pleasing information that they have started today for the Darling, their camels and horses all well and in good condition; we and our camels being just done up, and scarcely able to reach the depot have very little chance of over-taking them. Brahe has fortunately left us ample provisions to take us to the bounds of civilization, namely: flour, 50 lb., rice 20 lb., oatmeal 60 lb., sugar 60 lb. and dried meat 15 lb. These provisions, together with a few horseshoes and nails, and some castaway odds and ends, constitute all the articles left, and place us in a very awkward position in respect to clothing.

'Our disappointment at finding the depot deserted may easily be imagined; returning in an exhausted state, after four months of the severest travelling and privation, our legs almost para-lysed, so that each of us found it a most trying task only to walk a few yards. Such a leg-bound feeling I never before experienced and hope I never shall again. The exertion required to get up a slight piece of rising ground, even without any load, induces an indescribable sensation of pain and helplessness, and the general lassitude makes one unfit for anything. Poor Gray must have suffered very much, many times, when we thought him shamming. It is most fortunate for us that these symptoms, which so early affected him, did not come on us until we were reduced to an exclusively animal diet of such an inferior descrip-tion as that offered by the flesh of a worn-out and exhausted horse.

'We were not long in getting out the grub that Brahe had left, and we made a good supper off some oatmeal porridge and sugar. This, together with the excitement of finding ourselves in such a peculiar and unexpected position, had a wonderful effect in removing the stiffness from our legs. Whether it is possible that the vegetables can so have affected us, I know not; but both Mr. B. and I remarked a most decided relief and a strength in the legs greater than we had had for several days. I am inclined to think that but for the abundance of portulac that we obtained on the journey, we should scarcely have returned to Cooper's Creek at [all].'

So then, with this new supply of food, there was a chance of their getting through to Mount Hopeless, and after only one day's delay they began preparations for getting on the road again. King had broken the bottle that contained Brahe's letter and had put the pieces on top of the stockade, but another bottle was found, and with Burke's letter inside it was buried in the cache. One never knew, there was just a chance that someone might come looking for them. With a rake which he had found leaning against the stockade King smoothed over the ground above the cache, leaving it exactly as it was before. Afterwards he propped the rake against the coolibah tree. There was little, apart from the rations, for them to take away; King cut a large square from a hide that formed the door of the stockade, with the idea no doubt of making boots from it, but a bag of horse-shoe nails he rejected and scattered about on the ground. He also hung a few rags and pieces of leather for which they had no use on some nails driven into the stockade. The ashes of their campfires were left as they were.

At a quarter past nine on April 23 they set out in the opposite direction to Brahe's, a bedraggled little group with their weary camels and their tattered clothes, moving slowly back on their tracks down the south bank of the Cooper.

CHAPTER NINE

Back to Menindie

It would not have mattered to Brahe if he had left the depot on Cooper's Creek a day or two later; he might perhaps have even hung on for another week. But by April 18 he had absolutely made up his mind that he had to go, and he arbitrarily fixed on Sunday, April 21. Patton's gums were in a fearful state, and he was in great pain. He kept asking to be taken back to Menindie so that he could get medical attention, and it was apparent to all of them that if he stayed where he was he would die. Moreover, Brahe himself and both McDonough and Dost Mahomet had now become so weak and undernourished that they had difficulty in looking after the animals, and it was a severe strain when one day the horses strayed away for fifteen miles and had to be brought back.

By this time, too, Brahe had given up all hope of Burke's return; the rations he had taken with him could not possibly have kept him going for the four months he had been away, and so, Brahe reasoned, he must either be dead or have found his way out to Queensland.

There was another factor that helped Brahe to make up his

mind: he felt that he was bound to leave a cache of food behind, just in case by some miracle Burke and his companions did return, and now he had just enough provisions left to make this cache and to get his party back to Menindie. If he stayed longer he could leave nothing behind. Perhaps too, he was influenced by the fact that rain had recently fallen, and now they had better prospects of finding water on their way down.

Having made up his mind on April 18, Brahe and his men spent the next two days preparing for their departure. The provisions were divided, the cache was dug, camel dung was raked over it to disguise it from the natives, and the blaze was cut into the tree. Next he took out Burke's sealed letters and, in accordance with his instructions, burnt them.

It was strange that Brahe should have written in his note, 'We have six camels and twelve horses in good working condition'—those fatal words that decided Burke that he had no chance of catching him up—because two of the camels were suffering from scab, suffering so much that they died a few weeks later. Brahe was never really able to explain this; perhaps at the time he merely wished to put a good face on things. At all events, on the morning of April 21 the animals' packs were stowed, Patton was lifted up and strapped to the quietest camel, and at 10.30—just nine hours before Burke arrived—the little caravan filed out of the camp.

They headed upstream, intending to continue on the Cooper for several days and then strike directly across the desert to Bulloo. On this first day they took things easily, and at five o'clock Brahe called a halt. That night the two parties were camped only fourteen miles apart, and just possibly Burke might have caught up with them there. But next day it was too late: Brahe pushed his men on at a much faster pace, and by April 23 he was fifty miles away from the depot, and ready to begin his dash across the dry country that lay between the Cooper and Bulloo. Patton, strapped sideways on his camel, complained that he could not get a comfortable seat, but he managed to keep going. They went on steadily for four days, Brahe setting the course through the barren hills, and out on to the plains, with one of Wills' compasses, and on April 27 they struck the waterholes of Bulloo. They had been precisely 100 hours without water, and the horses plunged forward in frenzy to drink.

On the way to Bulloo Brahe noticed fresh tracks of horses and camels going in different directions, and they were not more than ten or twelve days old. While his party rested next day he went out by himself before dawn to see if he could resolve this mystery. His own horses had been allowed to stray in the night, and the diary he wrote later says: 'At about daylight I got in sight of them, at the same time observing smoke rising within 300 yards from me, and near the horses. There was not light enough to see well, and I thought I had dropped upon a camp of natives, and resolved to try to obtain some information from them respecting the Darling party. After going a few yards further I saw, to my great surprise, a European advance towards me. It was Mr. Hodgkinson. He led me to Mr. Wright's camp, and after bringing in our party, with horses and camels etc., I placed myself and my party under the orders of Mr. Wright.'

It was the first time the two parties had met for six months, and Wright had an appalling story to tell. After leaving Burke at Torowoto on October 29 in the previous year, he got back to Menindie in six days only to find that nothing was in readiness for the move to Cooper's Creek. Half the stores were still scattered about the settlement, and practically nothing had been done about transporting them to the new camp on Pamamaroo Creek. The animals that had been left behind were in poor condition, some of the men were ill, and all of them were plagued by flies. The news from Melbourne was disturbing: the banks were dishonouring the expedition's cheques. Burke had written dozens of cheques on the way up to Menindie, and now the word had got along the Murray and the Darling that none of them were good. Payment was being refused on even small amounts of a few pounds; the expedition was bankrupt. Later on this matter was cleared up, but at the time of Wright's return to Menindie it seemed that all their salaries were in jeopardy, and that the expedition had been abandoned and forgotten by its principals.

There was a fairly regular post between Menindie and Melbourne—letters usually arrived within a fortnight by way of Swan Hill—but no mail of any sort was received. Ludwig Becker sent off various packages to Macadam containing his drawings, notes and specimens, but there was no acknowledgement whatever.

All this put Wright in a quandary. How was he to move the stores up to Cooper's Creek with a team of sick animals and a party of men who did not know whether or not they were still employed by the expedition? His own position was ambiguous. Burke, it was true, had appointed him leader of the rearguard but only subject to the Committee's approval. How was he to know whether or not the Committee would give that approval? They might withhold it just as they were apparently withholding the men's salaries. And so he decided that the best thing to do was to post off Burke's Torowoto letter to Melbourne—that letter in which Burke had asked that Wright should be put in charge of the rearguard—and to await results.

Another matter delayed him. On the very day of his return to Menindie a trooper named Lyons rode in from Swan Hill saying that he had important dispatches for Burke from the Committee giving details of Stuart's progress, and that he was instructed to deliver them personally. Lyons was told that it might be dangerous to go on alone to Cooper's Creek but he insisted, and Wright felt it his duty to let him have four horses and the assistance of a saddler named McPherson. The two men set off on November 10 with a black tracker named Dick who was to guide them. Thus the strength of the rearguard was further depleted.

For the next six weeks nothing was heard from them, or indeed from anybody, and then, on December 19, the black tracker returned to Menindie with the news that Lyons and McPherson were stranded in the Torowoto district with their horses knocked up and themselves in danger of dying of starvation. They had never succeeded in reaching Burke.

Dr. Beckler had given in his resignation and was awaiting his replacement, but he volunteered to go out and rescue the two men. With Dick acting as a guide he found them in the last extremity, living on nardoo flour, and he led them back to Menindie. It was a very creditable performance and quite disproved Burke's contention that Beckler was afraid to leave the settled districts. Yet the incident greatly delayed them; Beckler did not return until January 5 and of course it was impossible to move without him.

All this time there had been no word from the Committee and

at the end of the year Wright decided to send off a second letter
to Melbourne with Hodgkinson, the young man who had now
become foreman of the base camp. 'As I have every reason to
believe,' he wrote (or rather, he dictated to Hodgkinson), 'that
Mr. Burke has pushed on from Cooper's Creek, relying upon
finding the depot stores at that watercourse upon his return,
there is room for the most serious apprehensions as to the safety
of himself and his party, should he find that he has miscalcu-
lated.' This was an odd communication from a man who,
despite all his problems, had really done nothing for two
months, even though he knew that Burke was expecting to be
followed up at once.

It was, of course, nothing new for a base camp to be a dismal
place, but the lethargy that had overtaken Menindie during
these months seems to have been quite exceptional. Wright did
not even move to Pamamaroo Creek when the new camp was
set up there. He lived with his wife and family in more comfortable circumstances at Kinchega station, fourteen miles
away. For as much as a week at a time he did not even bother
to visit the camp. It was said later that the other members of the
rearguard urged him to set out for Cooper's Creek before the
summer was too far advanced and the waterholes dried up. But
Wright did nothing; he simply let the days go by waiting for
news either from Cooper's Creek or from Melbourne. He kept
insisting that until his appointment was confirmed, or until he
could either buy more horses or Burke sent back to him some
of the camels he had taken to the Cooper, he could not move.

One rather wonders about all this. Wright, of course, should
never have been employed by Burke at all—not at any rate as
an officer of the expedition: he was too slow, too limited, too
venal, one of the kind whose horizons are no higher than their
salaries. But how hard did the others push him to move? How
much were they too worried about the unpaid cheques and
about the hazards of the journey? It might have been that they
were quite ready to shuffle off the responsibility upon Wright,
and when he did nothing they succumbed to the general inertia
of that hot, fly-ridden, leaderless camp on the Darling.

And so they pottered about the Pamamaroo Camp, tending
the animals, fishing in the river, cooking their dreary meals and
no doubt riding into Thomas Paine's pub in Menindie for a

drink. (Paine was well supplied; he had purchased the last twenty gallons of the camels' rum for £16.) One day a horde of white ants invaded the camp and demolished their supply of dried beef, whereupon crested pigeons appeared and ate the ants. Another day a boat arrived with twelve pack-saddles sent up from Melbourne (but no letters). As the heat increased they hung up canvas buckets on the trees to cool their drinking water. Ludwig Becker did his drawings and collected his specimens; Dr. Beckler made his botanical notes; Wright dropped in from time to time to see what was going on. These things were the minutiae of their daily lives, one day drifted into another, and the oppressive heat was a mighty leveller of enterprise.

On January 22, 1861 (when Burke and his men had almost reached the Gulf), Becker wrote wearily in his diary that he had now passed three months on the Darling, and that it was five months since they had left Melbourne; and in all that time he had not received one line from the Committee to acknowledge the specimens, drawings and diaries he had sent down.

It was Hodgkinson who set things in motion at last. He alone seems to have had some sense of urgency, for he rode the 400 miles to Melbourne from the Darling in eleven days, and when he arrived on December 31 he was greeted with some surprise. The Committee told him that they had had no notion that there had been any delay. They had had Burke's letter from Torowoto but had not replied to it because they had believed that Wright had set out long ago to follow him up to the Cooper. They now gave Hodgkinson £400 in cash—enough to buy 10 additional horses and 150 sheep (to replace the beef demolished by the ants)—and Hodgkinson rode off to Menindie that same night.

When he got back there on January 9 there was a stir in the camp at last; horses were bought from the surrounding stations, harness was found, and the packing of the stores began. It was decided that it was too late in the year to take the sheep—the grass had dried up—but the original stores that had been brought up from Melbourne proved more than ample; indeed, a great part of them was dumped with Thomas Paine and never left Menindie. Ten camels, all in good condition after months of idleness on the Darling, and thirteen horses were available, and on January 23, twelve days after Hodgkinson's return,

Wright dictated a letter to the Committee saying that he was setting out next day with the entire party: Dr. Beckler (who had apparently thought better of his resignation), Ludwig Becker, Hodgkinson, three men named Stone, Smith and Purcell, who had been engaged at Menindie, and the Indian, Belooch.

Actually it was January 26 when they got away,[1] and they started by night to avoid the excessive heat of the day. One would not have expected them to make the fast time to the Cooper that Burke had—twenty-three days—since they were more heavily laden, and now, at the height of summer, they were going to have difficulty in finding water. Moreover, they had no surveyor with them, and Wright was not the kind of man who would inspire much confidence in his followers. Yet even so one would have to search far through the history of Australian exploration for anything to match the futile wanderings and the bungling ineptitude of this journey. They seemed doomed from the start to do the wrong thing, and as it so often happens when affairs are mismanaged, they were made to pay for their mistakes by suffering twice the number of setbacks that would normally have occurred. Three horses died of exhaustion, rats broke into their stores, and five members of the party fell ill. Wright was quite unable to cope with all this. He himself kept thrusting ahead for water while the others straggled on behind him as best they could, getting slower and slower with every mile.

It was not until February 12 that they reached the half-way mark at Torowoto. Here they rested for two days, and then moved on again for eighteen miles until they were blocked by an apparently waterless plain stretching away to the horizon. Wright now went ahead with Smith, and when they found a puddle twenty miles away to the north the whole party was assembled there. The horses, however, mad with thirst, stampeded the puddle, turning it into a mass of mud, and the camels had to be sent back to Torowoto for more water. Then again Wright went on with Smith and Belooch, and eleven days later they reached Bulloo, eighty miles from Cooper's Creek. He then sent back for the others, but by now Becker, Stone, Smith, Purcell and Belooch—more than half of the entire party—were

[1] The additional delay seems to have been caused because Wright was waiting for a boat to take his wife and children down to Adelaide.

1 The inhospitable gibber desert near Innamincka

Kaufmann, M'Callum, and Co.

In accordance with the above requisition, I hereby convene a SPECIAL GENERAL MEETING of the CHAMBER for Friday next, September 3, at 3 o'clock p.m., at the Exchange Room.

(Signed) H. W. F RRAR, President.
Melbourne, August 30, 1858.

EXPLORATION OF AUSTRALIA.—A citizen of Melbourne having signified to Sir William Stawell, President of the Philosophical Institute. his in'ention of subscribing £1,000 to the purpose of the Exploration of Australia, on condition of a certain further sum being subscribed by the public towards the same object, a PUBLIC MEETING will be held ot the Mechanics' Institute on Tuesday, August 31, at 4 o'clock p.m., to consider the above proposal. Sir W. Stawell will be present.

LICENSED VICTUALLERS' SOCIETY, Melbourne.—The Members of the Melbourne Licensed Victuallers' Society invite a GENERAL MEETING of the TRADE on TUESDAY, SEPTEMBER 7, at the Bull and Mouth Hotel

2 Notice from the *Argus*, August 1858

3   Theatre ticket for the performance in aid of the Exploration Fund

4   Robert O'Hara Burke, 39, and William John Wills, 26

5   John King, 19, the expedition's camel expert
and sole survivor of the party who reached the Gulf

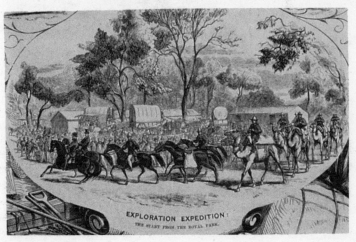

EXPLORATION EXPEDITION:
THE START FROM THE ROYAL PARK.

6   The start of the Expedition leaving Royal Park

7 'The Departure of the Burke and Wills Expedition'. Painting by C. Summers

8 The Melbourne *Punch* cartoon, 8 Nov. 1860

Articles required for the
Equipment and provisioning of twenty
men for twelve months

No.	Article	Remarks	Cost
1320	Ho. meat reduced to pemican	Equal to 3½ ton flesh	112 . .
1800	„ Bacon		90 . .
7100	„ Flour		76 6 6
2600	„ Rice		53 6 8
1600	„ Sugar		31 13 4
300	„ Tea		45 . .
250	Tobacco		45 16 8
200	Salt		1 5 .
1000	Coarse Flour or Oatmeal	For Camels & Drivers	16 13 4
1000	Ghee (clarified butter)	Do.	125 . .
500	Soap		
10	Gall. Vinegar		
1	Cheese		
20	Gall. Lime juice (in Kegs)		
	Sundries		
10	lb. Dates		
20	lb. chocolate		
40	„ Coffee in tins		
	Stationery		
	Ink powder		

9   One of the original lists of supplies for the Expedition

10   'The Burke and Wills Expedition; the first day's march (drawn from nature) 1862'. Painted by William Strutt

11 William Wright was left in charge of the depot at Menindie. He was expected to follow Burke's party with supplies but was prevented from doing so

12 A trooper riding after Burke with a message from Melbourne. Painting by S. T. Gill

13 Dick, the Aboriginal guide who accompanied Trooper Lyons.
Painting by Ludwig Becker

14 William Brahé, 25, was left in charge of Cooper's
Creek depot after Burke's party set off for the Gulf.
Painting by William Strutt

15 'The Pioneer Party leaving Cooper's Creek'. Painting by
S. T. Gill

16 Burke and Wills at Camp 119 near the Gulf of Carpentaria.
Painting by S. T. Gill

seriously ill with scurvy and from the effects of drinking bad water. All March went by while they dragged themselves miserably forward.

Finally by mid-April they were all gathered at Bulloo, but Ludwig Becker, Stone and Purcell, were too weak even to raise themselves from the ground, and it was clearly impossible for them to continue any further. They were now an incredible sixty-nine days out of Menindie, and the whole caravan was in a state of near-desperation.

Up to this time the blacks had not been troublesome. On February 13, Wright says in his diary, a group of them had appeared, each man with a tassel tied to his loins and a bunch of emu feathers dangling from his chin. 'In the evening they brought their women to the camp and freely offered them as presents in return for the few things we had given them.' But at Bulloo 'bands often visited the camp signifying the ground to be theirs and ordering us to move away'. Every time Wright rode out he was surrounded by signal fires and the blacks gathered threateningly before him; once they had 'tried to entice Smith by means of their women'. Towards the end of April they had become still more menacing. Led by 'a strapping lubra bearing a boomerang with considerable grace' they advanced right into the camp, pilfering any article they could find. A stockade had been built and two tents had been erected outside it for the sick and dying men. These tents now attracted the attention of the blacks. Wright says: 'Dr. Beckler reporting to me that he saw natives creeping on their hands and knees near the fire, I took Smith down with me to clear them away. It was indeed high time—several of them were fingering their boomerangs as if impatient for a shy; and lifting up the lappels of Purcell's tent, commenced unpacking the medicine basket, while a third [man] with an armful of boomerangs was throwing them carelessly upon the ground near his brother warriors. However, they were not quite resolved upon hostilities, as when Smith and I pointed our pieces at them they very quietly moved off before us, and retired without any further manifestations of hostility. Throughout this scene Stone, though dying, behaved with great intrepidity, raising himself upon his bed and aiming his revolver at the natives when they approached him. About 2 pm just as the blacks moved off, I was called by Stone, who, grasping me by the hand, said "I am going". He then spoke a few words, and repeatedly asked that cold water should be thrown over him, as he could not breathe. Within ten minutes from the time he first called me, he turned upon his face and died.'

Two days later Purcell was also dead and the tribesmen came on again: 'The whole body clustered around Stone's grave and became most insulting in their demeanour. Taking up a dead rat one of them made a harangue upon it, and concluded by flinging it contemptuously at us. Finding we did not notice this, they threw the earth from Stone's grave in the air and after carrying logs as if mocking the erection of the stockade made signs that we should all meet the same fate as those dead.'

On April 27 things had come to a crisis: 'About eleven o'clock the cry of "Natives" started us to our feet, and every article near the fire was carried into the stockade with the utmost celerity. On looking out a body of natives numbering between forty and fifty could be seen advancing towards us from the west, not seeking any cover, but marching in good order straight across the open plain. On this occasion I saw plainly that they meant mischief, as they were all painted, and bore more spears than we had seen on any former occasion. Most of them were painted with a deep red band, from the neck down to the centre of the chest, crossed by similar bands at right angles to it. When within a couple of hundred yards, they quickened their pace into a run, exciting each other with war cries, and placing their arms in position ... despite all my motions for them to stop, they approached within a few yards of us before I gave the order to fire. A few discharges repulsed them, but as they collected again some 600 yards off I fired a rifle at them and eventually dispersed them. As soon as they disappeared we visited Mr. Becker in his tent, and found that he was quite unconscious of any unusual occurrence.'

Wright does not say how many blacks were killed or wounded.

The scurvy in the camp is something of a mystery. Ludwig Becker was in his fifties and perhaps might not have been able to offer much resistance to the disease, but Stone and Purcell were station hands who had been enlisted on the Darling; they were accustomed to the tough life in the interior, the bad water, the poor food, the devastating heat. This march of a couple of hundred miles or so was probably no worse than other marches they had done before; yet they succumbed, and all the attentions of a trained doctor could not save them.

Dr. Beckler subsequently wrote a medical report on the expedition, and in it he gives a description of what it was like to die in central Australia: the patient lying speechless in his tent through the awful silent heat of the day, too weak to move, husbanding his ration of water, the flies settling on his face and at night the mosquitoes attacking him. Scurvy is the easiest of diseases to cure, but in the absence of fresh fruit and vegetables there was nothing to be done; the patient simply lay there dumbly, while the will to live ebbed slowly away.

All this is obviously and terribly true, and yet one feels that it was not entirely the lack of vitamins that made these men die one after another, so inconsequentially, almost as though they were playing a part in some Elizabethan tragedy in which the minor figures are perfunctorily dispatched and, in a moment, are forgotten. It was a much tougher age than this, and the conditions of exploration are nearly always harsh—presumably they all knew that when they enlisted—and yet there is a certain unexplained callousness here. They were much too tough with one another. Burke says of Becker away back on the Murray, when they were making a forced march, 'The first two days of it nearly choked poor B——, and I think he will not be able to stand it much longer.' They thought Gray was gammoning on the journey down from the Gulf. Stone, and then Purcell, we now hear, just 'die'. But would they have died had there been a little less indifference to start with, a little more attention given to their first symptoms of weakness? Might it not have been better for the expedition to have kept together as a team, instead of the leaders pressing on ahead, leaving the devil to take the hindmost?

Now it was Becker's turn. On April 28 Wright had decided to beat a retreat to Torowoto, carrying the unconscious man with them on a camel. They were actually packing up to move when Brahe made his providential appearance. Brahe was not really able to improve the position very much—he had his own dying man with him, and he himself and his other two companions were far from well—but it seemed to the blacks that

Wright had received an impressive addition of strength, and that night they finally withdrew. Becker was not aware of all this; he lay prone and speechless in his tent all day, and that night he died without regaining consciousness.

Poor Becker. He was a mild and willing man, and he was the most gifted and sensitive member of the expedition, the best able to take a detached view of the scene. There was really no place for him in this adventure from the start; he thought they were out to observe what they saw, to open up new fields for science, to take careful notes as they went along, and instead he found himself engaged in a race and a struggle for survival. He was too gentle a man to engage in all this violence. They buried him beside Stone and Purcell on April 30, and then next morning set out for Menindie, a weary and dispirited group. It was more like an ambulance train than an expedition, Patton still strapped to his camel, several of the others hardly able to walk, and some of the animals visibly failing. They made camp beside the Koorliatto waterhole that night, just south of Bulloo, and Wright decided that he would have to give the sick a rest.

Brahe was now beginning to have doubts about Burke. Was it just possible that Burke had come back to the depot on the Cooper? Should he not go back to make sure? Should he not satisfy himself that the blacks had not disturbed the cache? They were still only eighty miles from the creek. Brahe put it to Wright that the two of them should make a visit to the depot while the sick were recuperating at Koorliatto, and Wright, surprisingly, agreed. Probably he wanted to be able to say when he got back that he had actually reached the depot. Taking three horses with them the two men set off on May 3, and after three days' hard riding arrived at the nearest part of the creek. Early in the morning of May 8—fifteen days after Burke had left it— they rode into the depot.

The place was silent and deserted. They tethered their horses to the trees and went inside the stockade. The cache appeared to be undisturbed, the camel-dung raked over the ground as it had been before. They saw camel tracks about the camp, but Brahe presumed that these had been made by his own animals before he left the depot. It was true that there were the ashes of three fresh campfires on the ground, but the blacks were always making such fires, and no doubt, Brahe decided, some of them had camped here since his departure; indeed, it would have been strange had they not visited the place. Brahe did not notice that the rake had been moved, nor the glass of the broken bottle on the top of the stockade, nor the bits of rag that King had hung there, nor the square that had been cut out of the leather door. He did not see the billy that King had left behind, or at any rate placed no significance upon it. The blazes were there on the trees with nothing added. In other words, Brahe saw what, no doubt, he wanted to see: that nothing had been disturbed, that he had been right to come away from the depot when he did.

They decided not to dig up the cache because the freshly upturned earth might attract the attention of the natives, and they did not think of adding another note to the bottle—what was there to say? Nor did there seem to be any point in adding a fresh blaze to the tree indicating that they had made a return visit to the depot. After fifteen minutes they decided that they had seen enough. They got on their horses and rode away.

It is tempting at this point to pause and consider what they would have done if they had dug up the cache and discovered Burke's letter there, and the rations gone. There is only one answer to this: they would have got on to Burke's tracks and followed them down the creek. Their horses were capable of at least twenty miles a day, while Burke and the others were on foot and very weak, and so there is no reason why they should not have overtaken them. Brahe and Wright did not have much food with them, but Burke's party still had most of the supplies they had got from the cache; and in any case they could have sent back to Koorliatto for more.

As things were, however, Brahe's conscience was clear: Burke's party had now been gone nearly five months, and he went off with Wright feeling that, for the moment, he could do no more. They got back to Koorliatto on May 13.

There now began the long agonizing ride home. For four weeks they wandered slowly southward, finding very little water; in fact, at one moment they might all have died but for a providential fall of rain. Two of the camels collapsed and were abandoned, and scab spread among the rest. Patton managed to hang on until early June, and then, having buried him, they went on again. On June 18 they straggled into Menindie.

Of the original party that had made this journey from Bulloo, four were dead, and only Wright, Brahe, Beckler, Hodgkinson, McDonough, Smith, Dost Mahomet and Belooch were left. They still had thirteen camels and twenty-three horses, and the bulk of the stores had been returned to Menindie.

On the way down Wright had railed constantly against Burke. He had been mad, he said, to go rushing off blindly like that to the north in midsummer, relying only upon surface water. He was lost, there was no question of it. 'What would have been the good?' he said to McDonough, 'of my waiting up there at Cooper's Creek with three or four months' provisions?' The others did not agree with 'him about this; they still thought that the lost party might have been picked up by a vessel somewhere on the northern coast, or that, by now, they might be in Queensland. But Wright was adamant. Burke, he said, was dead.

He did not, however, express these views quite so strongly in the report to the Committee which he dictated to Hodgkinson on his return to Menindie. Burke, he said, 'took with him but 12 weeks' rations, and I think it my duty to urge the Committee to dispatch a party for his relief without delay, unless they have received information of his arrival in the northern squatting districts. I would suggest the dispatch of a party overland, and a vessel to the Gulph [*sic*] shores, as it is not improbable that Mr. Burke, or a portion of his party, may be detained on the coast... In conclusion, I beg to remind the Committee, that any benefit to be derived from an attempt to relieve Mr. Burke will be rendered hopeless unless the party or parties are dispatched at eight weeks at the furthest.'

Wright did not propose to take part in either of the relief expeditions he so warmly urged on the Committee. Indeed, he proposed to do nothing more at all. He informed the Committee that his presence was urgently needed in Adelaide, and off he went there to rejoin his wife. It was Brahe who was left to go down to Melbourne and break the shocking news to the outside world.

CHAPTER TEN

Towards Mount Hopeless

Now in point of fact on May 8—the day that Brahe and Wright visited the depot on the Cooper—Burke, Wills and King were only about thirty miles away. They had intended, it will be recalled, to go back on their tracks down the creek for thirty or forty miles and then strike south-west to the homesteads which they believed existed near Mount Hopeless, about 150 miles away. That was the route Gregory had taken three years before and he had managed it, though admittedly in much better condition than Burke's party, in about a week. From Mount Hopeless it would be relatively easy to continue on through the settled districts to Adelaide.

At the start they had made very little progress, intending, as Wills says in his diary, 'to recruit themselves and the camels whilst sauntering slowly down the creek.' And so when they left the depot on the morning of April 23 they marched only five miles and then camped at a place where there was good feed for the camels. Next day they had a windfall. As they were about to start a party of blacks appeared, and in exchange for some matches and bits of leather strap gave them about 12 lb.

113

of freshly caught fish. They were greatly heartened by this, and again 'sauntered'—it seems a strange word, more indicative of a stroll through the park than this weary trudging—for a few more miles. That night they slept soundly despite the bitter cold and the dew on the ground in the early morning, and once again the blacks appeared with a gift of fish. 'They are,' Wills wrote in his diary, 'by far the most well-behaved blacks we have seen on Cooper's Creek.' He gave them some sugar which they ate with great delight. On this day, April 25, Burke called a halt after three hours on the banks of an immense waterhole several miles long. There were many birds feeding there, but they were shy and difficult to get at with a gun, and in any case none of the party had much energy for hunting. They had been a little shaken by a mishap that had occurred during the morning: one of the camels had fallen on a rocky stretch of path and had been cut and bruised before they had managed to get him up again. It was essential, as they all well knew, to keep the camels going since they themselves were quite unable to carry the food they had brought away from the cache in addition to their fire-arms and bed-rolls.

On the morning of April 26 they got up very early and the camels were loaded by the light of the moon. They followed a native path for a while, and then, after stopping for breakfast, continued on again through 'the most splendid salt-bush country you could possibly wish to see'. By noon they were back at their old camp from which they had made their tremendous thirty-mile walk into the depot on April 21. The journey had taken them four days this time, but they were not disturbed. 'This comparative rest,' Wills wrote, 'and the change in diet have worked wonders; the leg-tied feeling is now entirely gone, and I believe that in less than a week we shall be fit to undergo any fatigue whatever. The camels are improving, and seem capable of doing all that we are likely to require of them.'

They were ready now to make their forced march through new country towards civilization. Wills was still able to plot a course: he had a watch, a prism and a pocket compass in addition to a Réamur thermometer, and anyway they hoped to be able to follow the course of the Cooper nearly all the way.

The Cooper is an unpredictable stream. In a year of exceptional rainfall the head of water comes down with a roar,

17 Drawing of Burke and Wills in the mangroves off Flinders River, Feb. 1861

18 'The return to Cooper's Creek by Burke, Wills and King from the Gulf'. Painting by N. Chevalier

19 The 'DIG' tree photographed *circa* 1930

20 Rajah, the last camel, was killed for food when he was unable to walk. From illustrations by de Gruchy and Leigh in the *Diaries of Burke and Wills Expedition to Carpentaria*, 1861

May 30th 1861

We have been unable to leave the Creek. Both Camels are dead and our provisions are done.

Mr Burke & King are down on the lower part of the Creek I am about to return to them, when we shall all probably come up this way.

We are trying to live the best way we can like the Blacks but find it hard work.

Our clothes are going to pieces fast. Send provisions. and clothes as soon as possible.

William J Wills

The Depôt Party having left contin___ instructions ___ ___ ___ in this___

21   The note Wills left in the cache at the depot

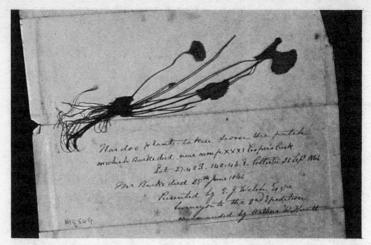

22 A sample of the nardoo plant collected by Howitt's search
party. The seeds of this plant provide a food source when ground

23 'Last hours of Burke and Wills'

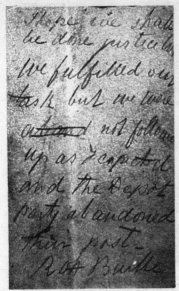
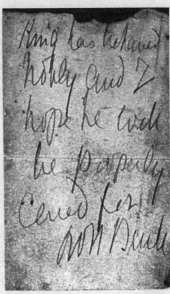

24 Notes written by Burke just before his death. King kept these fragments in a pouch around his neck until he was rescued

25 Dr Wills, the explorer's father, was active in organising a search party

26 Alfred Howitt, 31, led the rescue party which set
out in search of the missing explorers

27 'The Blacks inform John King that the Whitefellows are
coming'. 15 Sept. 1861. Illustration by de Gruchy and Leigh

28 'The finding of King', from *Illustrated Australasian News*, 1 Jan. 1891

29 'The Burial of Robert O'Hara Burke'. Painting by William Strutt

30 The funeral of Burke and Wills took place on 21 Jan. 1862. Alfred Howitt brought back the bodies of the explorers for a heroes' burial. From an engraving in *Illustrated London News*, 25 April 1863

31 The commemorative statue of Burke and Wills at its original site in Collins Street, Melbourne

picking up dead logs and debris of every kind, and for a dozen miles or more across the flat land there is nothing to be seen but a brown flood with the tops of the trees appearing above it. But this only happens every ten years or so. Normally the creek fans out into innumerable channels which run away in every direction, though generally towards the south-west, and these channels soon dry up into chains of waterholes and billabongs. Usually the water is drinkable, though it is very muddy and a slaty-greenish brown in colour. However hot the day it seems relatively cool to swim in, and in the opaque depths quite big fish can be netted. In the evening little turtles break the surface for an instant amid the screeching and shouting of the cockatoos. The banks of the waterholes can be twenty feet high or more, and are composed of fine grey silt that is scored by horizontal lines formed by the receding levels of the flood. Every branch of the creek is lined with timber and polygonum reeds which are very restful to the eye after a long hot day. These pleasant scenes, however, do not persist. The further you go down the Cooper towards Lake Eyre the drier it becomes, and in the end every channel peters out into rocks and sand. It does not matter which channel you follow; always you end up among sandhills and vast waterless plains of sharp red rocks with an occasional light covering of thorny bushes about a foot high. Nothing seems to move in this desert, not even a dingo (a native dog), and it is rare even to see a bird, except perhaps a wedge-tailed eagle overhead or a plover chasing grasshoppers on the hard ground. It is not sinister country in any way—it is too bright and open for that—but here the spaces are too vast, the sun too pitiless: time becomes an eventless continuum and the daylight hours pass in a torpor. Torpor, inertia—this is what overcomes the traveller in this country, especially if he is on foot, and his natural instinct is to recoil from the sun and to return to the nearest shade. There are, of course, days when clouds bank up and a cloudy sunset colours every object on the plain with a burning brilliant red. But then the pestilential flies redouble, a muffled windless heat brings a million crawling and flying insects out of the ground and often no rain falls.

Now, in late April, it was the beginning of winter, and the heat was not too bad—it was the cold by night that Burke and his two followers had to contend with—but it was not an exceptional year: no great flood had come down the Cooper. What they had to do then was to leave the creek and get themselves across this dry waste and somehow keep going until they reached the more fertile country around Mount Hopeless, a hundred miles or more away to the south-west.

The point from which they were about to strike out was a few miles to the west of the present homestead of Innamincka, and it was just about that part of the Cooper which Sturt had crossed and re-crossed sixteen years before. Sturt had had fairly fresh horses, sufficient food and a base to fall back on at Fort Grey, nor had he travelled so far as these men.

And so from now on we must picture them walking very slowly, exploring the dry channels of the Cooper one after another and constantly turning back when all signs of water gave out; a concentrated little group, walking in Indian file through the silent gum trees, pestered by the flies, not speaking very much, each one intent upon an inner world of his own discomfort—a chafing boot, a sore that would not heal, the thrusting off of a dead weight of lassitude—and no sound about them except the creaking of the camel packs. They were constantly on the watch, watching the flight of birds (as Sturt had done), watching for the signs of blacks and watching one another. They do not appear to have quarrelled or to have lost patience with each other, and this was no moment for hysteria. They were aliens in this hard indifferent country, this gaol of interminable space, and their only hope of escaping from it was by supporting one another to the limit. Burke was much older than the others—thirteen years older than Wills, eighteen years older than King—but he seems to have kept up very well, and they accepted him absolutely as their leader. Probably he took all the routine decisions of the march—when they should rest, where they should camp, what direction they should take. Since they went to bed soon after dusk, their bed-rolls laid out on the ground, they tended to get up early and do the first part of their march in the moonlight when it was cooler and there were no flies.

On Sunday, April 28—another of these fatal Sundays—a very serious thing happened: Landa, the better of their two male camels, got bogged in the mud beside a waterhole. This mud, as any present-day traveller on the Cooper can testify, is of a stickiness and tenacity that almost passes belief; it appears to be sandy and almost dry on top but even so light a weight as a man is sucked down at once into a morass and as he sinks black water oozes in upon him. Once fairly stuck into this mess even a vehicle with a four-wheel drive needs a tractor to haul it out, and for a camel thrashing about with his long legs the situation is much worse. 'Although we tried every means in our power,' Wills says, 'we found it impossible to get him out. All the ground beneath the surface was a bottomless quicksand, through which the beast sank too rapidly for us to get bushes or timber fairly beneath him, and being of a very sluggish, stupid nature, he could never be got to make sufficiently strenuous efforts towards extricating himself. In the evening, as a last chance, we let the water in from the creek, so as to buoy him up, and at the same time soften the ground about his legs, but it was of no avail. The brute lay quietly in it as if he enjoyed his position.' And indeed one feels that that soft cool bed may have been a welcome thing for poor stupid Landa after being driven for three thousand miles across Australia.

He lay all night in the mud and next day they made one more attempt to get him out. It was useless and they shot him. The rest of that day and all the next was spent in cutting off what meat they could get at and in drying it in strips in the sun. They were now left with only one camel, Rajah, and their position had taken a sharp turn for the worse. Now each man had to shoulder his own bedding and whatever else he could carry while the stores were loaded on the camel.

On May 2 they were still moving down the creek and still coming across parties of natives—more fish and nardoo cakes were exchanged for fish-hooks and sugar—and they went on until the water petered out in a forest of dry box trees. Then they turned back to the nearest waterhole to camp for the night. It had been a bad day. Rajah was trembling with exhaustion, and to lighten his load a little they took out a few small luxuries they had managed to preserve till now—some ginger, tea, cocoa, a few pounds of sugar and two or three tin plates—and threw them away.

They next went off in a northerly direction on another arm of the creek, and they stuck at it for two days before they were again confronted with the desert. Rajah was getting increasingly stiff; it was so cold in the mornings he could hardly get up with his load. On May 5 Wills left the others in camp and went out to reconnoitre by himself. He got himself on to the crest of a sandhill which gave him an all-round view. To the north and east there were lines of timber, but south and west, the direction in which they wanted to go, nothing but sand ridges and bare plains. 'This dreary prospect,' he says, 'offered no inducement to proceed.' He rejoined the others and they moved a little further up the creek to camp.

It was now two weeks since they had left the depot, and the possibility had to be faced that they would never get off the creek. 'The present state of things,' Wills wrote, 'is not calculated to raise our spirits much. The rations are rapidly diminishing; our clothing, especially the boots, are all going to pieces, and we have not the materials for repairing them properly; the camel is completely done up, and can scarcely get along, although he has the best of feed and is resting half the time. I suppose this will end in our having to live like the blacks for a few months.'

On the morning of May 7 Rajah was unable to get up off his knees even without his load, and Burke and Wills left him in King's charge while they went up the creek a little way to see what they could find. Towards midday they came on a native camp where they received a warm welcome; by now the tribes had taken strongly to these strange wandering visitors and were almost ready to adopt them. Burke and Wills were plied with fish and nardoo cakes till they could eat no more. They were also given pitchery—that strange drug that is made from roasting the stems of a native shrub and is still used by the blacks in the centre of Australia. King describes it thus: 'After chewing it for a few minutes I felt quite happy and perfectly indifferent about my position, in fact much the same effect as might be produced by two pretty stiff nobblers of brandy. After chewing it the natives do not throw it away but place it behind the ear, much in the same style as a sailor places his quid in his hat, until it has lost all goodness. Offering this pitchery pill to a stranger is the greatest expression of amity which, however, we did not at first understand and felt rather disgusted than otherwise when they used to press upon our acceptance their nasty dirty-looking balls of chewed grass, as it appeared to be. Young tribesmen were not allowed to use it.'

So now Burke and Wills forgot their plight for an hour or two and spent the night in a gunyah—a hut which the blacks had prepared for them. Next day, May 8, that same day that Brahe and Wright were at the depot a little further up the creek, Burke rejoined King while Wills went on alone with the reconnaissance, moving downstream this time. But again there was no way out: 'Finding that the creek turned greatly towards the north, I returned to the blacks' encampment; and, as I was about to pass, they invited me to stay. So I did so, and was even more hospitably entertained than before, being on this occasion offered a share of a gunyah, and supplied with plenty of fish and nardoo, as well as a couple of nice fat rats. The latter found most delicious. They were baked in the skins. Last night was clear and calm, but unusually warm. I slept by a fire, just in front of the blacks' camp. They were very attentive in bringing firewood and keeping up the fire during the night.'

When he got back to his own camp he found that Rajah, being unable to move any more, had been shot. Now they were entirely on their own resources. Burke and King spent the next two days cutting up the meat with their last two broken knives and a lancet, while Wills cast about for weeds and herbs to boil up into a soup. He experimented with a large bean the blacks called padlu, and found it not too bad, rather like 'a French chestnut'. But it was the native flour nardoo which was increasingly dominating their lives. The nardoo plant belongs to the Marsilea genus, a kind of fern, and it grows wild in crops about a foot high and chocolate brown in colour. When the seeds or spores are pounded on a flat, hollowed-out stone—and you see these stones by the hundreds in central Australia—a kind of flour is produced, and it can be worked up into a paste and baked in the ashes of a campfire. But it is an extremely long and monotonous business both to gather and grind the seed. A day's work will produce only a small handful of cakes, and there is not much nourishment in them. However, the blacks managed to survive on it, and Burke, seeing that they themselves would have to do the same, went back with King to the native encampment to find out all he could about the gathering and grinding of the seed.

Wills, left alone, made a note on May 11: 'I have now my turn at meat jerking, and must devise some means for trapping birds and rats, which is a pleasant prospect after our dashing trip to Carpentaria, having to hang about Cooper's Creek, living like the blacks.' Next day Burke and King returned with the depressing news that the blacks had disappeared. There was no longer now any question of the blacks 'giving trouble'; the party's very existence was beginning to depend upon them, and Burke and King set out once more on the search for the tribe, taking four days' provisions with them. They were back next day saying that no trace of them could be found; they were now entirely alone on this part of the creek. What then was to be done? Well, there was one thing: they could make one more determined effort to get off the creek and reach Mount Hopeless. If they could make a forced march of, say, thirty or forty miles across the plains surely they would find a creek or a waterhole of some sort. Then they would rest and go on again.

All May 15 was spent in planting the stores they could not carry and in getting ready, and next day they set out, each man with a 30-lb. pack on his shoulders, and Burke and King each carrying a billy full of water. They planned to live on nardoo cakes and three sticks of meat per man each day. At the very outset they made a most welcome find: a whole field of nardoo at the foot of a sandhill. This discovery, Wills says, caused 'a revolution in our feelings, for we considered that with the knowledge of this plant, we were in a position to support ourselves, even if we were destined to remain on the creek and wait for assistance from town'. For the moment, however, they were concentrated on this last effort to escape, and they made eight miles the first day. Their packs were too heavy, and next day they buried more of their stores, before pressing on again under a cold cloudy sky with a strange halo round the sun.

For the next six days there are merely jottings in Wills' diary; obviously the strain of the march left him with no energy to write. Perhaps had rain fallen they might have got through, but as things were they went on and on and there was nothing before them on the empty horizon, not a tree, not a sign of water. When they had marched about forty-five miles southwest from the creek—five miles beyond the point which they had estimated to be their absolute limit—they sat down among the sandhills to rest for an hour and then turned back.

Even across a gap of a hundred years it is difficult not to feel indignant. This was too hard; surely they might have been allowed, if not success, at least a little respite: a shower of rain, a pigeon such as Sturt had seen making for a waterhole, just one faint whisper of hope instead of this endless implacable rejection. The narrow margin by which they had missed Brahe at the depot had been, in the main, bad luck, and Brahe's failure on his return visit to realize that they had been there, though maddening, was a comprehensible twist of fate. But this remorseless hostility of the land itself was unfair, perversely and unnaturally so.

Yet still they were a good way from despair. When they had struggled back to their old camping ground on the Cooper on May 24 we get this note in Wills' diary: 'Started with King to celebrate the Queen's birthday by fetching from Nardoo Creek what is now to us the staff of life. Returned a little after two pm with a fair supply, but find the collecting of the seed a slower and more troublesome process than could be desired. Whilst picking the seed, about 11 am, both of us heard distinctly the noise of an explosion, as if of a gun, at some considerable distance. We supposed it to be a shot fired by Mr. Burke; but on returning to camp, found that he had not fired or heard the noise. The sky was partially overcast with high cum. str. clouds, and a light breeze blew from the east, but nothing to indicate a thunderstorm in any direction.'

It was, of course, impossible that it could have been a gunshot; sixteen days had passed since Brahe and Wright had visited the depot and they were now over a hundred miles off on their way down to Menindie. Like Sturt so long ago, what Wills and King undoubtedly heard was a piece of rock splitting off some distant cliff. But they did not know this, and their hope of a rescue party coming up to the Cooper was very strong. It seemed to them quite possible that someone had arrived at the depot and had fired a gun; and so it was decided that one of them should make a superhuman effort and walk back there to find out. The choice fell on Wills.

On May 27 he set off, carrying with him a few days' rations, a shovel, and his diaries which he proposed to bury in the cache. The journey began well. He found the ground 'quite black' with nardoo seed, and he came up with a group of native women and their children who were gathering it. Soon they were joined by a band of twenty men, and they led Wills off to their camp, promising him food. One man carried his shovel, another his swag. After eating with them Wills shared a gunyah with an old man of the tribe, and through the cold night fires were kept going so that they should be warm. Wills had completely altered his earlier opinion of the Cooper's Creek blacks—those mean-spirited and contemptible natives of six months ago; he refers to them now as 'my friends', and begins to compile in his diary a little vocabulary of their words.

He was not feeling very well next day after eating some freshwater mussels, but he pushed on again and presently he surprised a flock of crows squabbling on the ground over a freshly killed fish. He grabbed it from them and ate it for supper, together with nardoo porridge. That night he slept in a deserted hut and was fairly comfortable. He was now only eleven miles from the depot, and next day, May 30, he reached it at eleven in the morning. Again, nothing. No one there, no sign of any white man having been near the place. He dug up the cache with his shovel and found it just as they had left it on April 23, with Burke's letter lying in the otherwise empty box. So that was that: there was nothing more to be done. He sat down and wrote the following letter:

'Depot Camp, May 30.
    We have been unable to leave the creek. Both camels are dead, and our provisions are done. Mr. Burke and King are down the lower part of the creek. I am about to return to them, when we shall probably come up this way. We are trying to live the best way we can, like the blacks, but find it hard work. Our clothes are going to pieces fast. Send provisions and clothes as soon as possible.

                                        W. J. Wills.'

And then in a spasm of bitterness he added a postscript: 'The depot party having left, contrary to instructions, has put us in this fix. I have deposited some of my journals here for fear of accidents.'

When the letter was placed with the journals in the box he

shovelled back the earth again. It did not occur to him to add anything to the blazes on the trees, saying that he had been there, and that afternoon he turned back to rejoin the others.

He was now very weak, and perhaps his disappointment added to it. He had no food left at all. On June 2 he dragged himself into the last camp where the blacks had been so kind to him on the way up and found it deserted. He was desperately hungry and he gnawed at some fish bones he found lying about. Then he had a little luck on the next waterhole: 'I was so fortunate as to find a large fish, about a pound and a half in weight, which was just being choked by another, which it had tried to swallow, and which had stuck in its throat. I soon had a fire lit, and both of the fish cooked and eaten.' He slept that night under some polygonum bushes.

Next day he was hailed from across the waterhole by a native they had named Pitchery, and he was led into a camp where a large pile of fish was cooking. While the blacks stood round, two of them filleting the fish for him, he devoured the lot, and was then offered as much nardoo cake as he could eat. Strengthened by this he got back that night to Burke and King and gave them his dismal news.

Now at least the issue was clear. They could not leave the creek. Their only hope was to stay where they were and try with the help of the blacks to keep alive until rescue arrived.

CHAPTER ELEVEN

The Rescue Parties Set Out

The agitation in Melbourne about the fate of the expedition had been growing since March. In that month the *Argus* published a letter: 'What has become of the expedition? Surely the Committee are now alive to the necessity of sending someone up? Burke by this time has crossed the continent or is lost. What has become of Wright? What is he doing?'

This was soon followed by other letters and leading articles in all the Melbourne papers. It was pointed out that nothing had been heard from Burke since he had written his letter from Torowoto in October of the previous year, and that was five months before. People began to recall the fate of Leichhardt, who had disappeared in this very area in 1848; and it was also a matter of some chagrin that McDouall Stuart, the South Australian, had come back from *his* expedition safe and sound. It was true that Stuart had not quite succeeded in reaching the

Gulf of Carpentaria, but it had been a remarkable feat and in January 1861 this determined man had set out once more. Stuart was clearly going to win the great exploration race unless something was done.

Wills' father, Dr. William Wills, was very naturally concerned, and he kept writing to the Committee for news. Dr. Wills was not perhaps an impressive figure—people seem to have found him very tedious and interfering—but he was intensely proud of his son, and he was a pertinacious man. He had been very active at the start of the expedition, now having a word with Burke, now buttonholing the members of the Committee and generally interesting himself in all the arrangements. He is the sort of character Charles Dickens would have enjoyed writing about, the self-important figure who bobs up on every occasion and is determined to make himself felt. It is not hard to see where young Wills' sense of self-righteousness came from, for his father had it also and to the full; and when Dr. Wills' self-righteousness was aroused he was not easily to be turned aside. After the expedition was over he wrote a book about it, and either by innuendo or outright denunciation he demolished nearly everybody's reputation. There is something almost feminine in Dr. Wills' avenging single-mindedness.

Of Wright he says, 'a more ignorant being could not have been extracted from the bush. He was scarcely able to write his name.' Landells, he suggests, gave in his resignation either because he was frightened of going on into the unknown or because he wanted to displace Burke from the leadership. Dr. Beckler, he says, 'was neither a man of courage, energy, nor of medical experience.' Of Brahe and his deciding to leave the depot, he writes, 'the man was over-weighted; the position was too much for him, and he gave way when a stronger mind might have stood firm. The worst point about him seems to be his want of consistency and miserable prevarication. He even hints that Brahe was given written orders by Burke to remain indefinitely at the depot, and that he deliberately burnt them.

Ludwig Becker was 'physically deficient, advanced in years, and his mode of life in Melbourne had not been such as to make up for his want of youth. I do not mean to imply by this,' Dr. Wills goes on, 'that he indulged in irregular or dissipated habits. He possessed a happy gift of delineating natural objects with the pencil, but died before passing the bounds of civilisation, from causes unconnected with want or fatigue.' Of Dr. Macadam, the Secretary of the Committee, he says, 'I sincerely trust it may never be my fortune to come in contact with him again in any official business whatever. He is a man of unbounded confidence in his own powers, ready to undertake many things at the same time: and would not, I suspect, shrink from including the governorship of the colony, if the wisdom of superior authority were to place it at his disposal.'

No doubt there was a grain of truth in some of these judgements, but it is also clear that Dr. Wills was a marvellous indulger in prejudice. Even when one makes all allowances for his very natural anxiety he was too harsh. It is difficult to see what exactly he *was* trying to imply about Ludwig Becker—no one else has suggested that the poor fellow was an alcoholic—but at all events it was something unpleasant. And now in June 1861 Dr. Wills, with some justification, decided to make himself unpleasant with the Committee unless they bestirred themselves. He had received no answers to the letters he had written to Dr. Macadam, and so 'in the month of June, unable to bear the suspense any longer, with a small pack on my shoulders and a stick in my hand, I walked from Ballarat to Melbourne, a distance of seventy-five miles...'

He arrived just in time to attend a meeting called by the Committee to discuss what should be done. 'A chapter in the Circumlocution Office,' Dr. Wills says, 'painfully unfolded itself;' one after another the members made speeches about the finances of the expedition, the geography of the interior and the various routes that Burke might have taken. Dr. Wills warmly intervened to say that a rescue party should set out at once, and that he himself was ready to be a member of it. No one seems to have been much impressed by this; indeed, a Mr. Ligar, one of the Committee members, 'rather rudely asked me what I was in such an alarm about; observed that "there was plenty of time; no news was good news: and I had better go home and mind my own business".' Mr. Ligar was going to be made to regret those words.

Dr. Wills alone the Committee might have ignored, but not the Press; it was now in full cry, and at last, in the middle of June, it was announced that a 'Contingent Expedition' was to go out and make a search for the missing men. It was fortunate that, just at this moment, a really exceptional man offered himself as the leader of the rescue party. Alfred William Howitt came from a Quaker family; he was the son of the author, William Howitt, and he had arrived in Australia with his father in the early fifties to try his luck on the goldfields. Since then the young man had established himself as an explorer, at first in the country around Lake Eyre to the south-west of Cooper's Creek, and latterly in Gippsland in eastern Victoria, where he was leading a government expedition in search for gold. It seems strange that Howitt's name had never come up when the Committee was casting about for a leader of the original expedition, for he was a steady and intelligent man, an anthropologist, a geologist and an excellent bushman: a man in the Sturt tradition. He was just 31. It was now decided that with three others, a surveyor named Edwin J. Welch[1] and two assistants, Alex Aitkin and Weston Phillips, Howitt was to go to Menindie and make his way up Burke's track to Cooper's Creek. At this stage he was thought of as hardly more than a courier—a man to bring back news to the Committee.

On June 26 he set off with a minimum of fuss in Cobb's Coach for Swan Hill. Three days later the party reached an inn called the Durham Ox, on the Loddon River, and here they fell in with Brahe, who was on his way down to Melbourne. Directly he heard Brahe's news Howitt saw that the whole position was altered: a much more substantial expedition would have to be got together if Burke was to be found, and he wired the Committee in Melbourne saying that he was returning immediately with Brahe. They reached Melbourne on Sunday, June 30, and were at once taken off by Dr. Macadam to report to Barkly, the Governor, and Sir William Stawell at Government House in Toorak. Four men dead, Wright's party back at Menindie and Wright himself gone off to Adelaide, Burke missing since December 16 and now abandoned somewhere in the north—it was terrible news. Macadam rode off round the town to assemble the other members of the Committee and they all gathered in the Royal Society's rooms that afternoon. Now finally that the truth had reached them the

[1]Welch's father was wounded with Nelson in the *Victory*, and was later captain of the ship.

Committee were not at all complacent; they were very disturbed and everyone had something to say. Perhaps they also felt a little apprehensive about what the Press was going to print next day. Reading between the lines of the minutes of this meeting one detects a strained and harassed air.

Brahe was briskly questioned. Why had he left Cooper's Creek before his provisions were exhausted? Why had he not sent a message down to Menindie long ago? Why had he not kept a diary? Where did he think Burke was now?

Brahe appears to have answered these and a hundred other questions quite firmly and lucidly, and the Committee, though obviously looking for a scapegoat, calmed down a little as their knowledge was expanded. Brahe was sent off to write up a diary of the events on Cooper's Creek from such rough notes as he possessed, and Sir William Stawell remarked that there could be all kinds of explanations for Burke's absence: 'His men might have been attacked with scurvy, and be still alive without being able to move any distance; and they might be in some place waiting the arrival of the rainy season. That is but one of the thousand chances that might detain him ... Although we must necessarily feel anxious there is no ground for despairing at all.'

This was soothing. On the other hand, something had to be done and for an hour or more the members debated the matter back and forth without achieving much more than getting themselves into a muddle. It was Howitt who restored some direction to the proceedings. He submitted a letter which he had drafted on his way down to Melbourne from the Loddon, and in it he suggested that he should set out at once with a somewhat larger party. Brahe, he said, had offered to come back with him and his experience should be invaluable. They should go first to Menindie and pick up the camels and the horses there; by this time they must be recovering from their journey down from Bulloo. It now being winter he believed he could get up to the Cooper fairly quickly, taking five or six months' rations with him. He then proposed to get on to Burke's track and follow it, at any rate as far as Eyre's Creek, keeping a look-out for any documents that might be buried there. From that point on his subsequent actions would be guided by what he discovered.

The members fell upon this sensible document and debated it clause by clause. Stawell pointed out that speed was all: Wright's slow progress had enabled the natives to close in upon him. They should not adjourn the meeting 'having so unusually met on a Sunday' without passing a resolution to enable Howitt to get away at once. Others thought it more important to have his party properly organized than to gain a day. They decided that Howitt should have ten men in addition to Brahe, two of them black trackers, and one of them a doctor. He should have a supply of antiscorbutic medicines to combat 'the dreadful malady of scurvy'. A sub-committee should be formed to make the arrangements. Motion after motion was passed, and in the end it was agreed that they could do no more that night and that they should meet again on the following day.

Next day Dr. Macadam read out the diary that Brahe had written during the night, and although it threw little more light on the situation it helped the Committee to come to a decision: they agreed finally, more or less as they had done the year before in the case of Burke, to forget all about their motions and directions, and to give Howitt a free hand. No doubt they were prodded somewhat by an article that had appeared in the Melbourne *Age*: 'The unexpected news of Mr. Burke's expedition of discovery, which we publish this morning, is positively disastrous. The entire company of explorers has been dissipated out of being, like dewdrops before the sun. Some are dead, some are on their way back, one has come to Melbourne, and another has made his way to Adelaide, whilst only four of the whole party have gone forward from the depot at Cooper's Creek upon the main journey of the expedition to explore the remote interior ... The whole expedition appears to have been one prolonged blunder throughout; and it is to be hoped that the rescuing party may not be mismanaged and retarded in the same way as the unfortunate original expedition was. The *savans* [*sic*] have made a sad mess of the whole affair; let them, if possible, retrieve themselves in its last sad phase.'

The unfortunate *savans* of the Committee were also urged by the newspaper to send a second rescue party round by ship to the Gulf of Carpentaria.

Landells, the discredited camel-man, also intervened. He had been a good deal shunned since his return to Melbourne, and all his efforts to rehabilitate himself through letters to the Press had been unsuccessful. The Committee had refused to have anything more to do with him. He now wrote to Barkly (not the Committee) saying that he had managed to cure the six sick camels that had been left behind at Royal Park when the original expedition set out, and that he was willing to take them off on a search for Burke. Barkly appears to have taken no action over this; the letter was quietly filed in the Royal Society's archives and there it remains to this day. Attached to it is an indignant note from the man who was in charge of the animals at Royal Park, saying that Landells had never been near them and had nothing to do with their cure.

Howitt had hoped to get away on the Monday night's coach to Swan Hill, but it was not until three days later, July 4, that he managed to assemble his party. There were nine of them in all: Howitt himself, Brahe, a Dr. Wheeler, four assistants and two black trackers, Sandy and Frank. Welch, the surveyor, and the other two men had gone on to Swan Hill, and Howitt was to pick them up on his way through. The Government had indicated that it would put up £2,000 towards the expenses, and the salaries were fixed at £300 per annum for Howitt, £200 for Brahe, Wheeler and Welch, £120 for the six assistants, and ten shillings a week each for Sandy and Frank. Dr. Eades, the medical Lord Mayor, produced a supply of medicine to deal with scurvy, and the Committee gave Howitt a letter for Burke saying how concerned they were about him and informing him of Howitt's appointment. Howitt was very clear about this last matter: he insisted that if he did meet Burke he would not be under Burke's orders but would continue to control his own party. A second letter for Burke was given to Howitt to deliver. It ran as follows:

'Dear Sir,

It is with fear I now address you but I hope my fear will soon be allayed by hearing of you safe and sound . . . I daresay you almost forget me but if you scrape your various reminiscences of the past you may well recollect the laughing, joyous C. Cupid.

My sincere regards to you; all the citizens in and around Melbourne join in love to you, bless your little heart.

C.'

It was a kind thought, and indeed Julia Matthews had been anxious about Burke; she had even gone to the editor of one of the newspapers and had urged him to work up interest in a rescue party.

The *Age*'s suggestion was now taken up. In 1856 the sloop *Victoria* had been built in England and then sailed out to Australia. She was a fine vessel for her day, steam-driven, of 580 tons displacement, and she carried a crew of 158; indeed, she was something of a status-symbol, for she was the first war-ship to be built for any British colony. The *Victoria* was refitting just at this time, but her commander Captain W. H. Norman believed that he could have her ready within three weeks, and he was now ordered to proceed as soon as possible to the Albert River, on the Gulf of Carpentaria, taking in company with him the sailing-brig *Firefly*. Meanwhile a Mr. James Orkney offered the use of the *Sir Charles Hotham*, a little 16-ton steamer which he himself had built on the model of the *Great Eastern*. It was thought that the *Sir Charles Hotham* might be very useful in searching the shallow rivers on the Gulf, and so on July 6, with a commander and a crew of two, she gallantly set sail for the north, expecting to be overtaken by the two larger vessels later on. Mr. Orkney himself was footing the expense.

By now all the Australian colonies had been roused by the news of the missing explorers, and everyone wanted to help. Barkly wrote to his friend, Sir G. F. Bowen, the Governor of Queensland, asking whether his government would consider fitting out an expedition to look for Burke. The Queenslanders were more than willing. They voted £500, and under Gregory's supervision assembled two separate parties. One of these was led by William Landsborough, an experienced bushman who had emigrated to Australia in his youth and had taken up land on the outskirts of the Queensland settlements. Drought and hostile blacks had driven him out, and in recent years he had taken to exploration. It was now settled that Landsborough should have the assistance of two white men and two blacks, and that with thirty horses they should embark on the *Firefly* when it reached Brisbane. They were to be landed on the Albert River on the Gulf and thence strike southwards in search of Burke.

The other party was commanded by Frederick Walker, a very

tough character who had been in charge of a squad of mounted native police at Wagga in New South Wales. Walker had been so ruthless in his dealings with the tribes that he had been dismissed from the service, but latterly the white settlers had employed him and his band as a kind of private vigilante force in their skirmishes against the blacks. Walker was to march directly overland from Rockhampton, on the Queensland coast, in the hope of coming on Burke's trail somewhere in the interior. It was arranged that Captain Norman should keep an eye out for him and supply him with stores when he reached the Albert River; each evening at 8 p.m. the *Victoria* was to fire off a gun and half an hour later a signal rocket. At 9 p.m. a blue light was also to be sent up. The *Victoria* was to remain for six months as a base-ship in the Gulf, and Norman was to act as the co-ordinator of both these Queensland parties.

All this was very speedily and efficiently arranged. The little 16-tonner *Sir Charles Hotham* soon dropped out of the running—she was towed out of Port Melbourne by one of the coastal steamers but was cut adrift in bad weather and eventually ran aground north of Sydney—but the *Victoria* and the *Firefly* got away from Melbourne on August 4 and a week later reached Brisbane, where Landsborough's party was taken on board. They had trouble on the Barrier Reef north of Brisbane when the *Firefly* ran aground in a hurricane and the horses had to be swum ashore, but later she was refloated and taken in tow by the *Victoria*. The two vessels safely reached the Albert River early in October. By this time Walker was well on his way inland.

Still another rescue party was put into the field by South Australia. Its commander, John McKinlay, aged 42, was a huge man, six foot four inches in height, and like Landsborough he was a Scot who had come out to Australia as a young man and had worked and explored on the edge of the settled districts of New South Wales. McKinlay happened to be in Melbourne when Brahe arrived, and so had a thorough knowledge of all there was to be known of Burke's movements and of conditions in the centre. On returning to Adelaide to assemble his party McKinlay found that Hodgkinson had arrived there from Menindie, and he was at once enlisted as surveyor and second in command of the South Australian party. Four other men and some black trackers were also engaged. McKinlay intended to rely chiefly upon horses and he had twenty-four of them, but it so happened that two of the three camels that Wills had lost north of the Cooper eight months before had turned up in the settlements near Mount Hopeless; apparently they had wandered in a leisurely way down the creek and they had kept in good condition. The two animals were added to McKinlay's strength, and a pair of the Royal Park camels were also brought round by sea from Melbourne to Adelaide in the steamer *Oscar*.

McKinlay's instructions were plain: he was to get on to the Cooper and whether or not he met Howitt there he was to keep on going northwards. The South Australian Government also thought it would be a good plan if he kept a look-out for gold, minerals and precious stones along the way. On August 16 McKinlay led his little caravan out of Adelaide.

So now (not to speak of Stuart, who was already in the field), there were four expeditions headed into the centre: Walker and his mounted black trackers marching north-west from the Queensland coast, Landsborough striking south from the Gulf of Carpentaria, and Howitt and McKinlay coming up from the south. All four leaders were men who had lived for years in the outback and were accustomed to exploring in the bush. They had a firm base in the sloop *Victoria* on the Gulf of Carpentaria in the north, and a point of rendezvous on Cooper's Creek in the centre. In each case the parties were small, lightly equipped and very mobile; and it was now the cool winter season when water was to be found in the interior. The different colonies which had once been divided against one another and jealous of each other's explorations were now united, and the newly established telegraph lines between the capitals were kept fairly humming with messages co-ordinating the arrangements.

It is of course nearly always easier for a rescue party than for an original expedition: they have something definite to aim at, a track to follow instead of breaking new ground, and it is not so difficult to avoid errors when others have gone before. Even so it is surprising that these four expeditions were set up with such dispatch and with such professionalism in the matter of a couple of months. The explanation probably is that committees and governments behave much more sensibly and generously in a crisis than they do in the bumbling normal times of everyday life. The fate of a little group of lost human beings now seemed more important than all the mysteries of the centre, the hopes of gold, new farming lands and an inland sea; and tragedy—or at any rate the fear of tragedy—was proving a greater spur to action than either curiosity or ambition.

After Howitt had left Melbourne, Dr. Wills had come round to Adelaide by sea. He had a notion (which he dropped later) that he might offer himself as surgeon to McKinlay's party, and anyway Adelaide seemed as good a place as anywhere to wait for news. And in fact the first news of any interest did arrive at Adelaide. Towards the middle of September Dr. Wills received a note from Warburton, the commissioner of police, saying that he had important information and asking him to call.

'I hastened to him,' Dr. Wills says, 'and asked, "What news—good or bad?" He replied, "Not so bad," and then gave me the information which was made known in the House of Assembly that night.' It was a message from the police trooper in the little outpost of Wirrilpa, near Mount Searle, about halfway from Adelaide to Cooper's Creek, saying that a black named Sambo had come in from the north with a story that a party of white men were living on a creek in the centre. They were quite naked and had no stores or fire-arms of any kind, but they had camels with them. They kept alive by fishing with nets made of grass and they lived on board a raft. The local tribesmen were very frightened of them.

Well, it could be true; and anyway the police trooper had met McKinlay on his way north and had given him the news. He would investigate the matter. Dr. Wills went back to Melbourne, hoping that by now something had been heard from Howitt. After all, his had been the first rescue party in the field; he would be the first on to Cooper's Creek.

We hear nothing in all this about Wright, the man whose delay at Menindie had set the whole elaborate chain of events into motion. He was in Adelaide, lying low.

CHAPTER TWELVE

Howitt's March

Howitt made excellent headway on his journey northwards; by July 13 he was through Swan Hill, and on July 30 he swam his horses across the Darling at Menindie. Here he picked up sufficient stores for five or six months, and on August 14 he set out for the Cooper with thirty-seven horses and seven camels. They stuck to Burke's old route through Mootwingee and Torowoto and then, with Brahe showing them the way, they by-passed Bulloo and struck directly north to the Cooper. After the nightmare of Wright's meanderings this march was a model of precision and dispatch. They reached the creek in twenty-five days.

They were travelling, of course, at the best time of the year, when water was to be found at almost every halt, and indeed it was raining quite heavily during the last part of the journey. In this cool weather migrating birds teemed around the water-

holes, and everywhere the land was coming to life again, sometimes unpleasantly so, for they were harassed by flies and the
rain had brought out death adders and other snakes. On the
orange-coloured sandhills the pink mesembryanthemum was
in flower, and in the creek where Brahe and his men had not
bothered to fish they had no difficulty in hooking quantities of
perch. Howitt knew how to live off the land, and they made
good meals of pigeons roasted on coals, and of crayfish and
mussels dredged up from the waterholes.

Their purpose now was to make their way down the Cooper,
keeping a look-out for fresh camel tracks or any other signs of
Burke's return. On the face of it this search was a hopeless affair,
or rather it must have seemed so now that they were confronted
with the enormity of their task. Nine months had elapsed since
Burke had disappeared. Nothing whatever was known of his
route after leaving the Cooper; he could be anywhere within a
thousand miles and nearly all this country was unknown and
unexplored. Howitt speaks of 'the mysterious vastness of the
desert interior which held, somewhere, the secret which it was
our mission to discover'. One can imagine them plodding on
day after day with the black trackers marching in front and
stopping to examine the ground when there was anything
interesting to be seen. Once they came on what appeared to be
the tracks of a large cart, just such tracks as Wills had found on
the first march to the Cooper so long ago. Howitt followed the
tracks and found that they had been caused by heavy logs being
dragged along the ground during a flood.[1] But for the rest the
march up from Menindie was uneventful. The silent unreveal-
ing bush enfolded them, the dingoes loped away as they
approached, the kangaroos stared meaninglessly at the strange
procession, and nothing was communicated. Sometimes
strange double mirages quivered on the plains around them
and trees hung upside down in the empty sky. Where in all this
dreaming, floating space was Burke to be found?

There had been just one encouraging incident on September
6, when they were approaching the flat-topped hills and the
gibber plains of the Cooper country. A party of blacks—an old
grey-haired man, a younger man and a group of lubras with
their children—had come up to them on a dry watercourse.

[1]See page 63.

'They were in a very excited state,' Howitt says, 'waving branches and jabbering incessantly. The younger man shook all over with fright. Sandy could not understand them, and I could only catch "Gow" (Go on). At last, by the offer of a knife, I prevailed on the old man to come with us to show us the nearest water, but after half a mile his courage gave way, and he climbed up a box-tree, to be out of reach. Mr. Brahe rode up to him, when he climbed into the top branches, jabbering without stopping for a moment. Finding that he would not come down and kept pointing to the N.W. (our course) we left him.'

Whatever all this could have meant it was clear that the blacks were eager for them to follow down the creek, and the party marched onwards in the rain, the camels skidding awkwardly on the wet ground. On September 9 they were again approached by a group of blacks—'fine, well-built young men', with fishing nets wrapped round their waists, who called to them across the creek, waving their arms and beckoning them on. One of them on the following day came up to Howitt and offered him a plug of pitchery. He was very friendly, despite the fact that he had painted his body like a skeleton, but when they tried to find out from him if he had seen any white men with camels he could not understand.

On September 13 they rode into Depot LXV and Brahe declared that it was precisely as he had left it, the stockade still standing, no fresh blazes on the trees, nothing to indicate that anyone except blacks had been there. Incredibly they did not open the cache. The mute appeal of the word 'Dig' on the tree meant nothing to them: they had ample rations, Howitt explained later, and so there seemed to be no purpose in broaching the store Brahe had left behind. They stayed only a few minutes at the depot and then camped several miles further down the creek.

Next day they reached the place where Burke had made his last camp on the Cooper before striking north to the Gulf on his outward journey, and here at last they came on signs that within the past few months someone had visited the place. Around the camp there were camel droppings and tracks in places where Brahe was certain Burke's camels had never been on the outward journey. 'It looked very much,' Howitt wrote in his diary, 'as if stray camels had been about during the past four months. The tracks seemed to me to be going up the creek, but the ground was too stony to be able to make sure.'

Early next morning he set out with Sandy to cast about, and they had hardly gone a mile or two when they came on tracks running in all directions around the end of a large waterhole, and here on the ground Howitt picked up the handle of a clasp-knife. A little further on they came on very definite camel foot-prints going east, and the track of a horse. 'In about four miles,' Howitt wrote, 'this led me to the lower end of a very large reach of water, and on the opposite side were numbers of native wurleys (or huts). I crossed at a neck of sand and at a little distance again came on the track of a camel going up the creek; at the same time I found a native who began to gesticulate in a very excited manner, and to point down the creek, bawling out, "Gow! Gow!" as loud as he could; when I went towards him he ran away, and finding it impossible to get him to come to me, I turned back to follow the camel track and to look after my party, as I had not seen anything of them for some miles . . . Crossing the creek, I cut our track, and rode after the party. In doing so I came upon three pounds of tobacco which had lain where I saw it for some time. This, together with the knife-handle, the fresh horse tracks, and the camel track going east-ward, puzzled me extremely, and led me into a hundred con-jectures.'

And at this point messengers from the rest of his party, who had remained on another branch of the creek, came hastening towards him. They had tremendous news. King had been found.

It was Welch, the surveyor, who had discovered him. Welch had been hanging back in the rear of the party as they had made their way down the creek, and he had been very much on the alert as a crowd of blacks on the opposite bank of a waterhole had kept calling to him and urging him on. Suddenly, Welch says, his horse, Piggy, bolted towards them. The blacks scat-tered in fright leaving behind them 'one solitary figure, appar-ently covered with some scarecrow rags and part of a hat, and prominently alone on the sand. Before I could pull up I passed it, and as I passed, it tottered, threw up its hands in the attitude of prayer, and fell on the ground. The heavy sand helped me conquer Piggy on the level, and when I turned back the figure had partially risen. Hastily dismounting, I was soon beside it, excitedly asking:

' "Who in the name of wonder are you?"

'He answered, "I am King, sir." For the moment I did not grasp the fact that the object of our search was attained, for King, being only one of the undistinguished members of the party, his name was unfamiliar to me.

' "King?" I repeated. "Yes," he said. "The last man of the exploring expedition."

' "What, Burke's?"

' "Yes."

' "Where is he and Wills?"

' "Dead—both dead long ago." And again he fell to the ground.'

Welch fired a revolver to attract the attention of the others, and presently Howitt came up. It was difficult to make out what King was saying, and he was an appalling sight, burnt by the sun and half demented by starvation and loneliness. 'He presented,' Howitt says, 'a melancholy appearance; wasted to a shadow, and hardly to be distinguished as a civilised being but for the remnants of clothes upon him. He seemed exceedingly weak, and found it occasionally difficult to follow what we said. The natives were all gathered round, seated on the ground, looking with a most gratified and delighted expression.'

Howitt made camp at once and they carried King up to a tent on the bank beside the creek. Dr. Wheeler, who attended him, said afterwards that he could not have lived more than a few days had he not been found. What he craved for were sweet things and fat, and Wheeler fed him on a light diet of rice, sugar and butter. Next morning he was a good deal improved and little by little they got his story from him. Howitt sat beside him jotting it down in pencil in his notebook, secretly fearing that the patient would die before he got to the end. Brahe was also listening and no doubt was appalled. It is from Howitt's excellent transcription and from Wills' field-books (which were recovered from his grave a day or two later) that we can now piece together the story of how the explorers lived out their last weeks on the Cooper.

There had been an altercation with the blacks, King said,

while Wills was away at the depot early in June. The blacks had been very friendly, supplying them with fish each day, but they kept invading the gunyah of branches where Burke had stored the ammunition and the few articles of baggage they still possessed. 'One of the natives,' King said, 'took an oilcloth out of this gunyah and Mr. Burke, seeing him run away with it, followed him with his revolver and fired over his head, and upon this the native dropped the oilcloth. While he was away the other blacks invited me away to a waterhole to eat fish; but I declined to do so, as Mr. Burke was away, and a number of natives who were about would have taken all our things. When I refused one took his boomerang and laid it over my shoulder, and then told me by signs that if I called out for Mr. Burke, as I was doing, that he would strike me. Upon this I got them all in front of the gunyah and fired a revolver over their heads, but they did not seem at all afraid, until I got out the gun when they all ran away. Mr. Burke, hearing the report, came back, and we saw no more of them until late that night, when they came with some cooked fish and called out "White fellow". Mr. Burke then went out with his revolver, and found a whole tribe coming down, all painted and with fish in small nets carried by two men. Mr. Burke went to meet them, and they wished to surround him, but he knocked as many of the nets of fish out of their hands as he could, and shouted out to me to fire. I did so, and they ran off. We collected five small nets of cooked fish. The reason he would not accept the fish from them was that he was afraid of being too friendly lest they should always be in our camp.'

This was folly: they could not live without the help of the blacks, and Wills seems to have made this clear to Burke on his return. At all events, Wills went off to the blacks' camp to make peace with them. They were, King says, 'very hospitable and friendly, keeping him with them for two days. Then they made signs for him to be off. He came to us and narrated what had happened, but went back to them the following day, when they gave him his breakfast, and made signs to him to go away. He pretended not to understand them, and would not go, upon which they made signs that they were going up the creek, and that he had better go down. They packed up and left the camp, giving Mr. Wills a little nardoo to take to us.'

It was during this period, about June 5 (King was vague about dates), that the gunyah with the stores inside it was burnt. Burke was cooking some fish and a strong wind carried the sparks of the fire on to the dry branches of the hut. It blazed to ashes in a moment and they succeeded in saving only one gun and a revolver. It was now desperately important for them to rejoin the blacks and if possible live with them. Next morning they packed up their remaining things—30 lb. each was as much as they could carry—and trudged over to the blacks' encampment, only to find that it was deserted. However, there was a field of ripening nardoo nearby and they camped there to gather the seed. They were beginning now to move like automatons, dully and mechanically. 'Mr. Wills and I,' King said, 'used to collect and carry home a bag each day, and Mr. Burke generally pounded sufficient for our dinner during our absence, but Mr. Wills found himself getting very weak, and was shortly unable to go out and gather nardoo as before, nor even strong enough to pound it, so that in a few days he became almost helpless. I still continued gathering; and Mr. Burke now also began to feel very weak, and said that he could be of very little use in pounding. I now had to gather and pound for all three of us. I continued to do this for a few days, but finding my strength rapidly failing, my legs being very weak and painful, I was unable to go out for several days, and we were compelled to consume six days' stock which we had laid by.'

It was now the third week in June and thunderstorms began to crash above the creek. In the bitter cold at night the three men huddled together in a native hut, and they began to realize that they could not continue much longer. Wills in particular was failing rapidly for want of a stronger diet, and he insisted that there was only one hope left: he must be left behind in the hut while the two others, who were a little stronger, went off up the creek in search of the blacks. Wills assured them that if they left him a supply of food he would be able to hold out until they returned; it was the only chance for all three of them to survive.

In the end Burke agreed, and while Wills lay in the hut, the two others painfully set to work building up a store of nardoo.

'Night and morning very cold, sky clear,' Wills wrote in his diary on June 20. 'I am completely reduced by the effects of the cold and starvation. King gone out for nardoo. Mr. Burke at home pounding seed; he finds himself getting very weak in the legs. King holds out by far the best.' When the sun came out at midday Wills tried to give himself a sponge bath but found he could not manage it 'with any proper expedition'.

Next day he writes: 'Unless relief comes in some form or other, I cannot possibly last more than a fortnight. It is a great consolation, at least, in this position of ours, to know that we have done all we could, and that our deaths will rather be the result of the mismanagement of others than any rash acts of our own. Had we come to grief elsewhere we could only have blamed ourselves; but here we are, returned to Cooper's Creek, where we had every reason to look for provisions and clothing; and yet we have to die of starvation, in spite of the explicit instructions given by Mr. Burke, that the depot party should await our return, and the strong recommendation to the Committee that we should be followed up by a party from Menindie.'

June 24 was 'a fearful night'. A mad gale continued almost till dawn and they lay together 'shrivelled' with cold.

Wills was beginning to get the days mixed up and the next entry is dated June 23. 'Near daybreak,' he says, 'King reported seeing a moon in the E. with a haze of light stretching up from it; he declared it to be quite as large as the moon, and not dim at the edges. I am so weak that any attempt to get a sight of it was out of the question; but I think it must have been Venus in the zodiacal light he saw, with a corona round her. Mr. Burke and King remain at home cleaning and pounding seed. They are both getting weaker every day. The cold plays the deuce with us, from the small amount of clothing we have. My wardrobe consists of a wideawake, a merino shirt, a regatta shirt without sleeves, the remains of a pair of flannel trousers, two pairs of socks in rags, and a waistcoat of which I have managed to keep the pockets together. The others are no better off.'

By June 26 Burke and King had amassed enough nardoo for ten days—eight days' supply to be left with Wills and two days' supply for them to take with them on their search for the blacks. A sort of dreaming fatalism, a twilight of the mind, was beginning to overtake Wills. He notes calmly that the others are to set off next morning even though Burke is extremely weak. And he adds, 'I have a good appetite and relish the nardoo much, but it seems to give us no nutriment, and the birds here are so shy as not to be got at. Even if we got a good supply of fish I doubt whether we could do much work on them and the nardoo alone. Nothing now but the greatest good luck can save any of us; and as for myself I may live four or five days if the weather continues warm. My pulse is at forty-eight, and very weak, and my legs and arms are nearly skin and bone. I can only look out like Mr. Micawber "for something to turn up"; but starvation on nardoo is by no means very unpleasant, but for the weakness one feels, for as far as appetite is concerned, it gives me the greatest satisfaction.'

Wills had also written a last letter to his father, and it is astonishing now to examine this document; there is not a word misspelt, hardly a comma forgotten, or a fault in grammar or style. The firm, thin, sloping handwriting is wonderfully clear, and this trained pragmatical mind holds on to the end. He is full of grievance and self-justification, but it is genuine pathos rather than self-pity that comes through, and perhaps here we have a case of a limited man breaking through his bonds and becoming greater than himself at last.

The letter reads:

Cooper's Creek
Jun 27th 1861
My dear Father,

These are probably the last lines you will ever get from me. We are on the point of starvation, not so much from absolute want of food, but from want of nutriment in what we can get. Our position, although more provoking, is probably not near so disagreeable as that of poor Harry and his companions.[1] We have had very good luck and made a most successful trip to Carpentaria and back to where we had every right to consider ourselves safe, having left a depot here, consisting of four men, twelve horses and six camels. They had sufficient provisions to have lasted them for twelve months with proper economy. We have also every right to expect that we should have been immediately followed up by another party with additional provisions and everything necessary for forming a permanent depot at Cooper's Creek. The party we

[1] A reference to a cousin, Lieutenant Le Vescompte, who had died on an expedition to the Arctic some years before.

had here had special instructions not to leave until our return, unless from absolute necessity. We left the creek with nominally three months' supply, but they were reckoned at little over the rate of half rations, and we calculated on having to eat some of the camels. By the greatest good luck at every turn we crossed to the Gulf through a good deal of fine country, almost in a straight line from here. On the other side the camels suffered considerably from wet, and we had to kill and jerk one soon after starting back. We had now been out a little more than two months, and found it necessary to reduce the rations considerably, and this began to tell on all hands, but I felt it by far less than either of the others. The great dryness and scarcity of game and our forced marching prevented us from supplying the deficiency from external sources to any great extent, and we never could have held out but for the crows and hawks and the portulac. The latter is an excellent vegetable and I believe secured our return to this place. We got back here in four months and four days and found that the others had left the creek the same day. We were not in a fit state to follow them. I find I must close this that it may be planted but I will write some more, although it has not so good a chance of reaching you as this. You have great claims on the Committee for their neglect. I leave you in sole charge of what is coming to me, the whole of my money I desire to leave to my sisters; other matters I will leave for the present.

Adieu, my dear Father. Love to Tom.[1]

W. J. Wills

I think to live about four or five days. My religious views are not the least changed and I have not the least fear of their being so. My spirits are excellent.'

When Dr. Wills published this letter he suppressed the penultimate sentence, fearing, no doubt, that his son would be branded as an atheist. This solicitousness was not really necessary: the letters Wills wrote to his mother in England before the expedition set out make it clear that he was a Christian, although he had no time for what he called 'passive credulity'. He believed that, with an entire absence of fanaticism, one

[1] His brother in Australia.

should examine every religious belief for oneself and only accept faith when it came from inner conviction. It is perhaps relevant to repeat that he was just 27, and a scientist.

This letter, King said, was read aloud by Wills to himself and Burke so that they should see that he had written nothing to their disadvantage and only the truth. Wills also said he wanted his father to have his gold watch and both watch and letter were given to Burke. King promised that he would take good care of them if Burke died before he did. Once again Burke pressed Wills on the matter of their leaving him alone. Did he really wish it? Wills repeated that he did: it was their only chance. Wills' field-books from which the above quotations were taken were then buried near the hut; firewood, water and nardoo cakes were placed close to his hand, and the next morning, June 29, they left him there, lying on his bed, to fend for himself.

King did not get very far with Burke. All through the first day Burke complained of pain in his back and legs and he was distressed about leaving Wills behind. On the second day he said he felt better, but they had only marched two miles when he collapsed on the ground saying that he could go no further. 'I persisted in his trying to go on,' King said, 'and managed to get him along several times, until I saw that he was almost knocked up, when he said he could not carry his swag, and threw all he had away. I also reduced mine, taking nothing but a gun and some powder and shot, and a small pouch and some matches. On starting again we did not go far before Mr. Burke said he should halt for the night, but as the place was close to a large sheet of water, and exposed to the wind, I prevailed on him to go a little further to the next reach of water, where we camped. We searched about and found a few small patches of nardoo, which I collected and pounded, and with a crow which I shot, made a good evening's meal. From the time we halted Mr. Burke seemed to be getting worse, although he ate his supper. He said he felt convinced that he could not last many hours, and gave me his watch, which he said belonged to the Committee, and a pocket-book to give to Sir William Stawell, and in which he wrote some notes.'

King showed the pocket-book to Howitt; he had kept it all this time in a little canvas bag which he had hung round his neck, together with the two watches and Wills' letter to his father. Burke's notes were a rough disjointed scrawl written in pencil. They ran as follows: 'I hope we shall be done justice to. We have fulfilled our task, but we have been aban———. We have not been followed up as we expected, and the depot party abandoned their post. R. O'Hara Burke. Cooper's Creek, June 26th.

'King behaved nobly. I hope that he will be properly cared for. He comes up the creek in accordance with my request. R. O'Hara Burke. Cooper's Creek, June 28th.

'King has behaved nobly. He has stayed with me to the last, and placed the pistol in my hand, leaving me lying on the surface as I wished. R. O'Hara Burke. Cooper's Creek, June 28th.'

This last note was probably written a day or even two days later than the date given, for King says that Burke survived this second night after leaving Wills. He spoke very little through the night, and at dawn, when it was bitterly cold, King found him almost speechless. Burke managed, however, to make a Lear-like gesture at the end. He got King to put the pistol in his right hand, and since he knew that King was too weak to dig a grave he insisted that he should be left lying on the ground. It was probably at this moment that the last note was written. Through the early morning hours Burke prayed a little. At eight o'clock he was dead.

'I remained a few hours there,' King said, 'but as I saw there was no use in remaining longer, I went up the creek in search of the natives. I felt very lonely, and at night usually slept in deserted wurleys belonging to the natives.'

After wandering for two days he had a great stroke of luck: he came on some huts where the blacks had left a quantity of nardoo, enough to last him for a fortnight, and that night he succeeded in shooting a crow. He now rested for two days and then made his way back to Wills, bringing with him three more birds he had shot. He was too late, however; Wills was lying there dead. It was not possible to say just when he had died, just how many hours he had lain there staring up through the branches of his hut, but evidently he had never moved from his bed. Natives had been around the camp and had taken away some of his clothes. King buried the corpse in the sand.

And now, at the beginning of July, King entered into his

long, bemused struggle to keep alive. He remained dully around the camp for a few more days and then set off to track down, from their footprints in the sand, the blacks who had taken Wills' clothes. As he marched along he shot crows and hawks and presently the report of his gun brought the tribesmen out to meet him. King's account of how he was cared for during the next two months until Howitt arrived is one of the most moving tributes ever written to the kindness of the primitive people of Australia, and it makes perhaps the best epitaph for the now vanished blacks of Cooper's Creek. One must remember that they, too, were hard pressed for enough to eat, and an extra man who was a semi-invalid was a great burden to them.

'They took the birds I had shot,' King says, 'and cooked them for me, and afterwards showed me a gunyah, where I was to sleep with three of the single men. The following morning they commenced talking to me, and putting one finger on the ground, and covering it with sand, at the same time pointing up the creek, saying, "White fellow", which I understood them to mean that one white man was dead. From this I thought they were the tribe who had taken Mr. Wills' clothes. They then asked me where the third man was, and I also made the sign of putting the fingers on the ground, and covering them with sand, at the same time pointing up the creek.

'They appeared to feel great compassion for me when they understood that I was alone on the creek, and gave me plenty to eat. After being four days with them I saw that they were becoming tired of me, and they made signs that they were going up the creek, and that I had better go downwards; but I pretended not to understand them. The same day they shifted camp and I followed them; and, on reaching their camp, I shot some crows, which pleased them so much they made a breakwind in the centre of their camp, and came and sat round me until such time as the crows were cooked, when they assisted me to eat them. The same day one of the women, to whom I had given part of a crow, came and gave me a ball of nardoo, saying that she would give me more only she had such a sore arm that she was unable to pound. She showed me a sore on her arm, and the thought struck me that I would boil some water in the billy and wash her arm with a sponge. During the operation the whole tribe sat round, and were muttering one to another. Her husband sat down by her side, and she was crying all the time. After I had washed it I touched it with some nitrate of silver, when she began to yell and ran off crying "Mokow! Mokow!" (Fire! Fire!).

'From this time she and her husband used to give me a small quantity of nardoo both night and morning, and whenever the tribe was about to go on a fishing excursion he used to give me notice to go with them. They also used to assist me in making a wurley or breakwind whenever they shifted camp. I generally shot a crow, or a hawk, and gave it to them in return for these little services. Every four or five days the tribe would surround me and ask whether I intended going up or down the creek; at last I made them understand that if they went up I should go up the creek, and if they went down I should also go down, and from this time they seemed to look upon me as one of themselves, and supplied me with fish and nardoo regularly.

'They were very anxious, however, to know where Mr. Burke lay, and one day when we were fishing in the waterholes close by I took them to the spot. On seeing his remains the whole party wept bitterly, and covered them with bushes. After this they were much kinder to me than before, and I always told them that the white men would be here before two moons, and in the evenings, when they came with nardoo and fish, they used to talk about the "white fellows" coming, and at the same time pointing to the moon.

'I also told them they would receive many presents, and they constantly asked me for tomahawks, called by them "bomay ko". From this time to when the relief party arrived, a period of about a month, they treated me with uniform kindness, and looked upon me as one of themselves. The day on which I was released, one of the tribe who had been fishing came and told me that the "white fellows" were coming, and the whole of the tribe, who were then in camp, sallied out in every direction to meet the party, while the man who had brought the news took me over the creek, where I shortly saw the party coming down.'

This then was King's story as he related it, painfully and slowly, to Howitt while the two men sat together in the tent on Cooper's Creek.

CHAPTER THIRTEEN

Back to Melbourne

Within two days King had improved in health so much that he was able to lead them to Wills' grave, seven miles further down the creek. They found the place pretty much as he had described it to them—the two huts still standing on the sand between two waterholes—but the native dogs had been about and poor Wills' body was dreadfully mangled. The arms and legs were scattered about, his hair matted with the hair of the camel-pad on which he had died, and the skull nowhere to be found. They carefully gathered up the remains and made a new grave. Howitt had no prayerbook but he read from his Bible the fifteenth chapter from the first Corinthians, and how strange to hear in these wild surroundings:

> *O death where is thy sting?*
> *O grave where is thy victory?*

To mark the grave, they carved the following inscription on a nearby tree:

W. J. Wills
XLV Yds
W. N. W.

At the bottom of the blaze Howitt added his initials, A. H. They then dug up Wills' diary and came away.

King was exhausted when they got back to camp that night, and was not capable of further exertion during the following days. However, he managed to explain to Howitt where Burke's body lay, some eight miles away up the Cooper, and while Dr. Wheeler remained in camp with King, the others went off to the place on September 21. They had passed within thirty yards of the body on their outward journey without noticing it, and had actually camped 200 yards away. Here too, the dingoes had been scavenging, and the hands and feet were missing, but the rest of the body was entire. The Colt revolver lay on the sand a few feet away, corroded with rust, and still cocked and capped. Had Burke then meant to shoot himself?

They placed the bones in a Union Jack and lowered them into a grave. While they stood around bare-headed Howitt read aloud the eleventh chapter of St. John: 'I am the resurrection and the life; he that believeth in me, though he were dead, yet shall he live.'

On a gnarled box-tree close by they carved:

R O'H B
21 9 '61
A. H.

One detects after this a great lightening of spirits in Howitt's camp; they had accomplished their mission and King was picking up again. Yet Howitt in one way was disappointed: he longed to go on and explore the land himself, to cross the great wastes to the north and make a rendezvous with Captain Norman on the Gulf. And there is no doubt whatever that, had he not been bound to take King back, he would have done it; hardly since Sturt had there been such a man in central Australia. In later years Howitt was to become a distinguished anthropologist and a president of the Australian Association for the Advancement of Science. Now in his early thirties he was full of curiosity and vigour, everything on the Cooper fascinated him, the tribesmen, the rocks and plants, the meteors that kept trailing sparks through the night sky. He moved easily and confidently through this primeval world, and he possessed a quality that is very much lacking in the determined, embattled world of the Australian explorers—a touch of humour. There were no disagreements in his camp, he was very much the leader, and because of his knowledge of the bush they were all eating and living well. The condition of the horses and the camels had actually improved since they left the Darling. All at once the dark, threatening atmosphere of the Cooper is lifted, and this is now a place where white men can live in safety and look at the scene around them rather than at themselves.

Howitt's first concern was to get his news off to the outside world, and with this in mind he had brought up four carrier-pigeons from Melbourne. On opening the cages now, however—those cages which had been bumped about for hundreds of miles on the camels' backs—they found that the birds' tail-feathers had been worn away. Howitt shot three wild pigeons and with waxed thread spliced their tail feathers on to his own birds. This was an entire success: on being released in a tent the pigeons flew with perfect ease. Four separate messages were then placed in metal cylinders on their legs, and they were released next morning at dawn. For a moment things went splendidly; the birds wheeled up into the air in a flock at great speed, and began to cross the creek. Sturt could have warned them about what was going to happen next: out of the blue great kites descended, one pigeon was killed at once, and two others made off in panic over the sandhills with never a hope of getting away. The fourth bird gave up the struggle at once and lighted on a tree a mile off. When they reached him he was sitting on the ground under a bush with a kite narrowly watching him from close by.

In the afternoon they tried again with this last bird, but he was unwilling to expose himself a second time. He flew directly into a tree in the camp, and from that perch he could be induced neither to take off nor come down again. A day or two later the bird did descend to feed and they captured him. Reluctantly they untied the cylinder and abandoned him to his fate; the news would have to wait until they got King back to civilization.

Howitt's next concern was to make friends with the blacks on the Cooper. The tribe that had looked after King had decamped down the creek, but he followed their tracks and came up with them after a few miles. 'They made a great commotion when we rode up,' he says, 'but seemed very friendly. I unpacked my blanket and took out specimens of the things I intended giving them—a tomahawk, a knife, beads, a looking-glass, comb and flour and sugar. The tomahawk was the great object of attraction, after that the knife, but I think the looking-glass surprised them most. On seeing their faces some seemed dazzled, others opened their eyes like saucers, and made a rattling noise with their tongues expressive of surprise ... I made them understand that they were to bring the whole tribe up next morning to our camp to receive their presents, and we parted the best of friends.'

Next morning the tribe arrived in a long procession, about thirty of them, men, women and children, all of them quite naked except for girdles of fishing-nets, feathers and leaves round their waists. They announced their arrival from a mile away by bawling at the tops of their voices and by the time they reached the camp the uproar was deafening. Howitt seems to have arranged things as though he were presiding over a Christmas party.

'With the aid of King,' he says, 'I at last got them all seated before me, and distributed the presents—tomahawks, knives, necklaces, looking-glasses, combs—among them. I think no people were ever so happy before, and it was very interesting to see how they pointed out one or another, who they thought might be overlooked. The piccaninnies were brought forward by their parents to have red ribbon tied round their dirty little heads. One old woman, Carrawaw, who had been particularly kind to King, was loaded with things. I then divided 50 lb. of sugar between them, each one taking his share in a Union Jack pocket-handkerchief, which they were very proud of. The sugar soon found its way into their mouths; the flour, 50 lb. of which I gave them, they at once called "White fellow nardoo", and they explained that they understood that these things were given to them for having fed King. Some old clothes were then put on some of the men and women, and the affair ended with several of our party and several of the blackfellows having an impromptu "corroboree", to the intense delight of the natives, and, I must say, very much to our own amusement. They left, making signs of excessive friendship, carrying their presents with them.'

Later on Howitt had trouble with other tribes on the Cooper who pilfered things around his camp, but he managed to learn a few words of their language and he reasoned with them. Wheeler too was able to help. He set a young man's broken arm, and it was remarkable, Howitt says, how the patient submitted to the operation with perfect trust and composure. By such means the party continued on the best of terms with the blacks throughout their journey—nothing more different from Wright's experiences could be imagined—and Howitt could write in his diary with some confidence that the next white men who reached the Cooper would be welcome there.

While they were waiting for King to recover enough strength for the homeward march they shoed their horses and filled their days by shooting birds and making great catches of fish in the creek; on one day nearly 100 lb. were caught, all of them, Howitt says, delicious to eat. There was some difficulty with the camels. They could not be induced to cross the creek until a stratagem was hit on: they were made to sit down on the edge of the water and then were ordered to rise again. When they were off balance they were shoved in. Roaring and groaning they swam quite well to the other side, where they pulled their great splay feet out of the mud 'with a sound like drawing a gigantic cork'. But the real trouble was with the two male camels: they were constantly fighting each other over the females. The rivalry grew to such a pitch that the two animals ceased to feed and stood watching one another with hate. It was not until the females were kept entirely apart that peace was restored.

For the rest, they were finding the Cooper a marvellously peaceful country. There were no tribal wars, and except for the dingoes there were no savage wild animals to prey upon either man or beast. The violence of nature was apparent enough in the signs of the floods that had recently swept down the creek, and in the tremendous thunderstorms that roared above their heads, but the great emptiness of the land meant also that it had great powers of preservation. The mystery of the horse tracks that Howitt had seen on the lower part of the creek was cleared

up: they found a lone roan horse meandering across the plain,
and this was the very animal that Sturt had lost on the Cooper
sixteen years before. It had managed to keep alive through all
this time in fairly good condition, although when Howitt
caught up with it the beast was very wild and was suffering
from a broken rib—probably caused by a boomerang or a club
being thrown at it. Unfortunately the horse was injured when
it was being caught and soon died.

All this time King was getting better. He was still very weak,
but he was putting on weight at an astonishing rate, so much
so, Welch says, that he 'could hardly see, and for anyone who
had not seen him since he was found he might set recognition
at defiance'. They had to let out the clothes that they had given
him to wear.

By September 25 Wheeler decided he was well enough to
travel, and they turned homewards, leaving the sad last pigeon
perched on a tree. For the first few days they made easy stages
up the creek, so that King could get accustomed to his camel.
On September 28 they were at Depot LXV and now at last the
cache was dug up. Everything was intact: Wills' field-books, the
letter Burke had written when they had first returned from the
Gulf, the note Wills had deposited there at the end of May, a
few rough map tracings, one or two notebooks and a tin box
with letters inside. They filled in the hole again and went on.

There was a hot wind blowing, but it was superb spring
weather. Everywhere flowers and fresh vegetation were spring-
ing up on the sand, and always in the air the migratory birds
making to their waterholes. King was finding it difficult to get
a comfortable seat on his camel, so they gave him a day's rest
and changed him over to a horse. On October 4 they were ready
to make their forced march across the waterless country to
Koorliatto, and the animals were given a last drink in the creek.
It was hardly necessary; on this charmed journey they found
water nearly all the way, and this was fortunate, as King had
to be handled very carefully. More than once Wheeler ordered
a halt so that he could marshal his strength. He was quite cheerful and sometimes chatted freely with the others as they rode
along, but often he was dull and unresponsive, with an in-
valid's absorption with himself.

On October 11, when they were about a third of the way to

Menindie, Brahe and one of the men were sent on ahead to break the news to the outside world. The main caravan followed slowly on, and at last on October 28 they rode into Menindie. It was just over a year since King had left the settled districts. They gave him a week to recover from the journey, and then on November 6 he set out for Melbourne in Welch's charge.

Howitt did not go with them. He had no great liking for crowds and applause; he stayed behind at Menindie putting the expedition's camp into order and writing his dispatches, and then in his own good time he rode back to Melbourne when all the excitement was over.

And excitement there was, almost to a surrealist degree. When the news reached Melbourne on November 2—Brahe had sent a telegram from Bendigo—and it was known for the first time that the continent had been crossed, that Burke and Wills and Gray were dead, and that King alone was returning to tell the tale, there was a commotion such as we might have in our time at the news that just one survivor was returning from an expedition to the moon.

Here is Dr. Wills' account: 'I was staying at that time at the house of my friend Mr. Orkney [the man who had built the *Sir Charles Hotham*]. He had gone to the opera with Mrs. Orkney and another lady, and came home about half-past ten. I was surprised at their early return, and thought that something unpleasant must have happened. A servant came to say that he wished to speak to me privately, and then I received the terrible communication which had been announced at the theatre during an interval between the acts.

'As soon as I had sufficiently recovered from the shock, we proceeded in a car to the residence of Dr. Wilkie, the treasurer of the Committee. He had heard a report, but was rather incredulous, as nothing official had reached the Committee. At this moment Dr. Macadam, the Honorary Secretary, came in. He was perfectly bewildered, believed nothing, and had received no telegram. "But," I said, "when were you at your own house last?" "At seven o'clock," was the reply. "Good God!" I exclaimed, "jump into the car." We proceeded to his house, and there indeed was the telegram, which had been waiting for him for some hours.

'The next morning, Sunday, November 3rd, Brahe arrived at an early hour at Spencer Street station, having been sent in by Mr. Howitt with the journals and letters dug up in the cache at Cooper's Creek. I was anxiously awaiting his arrival. Dr. Macadam was also there, and appeared confused, as if he had been up all night. He insisted on dragging me to the Governor's house, four miles from Melbourne, Heaven only knows with what object. With some difficulty I obtained from him the possession of the bundle of papers, and deposited them for safety in the hands of Dr. Wilkie.'

And now everyone wanted to meet King, the one man who had been magically snatched from outer space, to see him, to cheer him, to press his hand, to make him know that there was to be compensation for the black, hopeless days. Poor King with his weak thumping heart received the first adumbration of all this when he reached Swan Hill on November 21. On the ride down from Menindie they had stayed quietly each night at outlying homesteads, but the colonists at Swan Hill let themselves go. They lifted King off his horse and brought him into town in a buggy to attend a public reception at the courthouse. There followed a drunken public dinner, speech after speech, toast after toast, and it went on until late in the night. King did not drink. He sat there, confused, tongue-tied and embarrassed, not knowing what to do with the wine they kept pouring out for him.

The following morning they bundled him aboard Cobb's Coach, and at Bendigo the gold-diggers rushed out, blowing horns, banging drums and firing their guns and pistols into the air. All the houses of the town were decked with garlands and flowers. 'I could not torture King out of his passive, dead-and-alive manner,' Welch wrote later. King shrank back into his seat in the coach, and so Welch was mistaken for the hero and a great crowd followed them into the centre of the city. A brass band playing 'Here the conquering hero comes' led the way.

Bendigo's leading citizens were gathered at the Shamrock Hotel and champagne was being opened by the case. King was induced to make a speech after they had toasted him, but he faltered when he came to speak of Burke and Wills and fell back into his chair in tears. Meanwhile the mob outside were threatening to break into the hotel to get a glimpse of him, and they were only held back when Welch promised that he would appear for a few minutes on the stage of the theatre close by. Everyone now surged towards the theatre, and in the confusion King was swept away by a group of frantic admirers. He was rescued at last, cowed and shaken, and locked in his bedroom for the night.

The coach that took them on again to Castlemaine was covered in decorations, and settlers came out to wave at them as they trotted by. At Woodend a train was waiting—flags on the engine, coloured bunting on King's special coach—and they had to fight their way through the crowds to get him aboard. At every station bouquets were flung into the carriage. The train was expected to arrive in Melbourne in the evening, and from early afternoon crowds began to gather at the principal station in Spencer Street. The Committee had made careful plans for King's reception; he was to be met at the station by Dr. Macadam and then conveyed in an open carriage to the rooms of the Royal Society, and here he was to meet Sir Henry Barkly, the Governor, the Committee members and their wives, and the political leaders of the colony. King's sister, a Mrs. Bunting, who was a wardress at the Melbourne Lunatic Asylum, was also to be there, and after the formalities was to take him off to her home in the suburb of St. Kilda.

That was the plan. It did not, however, take into account the resolute figure of Dr. Wills. As the bereaved father of one of the heroes Dr. Wills felt that he was not being given proper consideration by the Committee, and he was determined to get into the centre of this affair. Thus it was that King and Welch were a little startled when the train drew up for a few minutes at the station of North Melbourne—its last stop before the terminus— and Dr. Wills flung himself into the compartment. He greeted King with emotion, and grasping him by the arm tried to take him out of the carriage. He declared that he was the representative of the Committee and that he had been sent to convey King directly to the Governor. Cabs were waiting outside. Welch demurred at this; he said he had definite instructions to convey King to Spencer Street station where Dr. Macadam was waiting. According to Welch, Dr. Wills was furious and directed 'a volley of abuse' at him; did he realize he was flouting the direct orders of the Governor? Welch however remained adamant, and Dr. Wills, still in a very heated state, took his seat in the compartment and went on with the train to Spencer Street. As the train pulled in there was an outburst of cheering, and Dr. Macadam and his friends were swept away by the crowd. It pressed so fiercely around King's compartment that it was impossible for the porters to open the doors. In the end Welch forced his way out, and with his arms locked around King's waist battled his way through to the street outside. Here he managed to seize a cab and the two of them scrambled on board. Dr. Wills was close behind and jumped in too. They told the cabby to make for Government House as the nearest refuge.

Many of the people outside the station had lined the streets leading to the Royal Society, but when they saw King careering by in another direction they realized that a change of plan had taken place, and they set off in pursuit, some running, some riding, and others in their carriages. Dr. Macadam, who had King's sister with him, had extricated himself from the station by this time, and he too followed at a gallop. And so the whole cavalcade surged up Collins Street to William Street and thence to Government House. Here, after a short struggle, King was pushed inside the Executive Council Chamber and led into the Chief Secretary's office. He was shaking and scarcely able to stand. Presently his sister was brought to him here, and they were soon joined by Barkly, who had some difficulty in making his way to the room as the crowd was now swarming all over the building. Dr. Wills managed to get in by a side door. King and his sister had risen at the Governor's entrance, but Barkly told them to sit down, and it was quite apparent that King could do no more that day. When the hubbub outside had died down a little he was taken quietly away to his sister's house for the night.

'John King ...,' the Melbourne *Herald* wrote, 'is regarded with feelings similar to those which made the people say of Dante, "There goes the man who has been in Hades".'

He had not been in Hades. He had been living with the blacks on Cooper's Creek on an insufficient diet, and it could have been that there were now moments when he wished himself back there again.

CHAPTER FOURTEEN

The Royal Commission

There was not only hysteria in the colony over the tragedy
of the Burke and Wills expedition; moral guilt was also
agitating the public conscience. Somehow, it was felt,
society must atone for what had taken place. The loyal and
honest King must be rewarded and so must the dependants of
the dead men. A monument must be erected, a public funeral
arranged. It was not really possible to have a funeral without
bodies, but, someone suggested, why not send back for them to
Central Australia? That would be a gesture in the grand
manner. Howitt, who had slipped quietly into Melbourne a few
days after King, was approached and said he was quite ready to
go back and disinter the bones of Burke and Wills if that was
what the Government wished. The Government did indeed
wish it—money was now no longer any object—and presently
Howitt set off again. No one seems to have thought that he

might also have brought back the bodies of Ludwig Becker, and of Gray, and of the others who had died, but perhaps that would have been beyond even Howitt's powers.

There was another aspect of the prevailing mood of heroic gloom: somebody, it was thought, was to blame, the tragedy could not merely have been an act of blind implacable fate; some person or persons ought to be punished or at any rate exposed. Even before King had returned to Melbourne the Government had set up a Royal Commission of inquiry.

The five Commissioners were all eminent men in the colony, and one of them, Evelyn Shirley Sturt, was the Chief Magistrate of Melbourne and the eighth and youngest brother of Sturt. They were charged with inquiring into 'all the circumstances connected with the sufferings and death of Robert O'Hara Burke and William John Wills' and 'the true causes of the lamentable result of the expedition'. They were also 'especially to investigate the circumstances in which the depot at Cooper's Creek was abandoned by William Brahe and his party on the twenty-first day of April last; and to determine upon whom rests the grave responsibility of there not having been a sufficient supply of provisions and clothing secured for the recruiting of the explorers on their return, and for their support until they could reach the settlements; and generally to inquire into the organisation and conduct of the expedition'.

The Commission sat from November 18, 1861, to January 31, 1862, at twelve separate meetings, and since so many well-known men were involved the public interest was intense. The newspapers felt themselves free to comment very fully on the evidence as it was given and everyone took sides: some opposed Brahe, some supported him, and even Wright had his adherents. Others again were simply out for blood, and Dr. Wills adroitly dropped a bombshell into the proceedings by releasing to the Press that last letter from his son which indicted nearly everyone connected with the expedition. All in all it was an illuminating performance, much enjoyed by the whole colony, and the conclusions reached by the Commission were, as we shall see, very sensible.

There was some difficulty in getting the witnesses together. Wright refused to attend until he was given £100 for his expenses in coming from Adelaide, Hodgkinson was away in the centre somewhere with McKinlay and could not be reached, Dost Mahomet had been injured by a camel in Menindie, and some of the other members of the expedition had scattered to different parts of Australia in search of employment. However, in the end most of the vital witnesses were assembled, and induced to appear.

Dr. Macadam was the first to be summoned. He put in as evidence all the relevant papers: Burke's original instructions from the Committee, the field-books and letters which had been dug up from the cache at the depot and at Wills' grave, a copy of King's narrative as it was given to Howitt, the various diaries of Brahe, Wright and Howitt, and the correspondence that had passed between the expedition and the Committee.

Macadam moved briskly to the Committee's defence. At the outset, he said, Burke had approved of all the arrangements: 'Before leaving he expressed himself, both to the Committee and to the public, as satisfied that the whole thing was got up entirely to his satisfaction, and that he believed that the expedition was equipped such as no expedition had been before.' Burke had rejected Captain Cadell's offer to carry thirty tons of goods free by river to Menindie because he thought that some accident might happen in their transit, and he preferred to keep all the expedition's equipment under his own supervision. (Macadam might have added that Burke had quarrelled with Cadell and that the two men were not on speaking terms.) It had been the Committee's intention that Burke should not divide his party at Menindie but push on with his full complement, stores and all, until he reached Cooper's Creek, where he was to set up a depot.

Burke instead had vanished into the blue. He had left half his party and most of his provisions at Menindie and had gone ahead with Wright and a small group to Cooper's Creek. Wright had turned back at Torowoto on October 29, bringing with him a letter for the Committee from Burke (the letter that referred to Wright's appointment), and had reached Menindie on November 5. That letter did not arrive in Melbourne for over a month—on December 3.

The first they heard from Wright himself, Macadam went on, was when Hodgkinson turned up in Melbourne on December 31 with a letter from him dated December 19.

Did it ever strike the Committee [the witness was asked] that an immense deal of valuable time had been lost?—It was never made matter of comment.

It was the 5th of November Wright arrived [at Menindie], knowing what he had to do; and yet he does not appear to have taken any steps to let the Committee know what he was doing until the 19th of December?—Afterwards, upon looking into this matter personally, as one of the Committee, I noticed this great interval of time, but when the dispatches were brought down, as they urged great promptitude in our movements, this question of delay was overlooked and it was not mentioned at the time.

Has there been any explanation obtained since by the Committee with regard to this long delay?—None whatever.

However, Macadam went on, when the Committee did hear from Hodgkinson on December 31 that Wright and the bulk of the stores were still at Menindie, they had acted with rapidity. Hodgkinson was given all the money Wright had asked for and more, and had been immediately sent back to Menindie. Wright had finally set out for Cooper's Creek on January 26—three months after he had left Burke at Torowoto saying that he was going to follow him up at once.

The next thing the Committee heard about the expedition was when Brahe arrived in Melbourne five months later with his disastrous news: Wright, they now learned, had never reached Cooper's Creek with the stores, four of his men were dead, and the depot on the creek had been abandoned. Then too, for the first time, the Committee heard that Burke had set out for the Gulf of Carpentaria on December 16—six months before—and not a word had been heard from him since.

Once again, Macadam said, the Committee had been very prompt; even before they heard Brahe's news 'there was a sort of dread that something was going wrong'. Howitt was sent off and arrangements had been made to dispatch other rescue parties both by land and sea.

Macadam's evidence took up all of the first and a part of the second day's hearing, and on the whole he had not done too badly. There was just that awkward question of what the Committee had been doing during all those months when they had no news from Burke or indeed from anybody. Despite all Macadam's insistence on the Committee's promptness they seemed to have been somewhat idle, if not downright complacent. Clearly the Commission was going to take up this point again later on.

Brahe was the next man to give evidence. Perhaps it is only fair to recall here that he was still a young man in his twenties, and that he had been enlisted merely as an 'assistant' in the expedition. Yet Burke had put great responsibility upon him in leaving him in sole charge at Cooper's Creek. Then, too, Brahe was under fire from the Melbourne Press at this time; it was openly accusing him of having deserted his post at the depot. On the other hand, Brahe was a tough character; he had made the long weary trek back to the Cooper with Howitt and had behaved very well. There is also an interesting note in the Commission's report that he put in a bill for expenses as a witness which the Commission considered too high, and he was obliged to reduce it.

Obviously the key point of interest in Brahe's evidence revolved around just what instructions Burke had given him when he had been left in charge of the depot. The Commission questioned him closely on this:

Did Mr. Burke communicate to you what his plans were before he started—do you recollect any conversation that took place with you on the subject?—He intended to go from Cooper's Creek to Eyre's Creek [the Diamantina River] and try from there to go to Carpentaria if he could do it without running any risk.

Did he write anything?—The only writing I have had from Mr. Burke was the dispatch I delivered here in Melbourne, and a parcel of pocket-books he left with me and made me seal them in his presence, and he requested me to throw them into the water should he not return when I left the creek, and I told him I would burn them, and he agreed to that, and I burnt that parcel of books in the presence of McDonough.

And he communicated verbally to you his intention to proceed first to Eyre's Creek and then to the Gulf of Carpentaria, and that he would run no risk?—Yes; and he said he was bound to be back in three months since the provisions he took with him were scarcely sufficient for twelve weeks; we all knew that as well as he did himself; and he told me he would not run the slightest risk on account of provisions or scarcity of water, and on the morning he left us he called us round him and said that if he found any difficulties he might return in a month's time.

And on his finally leaving you did he make any observations?—That I was to follow him with dispatches if Wright should arrive within two days of his departure.

Then he expected Mr. Wright to arrive in two days?—He did.

Did you endeavour to find out why Wright did not come up?—I could not leave the depot. The first few weeks after Mr. Burke's departure large numbers of natives were continually about the depot, and one man was obliged to be minding the camels, we never allowed him to leave them, and another, Patton, used to look after the horses.

Did Mr. Burke give you any instructions about dealing with the natives?—Yes ... he told me if they annoyed me at all to shoot them at once.

Had you any conversation with Mr. Wright when you joined him as to his being so long coming up?—He expected me back at the Darling with the horses and the camels; Mr. Burke had told him that he would send me back from Cooper's Creek to meet him at the Darling ... Wright told me Hodgkinson had to be sent to Melbourne and that a great deal of time was lost getting answers to his letters.

You made up your mind finally to leave Cooper's Creek, in consequence, as you state in your diary, of the sickness of the men, and you were afraid of running short of provisions?—The sickness of one man, and that, by staying any longer I would consume the provisions, and could be of no service to Mr. Burke; I was then enabled to leave that small quantity of provisions, but I should have consumed them if I had remained longer. I did not think it possible that Mr. Burke should return to the place, from the provisions he had taken, and from what he had told me. I did not think that anything had happened to Mr. Burke but I made sure I should hear of him when I arrived at Menindie.

How did you suppose to hear?— That he had made

Queensland in perhaps a little more than three months after leaving Cooper's Creek ... On the day of his departure he made a remark to me and I mentioned Queensland. Then he said, 'If I am not back in three months' time you may consider me perished,' and I told him, 'Or on your way to Queensland,' and he said, 'Just so.'

What was the cause of Patton's illness?—I thought at the time it was caused by a fall from a horse; he was thrown by one of the horses about three months before.

Were the other men complaining at that time?—McDonough was kicked by a camel at the same time that Patton was thrown from the horse, and was laid up for some days and could not walk ... I myself had pains in my legs and sore gums, but not knowing what it was.

You did not suspect what was the matter with yourself and the men more than the hurts?—No. I did not understand Patton's leg at all, he got very bad on the 4th of April and had to take to his bed; he could not walk at all.

Did you get any fish [on the Cooper]?—Only once.

Is there not an abundance of fish in that creek?—We found some in shallow holes by baling out the holes; we had very large hooks and it required fine small hooks.

Could you not make any contrivance for catching fish?—Yes, but I had never been in the habit of fishing.

Were there any wild fowl about?—Yes, I shot a good many ducks at first, but we soon got careless about them and lost our appetite; very little food would do us, and the sepoy, who was very fond of going shooting for the first few weeks, could not be persuaded to do it afterwards.

Did you eat any of the nardoo?—No, I did not know of it.

Were you not in possession of certain seeds that you had instructions to plant in different places?—Yes, a great quantity was taken away from Melbourne.

Did you not plant any while staying at Cooper's Creek?—We did not take any from the Darling.

You deposited a note [in the cache] in case Mr. Burke should come back?—No, if I had expected Mr. Burke to come back I would have given him an explanation, or told him my reasons for leaving, and should have addressed the letter to him, but I did not consider that necessary. I left the note only for any party that should come up from the Darling [so that they should] know what had become of us. I was very likely to miss any party coming up.

You placed the note there not with the expectation that Mr. Burke would get it?—Certainly not.

Did you leave any things on the surface?—I left a rake, I believe, against the tree, and I found it there when I returned with Mr. Wright, still against the tree. I do believe that I put it there when I left the creek but I am not sure.

At this point the hearing was adjourned, and when it was resumed on the following day Brahe was again questioned about the letter he had left in the cache. Why had he said that only one man, Patton, was ill and the stock in good condition when in fact all of them were suffering from scurvy and two of the camels had scab? Could he really claim that his letter had accurately described the state of his party?

Brahe: It does in a very careless way ... I did not think it of any consequence to tell the exact state of our health.

Then the fact is that the paper you left with the provisions did not accurately describe the state of the party?—No, it did not: the doctor's statement of Wright's party must show that. McDonough was laid up shortly after our arrival at Wright's camp, and he was ill for weeks, and the same with Patton. I myself was very poorly when I returned with Wright to Cooper's Creek, and I suffered a great deal from pains in the legs and had sore gums. I had sore gums for three or four weeks before we left Cooper's Creek, but not knowing what it was I did not state it in the letter.

Was it a fact that you had 'six camels and twelve horses in good working condition'?—No, two of the camels were not in good condition, but I was told by the sepoy those camels were well able to go down, and I wrote it down.

The object of the question is to point out to you the discrepancy between the letter you left at the depot and the report written and signed by you after you came to town. [The report or diary which Brahe had written out for the Committee saying that all his men at the depot had been ill.]—I arrived here on Sunday morning; I had travelled very quickly from Menindie and was requested by the Committee of the Royal Society to write out a statement. I hurried home and I believe I handed it in that same Sunday afternoon, the day I arrived. I wrote it out as quickly as I could, and was tired and rather excited at the time.

In that journal of yours, April 15th, you say, 'Patton is getting worse and I and McDonough begin to feel approaching symptoms of the same disease.'—Yes, I wrote that out of my notebook—at least at that time I mentioned in my notebook, 'We have pains and do not understand what they are.'

That would be inconsistent with the paper you placed in the depot which states that two of your companions and yourself were quite well.—Yes, but I did not wish to give any uneasiness to any party in coming up on our account. It is very probable if I had stated we were ill that they would have thought that we should never reach the Darling.

Do you not see if you had reflected for a moment, you would have seen the difficulty in which Mr. Burke would be placed? If he had known you were ill and not very well able to make long journeys he might have been induced to follow you. But seeing you state you were quite well he did not do so.—I made so confident that Mr. Burke would not return.

In the letter to Dr. Wills from his son, who, it is regretted, is no more, it is stated that your party 'had provisions enough to have lasted them twelve months with proper economy'; that was not substantially the state of the case?—Certainly it was not, unless we were supposed to kill horses and camels, and I had no instructions to that effect.

It is stated also in this letter, 'the party we left here had special instructions not to leave until our return, unless from absolute necessity.'—I never received such instructions, and I do not believe that Mr. Wills at the time he left expected that I would receive such instructions, for on our way down [the creek] he asked me to remain at least four months if possible.

Would it not have struck yourself that you should not have moved from that depot unless in case of absolute necessity?—Certainly not ... The time Mr. Burke gave me was three months; he said that after three months' time I had no reason to expect him back, nor did I; I did not expect him back. But I might have stopped longer, and then used up those provisions I was able to bury.

Why did you not leave clothes behind as well as provisions?—I thought if they did return they were as well provided with clothing as we were. They were mostly shirts.

When you returned to Cooper's Creek with Wright how
long did you remain there?—I suppose—I could not exactly
tell—not more than a quarter of an hour.

Did you make an examination about to see who had been
there?—Yes; I tied my horse up, and so I believe did Wright,
near the cache, and went into the stockade and round it and
examined all the trees.

Could you not discover any tracks?—I saw camel tracks
but supposed them to be my own.

Did you see any impression of human feet?—No impression.

Why?—From the number of rats and the place being dusty.

Are you bushman enough to follow a track?—Yes.

Could you tell the difference between the track of a white
man and a native?—Certainly, unless they were bare-footed.

Even bare-footed?—I should not be able.

At whose instigation did you return [to the depot] after
meeting Wright; yours or his?—Mine.

What was the object of your return?—I had got right and
Patton was in the doctor's hands. I thought he required rest
and would get all right in a fortnight's time. Mr. Wright not
having been to Cooper's Creek I thought that we could not
be better employed than in going back there as a last chance
for Mr. Burke.

Had you a lingering suspicion he might be there?—Yes,
there was still a chance.

Can you give an opinion at all as to why Mr. Wills made
this death-bed declaration and also on two previous occasions had expressed so strongly that he expected to find you
there?—I cannot understand that. I do not know what reason
he had for it.

That was the end of Brahe's evidence-in-chief, and he had
come out of it rather well. But the question remained: was he
telling the truth when he said that Burke had told him to
remain only three months at the depot? There was no written
evidence to prove it. With Patton dead and Dost Mahomet in

Menindie (and unable to speak English), McDonough was the one remaining survivor of the depot party who could corroborate Brahe's word. McDonough was now called, and the question was put to him directly:

Did you hear Mr. Burke give any instructions as to the length of time your party were to remain?—I never heard him give instructions—I had a conversation with Mr. Burke relative to it.

What did he say?—About twelve o'clock the day before he left he came out—that was my watch with the camels—and had an hour's conversation about the matter. I referred to our stay on the creek and he told me we were to stay for three months or as long after as our provisions would last, leaving us sufficient to ensure our own return to the settled districts. He did not say what his instructions were but I just asked him how it was; and he told me that.

Then that was all he said on that point?—That was all on that point, but I beg to remark he told me with regard to Mr. Wright: 'I expect Mr. Wright up in a few days, a fortnight at furthest. I left him positive instructions to follow me' ... I understood at that time, by Mr. Burke giving those instructions, he thought they would be acted upon, and of course if Mr. Wright came up, there would be a permanent depot left there.

Then after Mr. Burke's departure did Mr. Brahe communicate the instructions he had received from Mr. Burke?—Yes.

What were they?—The day after Mr. Brahe returned, Patton asked him how long we were to remain. He said, 'Mr. Burke instructed me to remain three months or as long as our provisions would last.' But in going down the creek Mr. Wills asked him to remain four, and he made the same statement and repeated it in conversations more than once afterwards.

Mr. Burke must have been then somewhat doubtful as to Mr. Wright's getting to you?—No, I do not think he could have been.

Brahe (intervening): I recollect well what Mr. Burke said. On the morning he left he called us round him and said he expected Wright up that night or within two days, but perhaps he might not be able to come at all. He said, 'I cannot be sure of him; I cannot be sure of him; he may not come at all; he may be prevented by accident.'

To McDonough: Did you agree with Mr. Brahe in the proposal to return at the time he did?—When Mr. Brahe referred to me at first, a fortnight before we went, I said it might be as well to remain until the 1st of May, but then Patton was getting so bad; I knew him in my presence try to prevail upon Mr. Brahe to return or he said he would not have any chance of recovering.

Patton said so?—Yes, he had been in a very weak state for three weeks. I myself could have remained there, I think, with the usual exercise, many weeks longer and yet have been able to come to the Darling. We could have stayed four weeks longer if we left nothing in the cache for Mr. Burke.

Your great object, then, was to save Patton's life?—That was, I presume, Mr. Brahe's object. I had nothing to do with it. When he asked me, should we return, I said, 'Of course if it is a benefit to Patton to do so.'

Had you lost hope of Mr. Burke's coming back?—Wright was the only man who gave up hope. I thought it was more probable that he had gone to Queensland, though I did not know. I had a conversation at one time on the Darling with Mr. Burke with regard to clothing and that led me to suppose there would be a meeting [with him] at Carpentaria. In the first place I heard Professor Neumayer state: 'I hope to meet you, Burke, in the vessel.' On another occasion, when leaving the Darling, I was packing up Mr. Burke's clothing, and he was rather short of clothing, for he was very careless in that respect; whenever there was a blackfellow he would throw him a shirt or something, and I gave him two flannel shirts of my own. 'I do not care, McDonough,' he said, 'if I get on board the vessel with only a shirt on me, if I get through.'

What did you say as to Mr. Wright's desponding?—He always gave him up as lost: 'Neither gone to Queensland nor gone anywhere else; the man has rushed madly on depending on surface water, and the man is lost in the desert.' He never gave us any hope for him, in fact so much so I said I would wager. I offered to make a bet that he would be found at

Queensland or turn up somewhere.

Do you know that Mr. Wills said you were left with twelve months' provisions?—Not unless Mr. Wills meant that we should eat the horses and camels, he could not say that.

Did the blacks at Cooper's Creek alarm you much?—No, I have been with them. The first time we met them at the depot camp the sepoy came out in a very excited manner, and Mr. Burke sent me out. The sepoy stated that the black-fellows were outside, he was trembling all over. I went out, I had my revolver and my gun with me. There were about fifty of them, and they thought to feel my ribs to see if I was afraid, and I caught one and heaved him down and fired my revolver over his head, and they ran away.

Did you feel as a party, as you were weak, that you were less able to defend yourselves?—I was always able to defend myself until I went under Dr. Beckler's treatment.

Were you acquainted with Mr. Burke's family at home [in Ireland]?—Yes. He had a great deal of confidence in me and often told me many things since he came out; he was a particular friend of mine.

What was the state of Mr. Wright's party when you joined them?—They were in the most wretched state, everything thrown about in the greatest disorder.

Did Mr. Wright never think of sending any clothing or stores to the depot?—He did not, in fact he spoke very little to us; at the time he left to go back my impression was that he wanted to go back to see the creek, and not with a view to relieve Mr. Burke, simply that Mr. Wright's object was to go and see Cooper's Creek. I am confident that Mr. Brahe was anxious to relieve Mr. Burke.

Have you anything else you wish to say?—I wish to make a remark on Dr. Beckler's treatment of me and Patton. When I got under his charge I was quite able to work ... and then Dr. Beckler requested me to lay up until he had treated my knee ... I did not believe he was doing me any good, and I thought to take exercise, and then I found the sinews of my leg all shrunk in. And Patton, I should say, he was depending upon nothing but a pint of arrowroot morning and evening. Dr. Beckler had tins of fresh meat that he never used for Patton.

McDonough, having fired off this last salvo, retired. It was apparent that both he and Brahe were going to preserve a fairly united front. They must have had ample time beforehand to discuss what evidence they would give, but that did not necessarily mean that they were lying. Everything, of course, would have been a great deal clearer if Burke had written even one line of instructions to Brahe when he left him in charge of the depot. But then Burke had written no definite instructions to anybody throughout the entire expedition. There were just his last notes, composed in the bitterness of despair, saying that he had confidently expected to find Brahe at his post when he got back from the Gulf. Wills had amply supported his leader in this. But would they have both been quite so bitter if Brahe had made it clear in the note he had left in the cache that one of his men was dying, and that he himself and the other two men were suffering from scurvy? Might they have been a little more sympathetic to Brahe had they known something more of Wright's delay at Menindie? Perhaps King would be able to throw some light on this. Meanwhile the Commission turned their attention to the next witness, a Mr. Edward Wecker, who was the postmaster at Menindie.

Wecker was able to make one or two revealing comments on Wright's attitude during the long delay on the Darling.

> Did he state to you that he was waiting to get his command confirmed?—Yes, confirmed; and he was astonished that the command was not confirmed. He expressed it, not only to me, but to different parties there [at Menindie], because every party was astonished at Mr. Wright's conduct in staying so long at the Darling.
>
> That was the general remark?—That was the general remark—that it was a piece of folly of Mr. Wright's to stop and let the season pass, and go out in the summer, and Mr. Wright on every occasion said he was waiting for his appointment to be confirmed by the Committee in Melbourne ... He wished [this] so that he should have someone to fall back upon for his pay, because the name of the Committee at the time was in great discredit in consequence of small cheques that had been given, being dishonoured.
>
> You say Mr. Wright was generally blamed for losing so

much time?—Yes.

Allowing the summer to come on him?—Yes, he was generally blamed by all parties for losing so much time in starting out, but that was his excuse always. He was waiting for the confirmation of his appointment.

At the next hearing on December 5, John King took the stand. It was his 23rd birthday. He had recovered somewhat from his boisterous reception, and was, the Melbourne *Herald* says, an excellent witness. The newspaper adds, rather grandly, 'though his intellectual powers have not been highly cultivated he evidently possesses no small share of intelligence: a man who would mind his own business, and not given to ask very many questions, which, as things have turned out, is to be regretted; but with a memory capable of retaining everything within his knowledge.' The Commissioners treated King with much consideration, and led him gently up to the vital question:

Did you hear Mr. Burke give Mr. Brahe any instructions as to what he was to do?—None.

Mr. Burke told you on that last day before you started that Mr. Brahe was to be left in charge of the depot camp and that Mr. Wright was expected up in a very short time?—Yes.

Did he mention the time?—He said in a few days. He then shook hands with the different 'men, and when shaking hands with Patton, Patton, who was very fond of Mr. Burke, was shedding tears; he was disappointed in not being one of the party going with Mr. Burke, and Mr. Burke shook hands with, at the same time telling him, 'Patton,' he said, 'you must not fret, I shall be back in a short time; if I am not back in a few months, you may go away to the Darling.'

There was a much larger quantity of provisions left behind at the depot than you took on with you?—Yes.

Had you spirits of any kind?—There were none at all taken from the Darling.

Was the pork good?—Beautiful.

In fact Mr. Burke did not intend to take more than three months' provisions?—Just so.

And he could have taken more if he had liked?—Yes.

Mr. Brahe accompanied you part of the way?—As far as the first camp. He dined with us that evening, and when he was returning home to the depot he said, 'Good-bye, King, I do not expect to see you for at least four months.'

He made use of that expression?—Yes.

King then went on to describe their journey to the Gulf. Sometimes, he said, when they were crossing stony deserts they travelled by night, but otherwise by day. They had no tents and slept out. Wills was generally engaged for an hour or more writing up his notes when they made camp. He used to read these notes over to Burke, and Burke sometimes suggested additions but seldom, if ever, wrote anything himself. They had no particular difficulty in reaching the Gulf and found water almost all the way. Their rations were sufficient even though the journey took longer than they expected—two months instead of six weeks—and they were constantly surrounded by wild game, kangaroos, emus, ducks and turkeys, which, however, they did not stop to shoot; having enough food they 'kept their course'.

When you were nearing the Gulf did you not hear Mr. Burke express an expectation of getting relief there?—No.

Neither by land nor water?—No. Before Professor Neumayer left [Menindie] McDonough and myself were in the next tent to Mr. Burke's and McDonough heard some conversation between Professor Neumayer, Mr. Burke and Mr. Wills—something concerning a vessel. But it seemed Mr. Burke did not require a vessel, and would not give his sanction to it. Had we expected any assistance we would have crossed the Albert River [actually the Flinders] to the west side and there would have been no difficulty in reaching the sea. But as our provisions were getting so exhausted we were unable to do so. Mr. Burke thought he had quite fulfilled his task; we had the tide flowing, rising and falling to the extent of eight inches, and the water was quite salty.

There could be no doubt about the flow of the tide?—None whatever.

How did you ascertain that?—There were some rocks in the bed of the river, and we could see that these rocks were covered when the tide was up, and when it went down we could see the rocks.

You did not hear the sound of the sea?—No.

So now, King said, in pouring rain—ten or twelve tropical showers a day—and on greatly reduced rations, they had begun the long march home. Both animals and men were 'leg-tired', and Gray was complaining of pains in his back.

Did Mr. Burke say anything about the propriety of going to Queensland?—I never heard him mention anything of the kind.

Did .Mr. Gray get gradually worse?—Gradually worse as far as Mr. Wills understood; he [Wills] pretended to be a sort of doctor amongst us when any one felt ill, and he always gave medicine for any illness, and he said he thought the man's constitution was gone through drink, as he had lived in a public house at Swan Hill, and I have heard since he had drunk heavily there.

Then there had been the distressing incident when Gray was found under a tree eating some flour which he had stolen and made into porridge: 'Mr. Burke called him and asked him what he meant by stealing the stores, and asked him if he did not receive an equal share of the rations, which of course he could not deny. Mr. Burke then gave him several boxes on the ear, and not a sound thrashing as Mr. Wills states: Mr. Wills was at the other camp at the time, and it was all over when he returned. Mr. Burke may have given him six or seven slaps on the ear.'

Mr. Burke was not in the habit of striking his men?—No, it was the first time I knew him to do so.

The whole party were on very good terms were they not?—On very good terms; they were very social.

Even after that?—Even after that, though Mr. Burke abused Gray at the time.

For how long was Gray carried on the camels?—Some seven days ... He died the day before we struck the creek, some fifteen miles from the creek, and by it about seventy miles from the depot.

Had you not stopped to bury Gray you would have been there before Brahe left?—We should have been there all right.

Did you hear what Mr. Burke's expectations were on reaching the creek and whom he was likely to meet there?—Yes. We expected to find those we had left there and also the party from town ... Mr. Burke said he was sure of assistance coming up from town on account of his repeating it so often to the Committee that, under any circumstances, we should be followed up, and he had no doubt, until we saw our disappointment at the creek, but that there would be a party there.

Wright's party?—Yes, he expected Mr. Wright.

Once again King described the scene when they had found that Brahe had gone, and he was questioned closely about the state in which they had left the depot when they set off for Mount Hopeless on April 23.

Did you see the rake?—Yes.

Did you put it against the tree in the same position as you found it?—We found it against the stockade, and laid it against the tree that was marked.

It did not occur to Mr. Burke or anyone to leave any mark on the tree?—No, we did not expect the party would return. We thought the word 'dig' would answer our purpose as well as it would theirs.

Did Mr. Burke allude to any instructions Mr. Brahe had received?—No, the only doubt Mr. Burke had was, the day we struck Cooper's Creek the blacks were surrounding us, and Mr. Burke said that we must be very cautious in our dealings with them as we knew not what they might have done to the depot party.

Then he never dreamed that the party would have gone away?—We never thought of it, neither had we any right to expect it ... Mr. Burke some three or four days before we arrived at the depot asked me did I wish to remain at the depot or accompany him to town, as he thought there would be a permanent depot there [on the Cooper]. He said he would get me permission to remain a few weeks in town and then return to the depot, and Mr. Wills also made the same promise.

Was there as much [food in the cache] as you expected there would be?—We thought they might have left more. We considered they had nine months' provisions without stinting, and they had also instructions to kill the horses and camels if they required fresh meat.

Suppose Mr. Burke had been away five months he would still have expected to find them there?—Yes, we should still have expected to find the party there. Mr. Burke said they should have remained at any risk.

Mr. Burke, it is presumed, was exceedingly weak when you finally parted with him?—Yes, he walked till he dropped.

Did he express any intention in his wishing to have his revolver in his hand; did he give you any reason for it?—He said to me, 'King, this is nice treatment after fulfilling our task, to arrive where we left our companions where we had every right to expect them.'

King, at this point, was obviously getting tired and a little confused, but they had one more point to ask him about Wills' last letter to his father, and they handed it to him.

Did you see that letter?—That is the letter Mr. Wills read.

Did he read it out [to you and Burke] for the purpose of being corrected if there was any statement in it that was not quite correct?—I believe the reason was, in case the letter should be found, that he should not say anything to our disadvantage, mine or Mr. Burke's. He thought that we would see it was the truth and nothing but the truth.

The Chairman: The Commission will not trouble you further today and they are exceedingly obliged for the clear statement you have made.

Yet was it altogether clear? No one doubted that King was trying to tell the truth, but his devotion to Burke was apparent; what Burke thought, he thought, Burke's grudges were his grudges, and there were strong indications in his evidence that he was deliberately building up a case against Brahe. Had he and Brahe talked things over, one wonders, on their long journey down from Cooper's Creek? Had they quarrelled then, in private, as they were now quarrelling in public?

Brahe was now brought back into the box to be confronted with King's evidence, and he hedged a little. He was asked:

The last day of our meeting, you were asked about this letter from Mr. Wills to his father, in which Mr. Wills states, 'The party who were left here had special instructions not to leave until our return unless from absolute necessity.' You

said you never had those instructions?—Until I was compelled to leave.

You never had those instructions you said?—Not in those
words.

Did you consider it was absolutely necessary you should
leave when you did?—Yes.

For the reasons you have given to the Commissioners,
namely, illness?—Patton's illness.

And you would still have left, even if those instructions
had been given you?—Perhaps. It is impossible for me to say
whether I would or not.

No talk here of three months, or even of four. Yet even King
had admitted that Burke had taken only three months' rations
with him to the Gulf. What else could that mean except that
Burke expected to be back in three months? And presumably he
had told Brahe so. Curiously, the letter which Burke wrote to
the Committee from Cooper's Creek on December 13, 1860, was
never mentioned during the inquiry, and it was vital. It contained the words, 'it is my intention to return here within the
next three months at latest. I shall leave the party which remain
here under the charge of Mr. Brahe, in whom I have every confidence. The feed is very good. There is no danger to be apprehended from the natives if they are properly managed, and there
is, therefore, nothing to prevent the party remaining here until
our return, or until the provisions run short.'

Howitt, now about to return to the Cooper for Burke's and
Wills' bodies, was the next witness examined. He proved curiously ungiving, almost as though he was reluctant to involve
himself in any way, and he added nothing to what was already
known.

And now William Wright was called. One can imagine that
there was something of a stir at his appearance, for this was the
first time that he had come to Melbourne; now at last they could
have it out with him about his long delay on the Darling. On
the face of it there seemed to be very little that Wright could say
for himself. He had hung about for three months at Menindie
when he knew that Burke on the Cooper was in need of
supplies. He had bungled utterly by taking his party out in
midsummer, by quarrelling with the blacks and by allowing

four of his men to die. He had not even been bushman enough to notice on his visit to the depot that Burke and Wills had been there, nor had he even looked around for their tracks. And at the end of it all he had bolted down to Adelaide to escape the music.

What was he then? A villain or a fool? An illiterate who should never have been given command, or merely an unfortunate man dogged by bad luck?

Surprisingly Wright gave his evidence pretty well. Had the Commissioners been expecting to see a crestfallen, tongue-tied man they must have been disappointed, for he was quite definite in his replies to their questions, and although they cornered him once or twice it was extremely difficult to know just where and how far he was lying. His case, briefly, was that he had been overtaken by obstacles that were not of his making. Burke, he said, had promised to send Brahe back from the Cooper with some of the horses and camels to help in getting up the stores, but Brahe never arrived. At Menindie one thing after another had delayed him: first he had lent Trooper Lyons four horses and he had to wait for them to return, which they never did. Then he had to send Beckler out with three camels to find Lyons and he could not move until he returned. The Committee had never confirmed his appointment—never even answered his letters—and so he had had to send Hodgkinson down to Melbourne to get a yes or a no out of them and to obtain permission to buy more horses; and naturally he had to wait until Hodgkinson got back. And so one thing had led to another, and it had been impossible for him to move.

Certainly, Wright said, they had discussed the matter of Burke being left in the lurch, they had been very worried about it; but what could he have done at Menindie with no power to take command and not enough animals to shift the stores? Then, when finally he was able to set out for the Cooper a combination of forces—the hostility of the blacks, the sickness of his men, and the lack of water—had prevented him from reaching his destination.

There were obvious flaws in this argument, and the Commissioners set out to extract from Wright an admission that what had really delayed him was plain ineptitude and irresponsibility, plus a determination to see that he got his salary. From November 5, when he got back to Menindie from Torowoto, until December 19 when he sent Hodgkinson down to Melbourne, an enormous amount of time had gone by. What had he been doing all that time? 'Just merely looking after the stock,' Wright said. 'I did not know rightly what to do or how to act as I had no instructions whatever from the Committee.'

He had told Burke plainly, he went on, that he would not set out from Menindie until he did get those instructions and his appointment confirmed.

Burke expected you to have followed him up so closely as to have reached Cooper's Creek two or three days after he started [for the Gulf].—I do not see how he rightly could have expected that.

Knowing that 28 days at least must elapse from the time of sending a letter from Menindie before you could get an answer [about your appointment] from Melbourne, how can you reconcile that with this idea that you would be only two or three days after him?—I cannot reconcile it at all.

How is it that you felt it indispensably necessary to have the confirmation of the Committee?—I really did not know whether my appointment would be confirmed or not, or whether I would get any remuneration for it.

Your instructions were plain. Mr. Burke gave you them. Were you afraid of your salary?—I was not at all afraid of that.

Did any of the party rebel against your appointment?—No.

In Mr. Burke's letter [from Torowoto] he says this, 'Perhaps I might find it advisable to leave the depot at Cooper's Creek and to go on with a small party to examine the country beyond it; under any circumstances it is desirable that we should be soon followed up.' So that it is quite evident from this that he expected no delay. You cannot reconcile that?—I cannot ... When he was reading over the dispatch to me I did not take particular notice of it; in fact Mr. Burke used to alter his mind so very often, it was not possible to understand what he really did mean at times.

You adhere strictly to that statement, that you would, under any circumstances, have stayed at Menindie until your appointment was confirmed?—Yes.

Therefore if you had had fifty horses and fifty camels you would not have started until your appointment was confirmed?—I should not.

Well then, why had he not written to the Committee asking them about the matter. He *had* written, Wright replied. When? In November, when he had returned to Menindie from Torowoto.

Macadam was called at this point and he flatly denied that the Committee had received such a letter.

Have you a copy of that letter [Wright was asked]?—I have not.

You wrote it?—I wrote that with my own hand. Just a few words.

Could your memory serve you sufficiently to write the purport of that letter?—It would not.

Have you any objection to write a letter similar to that one, as nearly as you can remember it?—No. I write a very indifferent hand.

The Commissioners next turned to the letter from Wright to the Committee that *did* exist—the letter which he sent down to Melbourne with Hodgkinson on December 19. He was referred to the passage in which he had said that he had 'delayed starting merely because the camels [nine] left behind by Mr. Burke were too few in number and too inferior in carrying powers'. There had been no reference in that letter to his awaiting confirmation of his appointment. So which of his two statements was true? Had he delayed because he needed camels or because he wanted his appointment confirmed? Wright answered that he *had* raised the matter of his appointment in his letter.

Will you be good enough to find that? It does not appear to be in the letter.—I am almost certain from what I gave Hodgkinson to copy that I stated it.

There is no mention of it?—I thought I mentioned it distinctly, but it is not worded as I intended at all.

How can you reconcile the two statements?—The only answer I can give to it is the answer I have already given.

It should be pointed out to you that unless you can answer

that question satisfactorily you stand in an awkward
position before this Commission.

Wright made no reply.

In the rest of his evidence he was somewhat less muddled, or
at any rate less evasive. He had urged Burke to take the whole
expedition up to the Cooper in the first place, he said, but Burke
would not listen to this; he had wanted to push on. Then when
he did at last try to follow up Burke's tracks in January they had
all disappeared and the surface water had dried up. Even so he
might have got through to the Cooper if the blacks had not
hindered him and if his men had not fallen ill. When Brahe had
joined him at Bulloo there had been no possibility of going
back to the Cooper and of setting up a permanent depot there.
The men were ill and demoralized; they had actually 'cried,
begged and prayed' him to take them back to Menindie. Dr.
Beckler had said to him, 'You see the position you are in and
the responsibility in your hands. So sure as you go back to
Cooper's Creek, here are three men will die. You have buried
three men already ... You will be sacrificing these other men's
lives for the chances of a man who, more than likely, will never
come back this way.' They had all thought that Burke had gone
to Queensland.

Why then had he himself returned with Brahe to the depot?
'I thought,' Wright replied, 'that by my going back it would
still give Burke two or three weeks longer over the time in which
he had stated he expected to return.'

When Brahe and he had reached the depot, he went on, 'there
was no mark above the ground showing that any white man
had been there. There were two or three fires about the place
which I supposed had been made by blacks. I looked at those
fires particularly, and there was not a stick of wood as large as
one of the pen sticks on the table [here] which was not burned,
just as a blackfellow makes a fire: he just brings what is enough
to keep a fire and no more.'

Did you leave any record at Cooper's Creek of your having
been there?—No, I did not. I intended doing so but I thought
if I disturbed the place where the things were buried and took
the bottle up, the chances were the blacks, as I supposed they
had been at the depot, would discover them. I was not very

sure whether they were watching us—we had seen a smoke the night before—and being over-cautious I would not take the bottle up to put a note in it.

Would there have been any difficulty in putting W for Wright and the 8th of May under the 21st of April [on the marked tree]?—I could have done that with a knife if I had had the presence of mind to do so.

You did not make any search at all in fact?—I just stayed there and had a look round about the place. In fact I first thought of camping there that night, but the horses I had taken with me, being horses that had been at Cooper's Creek with Mr. Brahe, he said, 'If we stop here tonight the horses will certainly go back five miles up the creek, to the place where they used to run, and we shall have to walk up there in the morning for them;' and I thought it just as well to camp where the horses used to stop.

And so Burke's and Wills' last chance had gone.

Wright had not been altogether discredited by this examination. It was fairly clear that he was lying when he said that Burke had agreed that he should wait at Menindie until his appointment was confirmed. It was positively clear that he was lying when he said that he had written a letter to the Committee about the matter early in November; indeed, there was a strong supposition that Wright had cooked up this whole business of the confirmation of his appointment as an afterthought. Nevertheless Burke *had* been excessively vague about his orders all through. And it was certainly a fact that the Committee had been lax in not replying to the letters they did receive; nor had they done anything to push Wright into action even though they knew as late as December that he was still loitering on the Darling.

Sir William Stawell now came forward to defend the Committee's good name. As Chief Justice of the colony he was treated with even more deference than King had been, and he gave his evidence with an air of magisterial authority.

Burke, he said, had been instructed to cross the continent if he could do so with safety, and then fall back on to the Cooper so that he could continue his discoveries in other directions. There was no question of Burke having been urged to get ahead of McDouall Stuart; he himself, as chairman of the Committee, had written a private letter to Burke warning him against unwise haste.

> Do you remember the nature of the dispatch sent to Mr. Burke by Lyons, the trooper?—It was substantially to inform him of Stuart's having reached so far as he had then gone across the continent.
>
> That could not have had any influence on Mr. Burke in urging him forward?—On the contrary ... there was nothing in the official dispatch that would urge him on. The Committee's object was, throughout the whole affair, to insure no risk being incurred. They were only afraid that an anxiety to get on might produce disaster ... So far from anything calculated to urge on the expedition emanating from the Committee, they always took the opposite view.

Now this was a good deal less than frank. Burke had very definitely been urged on. When he left Melbourne he knew all about Stuart's expedition and it had been made clear to him that, for the honour of Victoria, it was up to him to be the first to reach the Gulf. All Melbourne had been talking about this rivalry; *Punch* had published its cartoon about 'The Great Exploration Race', and there is no doubt that one of the reasons why Burke had been appointed leader of the expedition was that he possessed those very qualities of dash and initiative that would make him get ahead. Stawell's own letter to Burke was not nearly so cautionary as he now tried to make out. In fact, the whole tenor of Burke's instructions had been, 'Don't do anything rash but push on as fast as you can.'

Indeed, the really baffling thing was that the Committee, having shown all this zeal in the beginning, seemed to have lapsed into a quite inexplicable lethargy. This was what the Commission now wished to investigate. Why, Sir William was asked, had the Committee not taken àny action on December 3 when they had Burke's letter saying that he should be followed up at once and asking them to confirm Wright's appointment?

Sir William replied that the Committee never for a minute imagined that Wright would want his appointment confirmed. Wright himself had not written to them about it. By December

3 they presumed that he had already left Menindie with the stores and so there was no point in writing him a letter—they thought he was already beyond the reach of the post.

It was pointed out to Sir William that the Committee had had two other letters from Menindie, which they had never even acknowledged; one from Dr. Beckler dated November 13 and the other from Ludwig Becker dated November 27, and these letters made it quite clear that, in point of fact, Wright had not set out at all; he was still at Menindie. What had the Committee done about that?

> *Sir William:* Nothing was done for the reasons I have already stated, and it being considered that nothing could be done ... The Committee were of the opinion that they had started the expedition and supplied it liberally with all means and appliances, and that unless they were asked to do anything, or the necessity for doing anything was brought before them, their hands were relieved.

And so it was not until Hodgkinson had arrived in Melbourne on December 31 that they learned for the first time that Wright was still in Menindie waiting for the confirmation of his appointment. They had then immediately given the confirmation and had supplied Wright with money to buy additional horses.

'This question of confirmation,' Sir William went on, 'always seemed a mere afterthought; that was the conclusion I believe the Committee arrived at. I do not know whether I judge him [Wright] harshly or not.'

All this was very well, but it did nothing to explain why the Committee had not prodded Wright on. Even when they heard from Hodgkinson on December 31 that he was still in Menindie, they took no particular steps to urge him forward; all that was done was to express, in a letter to Wright, a hope 'that your endeavours to remove the stores from your present depot to Cooper's Creek will be early and successfully accomplished'. That letter was written on December 31. Thereafter nothing whatever was done by the Committee to find out what was happening until the following June when they decided to send Howitt out. Thus six months had slipped by, and it was hard to say where the inactivity was most pronounced—in Menindie or in Melbourne.

Dr. Macadam did not make matters any better by returning to the witness box to say that Dr. Beckler's and Ludwig Becker's dispatches had not been acknowledged because they were 'inferior officers', and had been instructed that they should only communicate with the Committee through their leader. Macadam was curtly told by the Commission that that did not alter the fact those letters had revealed to the Committee that Wright was still at Menindie at the end of November, and they had done nothing.

The Commission was now treated to an absurd incident: George James Landells, the camel man who had resigned at Menindie, had been summoned to give evidence and he was evidently in a state of some emotion. The following confused dialogue took place:

You started with Mr. Burke from Melbourne originally?—Yes.

How far did you go on the journey?—I may mention that I should be very happy to give any information that lies in my power if the members originally composing the expedition were present here, and until I do so I cannot exonerate myself.

You know it is impossible to have the members of the expedition here. It is not a question of exoneration or otherwise, but we wish to obtain any information we can, to supply any missing link.—Details would come in, and I consider that I have been extremely ill-used, and I require to have evidence to disprove the statements that have been brought against me by different members, but which can be cleared up, I feel confident, as my character has been traduced.

This Commission is not appointed to inquire into that.—I would be very happy to give any information in my power; at the same time unless the members originally composing the expedition were present I could not do it.

Then will you be good enough to retire?—I am to understand that justice is not to be had. The doors of the Royal Society have been shut against me and I have not been able to get justice from them.

With this Landells withdrew, and he was replaced in the box by Mr. Thomas Dick, the publican who had employed Charley Gray at Swan Hill. Mr. Dick felt strongly about King's statement that Gray was reported to have ruined his constitution through drink. It was not true, he said; in all the eighteen months he had employed Gray 'his sprees were about six or seven', no more.

The Commissioners were moved to be jocular: 'That is tolerably good, is it not?'

Yes, Dick thought it was, and he had come here to clear Gray's name. It was kindly meant and the Commissioners thanked him.

King by now had had some afterthoughts and was invited to take the stand again. 'I wish to state,' he said, 'that there is no sign of religion recorded in any part of [Wills'] diary. We each had our Bible and prayer-book, and we occasionally read them going and coming back; and also, the evening before the death of Mr. Burke, I am happy to say, he prayed to God for forgiveness for the past, and died happy, a sincere Christian.'

King had also been thinking about the cache at the depot, and he said now that he believed Brahe and Wright on their return there could have seen that it had been disturbed; they should have known by the ashes of the fires that Europeans had been there.

How was a European to know whether it was a European or a native fire? There was not a stick of wood to show; could you yourself tell the difference?—We left wood there. He [Wright] states that there was no wood there.

There was plenty of wood about?—The wood was scarce. We had to burn some of the small stools which the depot party left there, and left some partly burned; from the position of our fires the difference might be distinguished.

There was only one other thing he wished to say, King went on: 'If Mr. Landells is to be examined then I shall have to defend Mr. Burke's character, as I am happy to say it is in my power to do so.'

At this point Dr. Wills was allowed by the Commission to put a point to Brahe:

I wish to know whether a portmanteau was left with you belonging to Mr. Wills, my son?—A bag, a calico bag, containing clothes.

You were aware that it was his own property?—I was.

What made you take those clothes back to Menindie, and not leave them in the cache?—Mr. Wills was as well supplied with clothes as any other member of the party, and I certainly did not think that they would be in want of clothes.

Are you not aware that those clothes might have saved his life?—I know a great many things now that I could not know then. If I had known that they would have returned the night they did I should have remained there certainly. If I had had any reason for expecting them back at all, I would certainly have perished rather than have left.

There remained now just one more witness of any importance, Dr. Herman Beckler, and he soon revealed that he was a pro-Wright man, or at all events he was anti-Burke. Burke, Dr. Beckler said, had used 'expressions' both to himself and to Landells on the way up to Menindie from Melbourne which he thought were unjustified. He had found that he was quite unable to please Burke, and he had finally resigned, partly because of Burke's treatment of Landells and partly because he was not allowed to get on with his scientific work. And so he had been left behind at Menindie. Later on he had thought better of his resignation and had volunteered to accompany Wright to the Cooper.

All the party were in good health?—Yes, so far as I could see.

But very soon after you started some of them got sick?—Yes, the first symptoms were exhibited at Torowoto by Stone. He had been engaged by Mr. Wright only one or two days previous to our leaving Menindie, and he had only just returned from Adelaide, and had been attended by a physician in Adelaide.

What was the matter with him?—He was suffering from what is here called chronic bronchitis.

Then in fact he was not a healthy man to take?—I do not think so. But his general outward appearance was not so that you could take him as suffering from any disease at the time.

You did not examine him to see if he was a fit man for the expedition?—I did not.

You were in medical charge at that time were you not?—I was so far as I had offered to accompany Mr. Wright. I had no authority to refuse anybody whom Mr. Wright had engaged.

Do you not consider that the inaction of remaining so long at Menindie without any occupation predisposed the men to disease?—I think so, or at least it predisposed Mr. Becker.

Was scurvy the complaint the men died of that did die?—Mr. Becker died of dysentery and the exhaustion consequent upon it—of course with some peculiar symptoms which were principally owing to the affection of scurvy, and Purcell died of exhaustion in consequence of scurvy.

Scurvy was the primary cause?—Yes, scurvy was the primary cause of all the deaths that occurred in our party.

Did you deal out preserved vegetables pretty liberally to those who were affected with scurvy?—We had no time to prepare those vegetables which we had with us; they are quite hard and they require dissolving or being kept in water for some time.

You took a number of seeds with you on the expedition, did you make any use of them?—The first we planted was at Bulloo, they were planted quite near the creek, but as soon as the young shoots of the plants appeared they were eaten off by the rats.

McDonough's statement that he had starved Patton was quite untrue, Beckler continued. He personally had prepared Patton's meals for him—porridge for breakfast and rice and apples for the other meals. He also had soup made from pounded meat-biscuit, but the preserved vegetables were too hard for him.

★

This last hearing of the Commission was on December 30, 1861, and a month later they were ready with their report. It read as follows:

'The expedition, having been provided and equipped in the most ample and liberal manner, and having reached

Menindie, on the Darling, without experiencing any difficulties, was most injudiciously divided at that point by Mr.
Burke.

'It was an error of judgement on the part of Mr. Burke to
appoint Mr. Wright to an important command in the expedition, without a previous personal knowledge of him; although, doubtless, a pressing urgency had arisen for the
appointment from the sudden resignations of Mr. Landells
and Dr. Beckler.

'Mr. Burke evinced a far greater amount of zeal than
prudence in finally departing from Cooper's Creek before
the depot party had arrived from Menindie, and without
having secured communication with the settled districts as
he had been instructed to do; and, in undertaking so
extended a journey with insufficient supply of provisions,
Mr. Burke was forced into the necessity of overtaxing the
powers of his party, whose continuous and unremitting
exertions resulted in the destruction of his animals, and the
prostration of himself and his companions from fatigue and
severe privation.

'The conduct of Mr. Wright appears to have been repre-
hensible in the highest degree. It is clear that Mr. Burke, on
parting with him at Torowoto, relied on receiving his imme-
diate and zealous support; and it seems extremely improbable that Mr. Wright could have misconstrued the intentions
of his leader so far as to suppose that he ever calculated for
a moment on his remaining any length of time on the
Darling. Mr. Wright has failed to give any satisfactory explanation of the causes of his delay; and to that delay are mainly
attributable the whole of the disasters of the expedition, with
the exception of the death of Gray. The grave responsibility
of not having left a larger supply of provisions, together with
some clothing, in the cache at Cooper's Creek, rests with Mr.
Wright. Even had he been unable to convey stores to Cooper's Creek, he might have left them elsewhere, leaving notice
at the depot of his having done so.

'The Exploration Committee, in overlooking the importance of the contents of Mr. Burke's dispatch from Torowoto,
and in not urging Mr. Wright's departure from the Darling,
committed errors of a serious nature. A means of knowledge

of the delay of the party at Menindie was in the possession of the Committee, not indeed by direct communication to that effect, but through the receipt of letters from Drs. Beckler and Becker at various dates up to the end of November—without, however, awakening the Committee to a sense of the vital importance of Mr. Burke's request in that dispatch that he should 'be soon followed up'—or to a consideration of the disastrous consequences which would be likely to result, and did unfortunately result, from the fatal inactivity and idling of Mr. Wright and his party of the Darling.

'The conduct of Mr. Brahe in retiring from his position at the depot before he was rejoined by his commander, or relieved from the Darling, may be deserving of considerable censure; but we are of the opinion that a responsibility far beyond his expectations devolved upon him; and it must be borne in mind that, with the assurance of his leader, and his own conviction, he might each day expect to be relieved by Mr. Wright, he still held his post for four months and five days, and that only when pressed by the appeals of a comrade sickening even to death, as was subsequently proved, his powers of endurance gave way, and he retired from the position which could alone afford succour to the weary explorers should they return by that route. His decision was most unfortunate; but we believe he acted from a conscientious desire to discharge his duty, and we are confident that the painful reflection that twenty-four hours' further perseverance would have made him the rescuer of the explorers, and gained for himself the praise and approbation of all, must be of itself an agonising thought, without the addition of censure he might feel himself undeserving of.

'It does not appear that Mr. Burke kept any regular journal, or that he gave written instructions to his officers; had he performed these essential portions of the duties of a leader many of the calamities of the expedition might have been averted, and little or no room would have been left for doubt in judging the conduct of those subordinates who pleaded unsatisfactory and contradictory verbal orders and statements.

'We cannot too deeply deplore the lamentable result of an

expedition, undertaken at so great a cost to the Colony; but, while we regret the absence of a systematic plan of operations on the part of the Leader, we desire to express our admiration of his gallantry and daring, as well as of the fidelity of his brave coadjutor Mr. Wills, and their more fortunate and enduring associate Mr. King; and we would record our feelings of deep sympathy with the deplorable sufferings and untimely deaths of Mr. Burke and his fallen comrades.'

It was well done, a balanced and fair judgement, and it pleased nearly everyone with the exception of those like Dr. Wills (who thought that Brahe should have been censured), and the Committee (who were hurt), and the partisans of Burke (who regarded all criticism of him as sacrilege). There was no basis here for criminal proceedings against Wright, but he had been publicly condemned as the man on whom the guilt chiefly lay, and that was a reputation that he was unlikely ever to live down. He retired to obscurity in Adelaide, leaving behind him still a slight, persistent mystery: why had he really delayed? Was it only because he wanted to make sure of his salary? Was it because he did not want to leave his wife and family and the comforts of the settled districts? Was it merely that he was stupid, lazy and indifferent: a man too mean-spirited to think of anyone but himself? Or was it just possible that he was the victim of that same fated chain of errors that had bedevilled the expedition from the beginning? These were questions that would never be fully answered.

CHAPTER FIFTEEN

The Public Penance

The graves on the Cooper were dug up. At the height of just such a summer that had defeated Wright, Howitt rode back to the Cooper and there he disinterred and boxed the scattered bones (minus Wills' skull, minus Burke's hands and feet) and loaded them on to his camels. This time, for a change, he came down by way of Mount Hopeless, and in just two weeks he crossed that terrible stretch of arid country that had doomed the explorers in the last few weeks of their lives. He then marched uneventfully through the settled districts to Adelaide and continued on to Melbourne by sea.

The funeral was held on January 21, 1863, and was a tremendous affair. Invitations to take part in the official cortège were sent all over the colony and no one was forgotten; the clergy and members of both houses of parliament, the Freemasons, the Foresters and the Rechabites, the army and the police, the mayors and corporations of the provincial towns. These last were provided with free railway tickets to Melbourne, and only the councillors of the town of Beechworth (Burke's old town) were unable to avail themselves of this generosity, owing, they said, 'to the absence of the railway itself'. The chief clerk of Geelong made a complaint about the inferior position allotted to the Geelong contingent in the funeral procession, but was placated in the end, and Castlemaine (another of Burke's old stations) sent down its Light Dragoons together with their horses. The funeral car was a replica of the one in which the Duke of Wellington had been carried to his grave in St. Paul's Cathedral in London ten years before. It was an enormous built-up carriage with decorated wheels and an open canopy above the coffins, and it was drawn by six black horses with plumes on their heads. King was one of the pallbearers, and among the distinguished men who took part in the march was the Governor himself. A military band led the way and the houses and shops along the route were draped in purple and black. Soldiers with reversed arms were posted on either side of the street, and some forty thousand people stood and silently watched the long procession go by.

On the grave in the Melbourne cemetery there was presently set up a 34-ton monolith of undressed Harcourt stone, and this was inscribed: 'In memory of Robert O'Hara Burke and William John Wills ... comrades in a great achievement, companions in death, and associates in renown. Leader and second in command of the Victorian Exploring Expedition died at Cooper's Creek, June, 1861.'

No one could be absolutely sure about the date—was it the end of June or the beginning of July that Burke had collapsed and Wills, unobserved, except perhaps by the blacks, had quietly stopped breathing?—but it hardly mattered.

The monolith by itself was not considered to be a sufficient tribute: a public fund for a monument was opened and the government contributed £4,000 to it. The sculptor, Charles Summers, was commissioned to execute this work and he produced a group of colossal proportions; the figure of Burke stood twelve feet high, a hatless, bearded giant in his shirt-sleeves gazing out into the distance, and his right hand rested on the shoulder of Wills, sitting beside him with his diary in his hand. On the granite pedestal below there were four bronze bas-reliefs depicting the start of the expedition, the return to Cooper's

Creek, the blacks weeping over the dead Burke and the finding of King. For a long time this somewhat ponderous work stood on the hill at the corner of Collins and Russell Streets in the heart of the city, but it impeded the increasing traffic, and in 1886 it was removed to its present site[1] outside Parliament House where hardly one man in a thousand bothers to look at it any more.

Other monuments and memorial stones were erected in the Victorian provincial cities and along the explorers' route into the interior, as well as in Totnes, Wills' birthplace in Devon. There was a proposal at one time (put forward by Barkly the governor) that the Carpentaria area of northern Australia should be called Burkeland, but nothing came of this, and now only a district there bears his name. However, the flourishing mining region of Cloncurry in Queensland—so called by Burke after those wealthy connections in Ireland—still bears its original name. Most of the other place-names chosen by the expedition—King's Gap, Gray's Creek, Boocha's Rest and so on— have long since been supplanted and forgotten.

In London the Royal Geographical Society bestirred itself. These were *anni mirabiles* for the Society, with Dr. Livingstone and Stanley in Africa, Speke and Grant at the source of the Nile, and Richard Burton and so many other British explorers making their great journeys round the world. The Society now presented its gold medal to Burke's family in London, and a gold watch was sent off to King. There was a feeling, however, that Wills ought to have had a gold medal as well—after all he was the only geographer on the expedition—and Dr. Mueller wrote to Sir Roderick Murchison, the president of the Society, about it. Hearing that Dr. Wills was in London, Murchison wrote him a charming letter saying that, under the Society's rules, only one medal could be granted for any one expedition, and that nothing less than a medal could have been given to so good a geographer as Wills was. 'Rely upon it,' he added, 'that his merits will never be forgotten by my associates and myself.'

Dr. Wills replied: '... It is not strange that Dr. Mueller and my friends in Australia should feel somewhat annoyed in the

[1]Since original publication, the statue has been moved twice: firstly, to facilitate construction of an underground railway station outside Parliament House, to the Treasury Gardens; and yet again to the newly formed City Square.

matter of the medal ... The clothes, for the want of which my
son died, so amply provided by himself, were worn by others;
the land discovered has been called exclusively by another
name—the Gold medal should follow. Still I am grateful for
your well-expressed remarks.'

It took a long time for this sort of rancour to die down. Even
on the day of the funeral itself there was an angry scene. After
the ceremony was over some three or four thousand people
gathered in St. George's Hall to hold a sort of post-mortem on
the expedition. Barkly made a speech, and then Macadam got
up to deliver an apologia for the Committee. He was received
with a storm of groans and hisses and nobody was disposed to
listen to him at first. But Macadam was an experienced politi-
cian, and he persisted in his speech—a very long one—until he
had won his audience round. The unfortunate Landells then
attempted to make an address but was howled down and the
meeting broke up in confusion.

In the midst of these strong feelings King was not forgotten:
a sum of £3,135 was invested for him, sufficient to bring him
in an income of £180 a year, an adequate amount to live on at
the time. The Victorian government also voted £2,090 to Wills'
mother in Devon, and £500 each to his two sisters, in addition
to £150 for Dr. Wills to pay his passage to England. Dost
Mahomet, who had lost an arm at Menindie, got £200, and
another £200 went to Welch, the surveyor, to compensate him
for an injured eye. A further sum of £1,045 was given to Ellen
Doherty, Burke's old nurse who had followed him out to
Australia soon after the expedition started. (Burke himself was
found to have left only seven shillings and eightpence in his
bank account, and for a long time the Melbourne Club pressed
the Committee for a sum of £18 5s. 3d. which he owed them.
They were eventually paid.)

The government accountants now prepared a statement of
the total bill—all the money spent on the original expedition
and the rescue parties, on the funeral, the monuments and the
pensions—and it was devastating, a sum of just under £60,000.
Even Stanley in Africa, a mighty spender in this great age of
exploration, had been unable to get through as much money
as this. And yet it was not long before people began to feel that
it had all been worth it. Despite its mismanagement and its

tragic result, the Burke and Wills expedition was one of those incidents that, in a quite unpredictable and unexpected way, set fire to a chain of events, and give colour and movement to an age. It had the quality of a myth, of a genuine and wholly Australian legend, and that was enough to inspire others to accomplish things which were far beyond the achievements of the original expedition.

The rescue parties that went out to look for the lost men increased the knowledge of the inland enormously. Quite apart from McDouall Stuart (who perhaps has not been sufficiently noticed in these pages), the continent was twice more crossed within a year, and huge areas were opened up for settlement; and all this was done without loss of life or any serious mishap. McKinlay's journey took him northwards across the Cooper to Gray's grave (which he thought to be the burial place of all Burke's party), and he then continued on at a fine pace to the Gulf. Like Burke he was unable to get through the mangrove swamps to the sea so he turned east, hoping to find Captain Norman in the *Victoria* at the mouth of the Albert River. In this he was disappointed—Norman had already sailed away—but he held on towards the east and eventually emerged on the Queensland coast whence he returned to Adelaide by sea. This vast march took him just a year, and almost the only casualty was one of those strayed camels of Burke's, which he was forced to kill and eat on the shores of the Gulf.

Landsborough meanwhile came down from the north, where he named and explored the Barkly Tableland in Queensland, and he then marched south to the Cooper to come out at last, safe and sound, at Menindie. Walker with his tribe of mounted black trackers also accomplished his mission. He found Burke's last camp on the Flinders, reported the fact to Captain Norman, and then, almost as though he was out for a casual stroll, went home to the east coast again. The indomitable McDouall Stuart, unaware of all these comings and goings, also reached the northern coast near Darwin in 1862. When the results of these expeditions were put together the mystery of central Australia was a mystery no longer. It was now known for certain that there were no mountains there really worth the name and no inland sea, but those flat horizons were not all desert by any means; there were valuable grazing lands stretching over tens of thousands of square miles, intermittent but considerable rivers with forests on their banks, and a very lively prospect of discovering all kinds of mineral ore. Even before Burke and Wills were finally buried in Melbourne, settlers were spreading up to Bulloo with herds of cattle and sheep, and within ten years there were station homesteads on the Cooper itself.

Soon a township with a pub, a police station and a customs post (that grim harbinger of civilization) was established on the creek at Innamincka, not half a dozen miles from Burke's first grave, and it became an important staging post for the herds of cattle being driven down from central Queensland to the Adelaide market.

Then in the eighteen-seventies the overland telegraph was built from Port Augusta to Darwin, a distance of 1,800 miles. It followed McDouall Stuart's route and the work was completed in two years, a tremendous achievement. Now for the first time Australia was directly in touch with the outside world and another of Sturt's dreams had come true.

There were other enterprises inspired by the Burke and Wills expedition. Lutheran missions established themselves on the Cooper and began to spread out through the interior. This was the beginning of a better and more humane knowledge of the blacks. Later the Flying Doctor Service arrived. The camel, having proved himself on the Victorian expedition, was imported into Australia in large numbers from India, and by the end of the century there were 6,000 of them. In the wet seasons they still bogged most fearfully in the waterholes, and poor Landa's cries and moans in the grasping mud of the Cooper were a lament for them all. The animal nowadays is rarely seen.

The greatest rewards were reserved for the miners. Working up Sturt's and Burke's routes they found that Piesse's Knob, to the north of Menindie, was in fact the site of a rich deposit of silver, lead and zinc, indeed the richest such deposit in the world; and so, under its new name, the Broken Hill commercial empire started on its way. By 1958 its earnings were estimated at £400,000,000. Then, further to the north in the Cloncurry area, there were other finds almost as valuable; Mount Isa with its copper, and the uranium mine with the delightful name

Mary Kathleen. Compared with the millions of pounds earned every year by these enterprises the £60,000 spent on the expedition does not appear to be a very great sum.

Geologists too followed in the wake of Burke and Wills, and they were soon able to prove that Sturt's vision of an inland sea was not at all a fantasy; in fact upon several counts it was a reality both in the past and at the present time. In the Cambrian age such a sea extended south from the Gulf of Carpentaria over western Queensland and South Australia, and even when this sea retired a great lake remained in the centre, and it collected the waters of the Diamantina and the Cooper when they were much more considerable streams than they are now. At the present time this lake—Lake Eyre—is only a fraction of its former size and it is usually as dry as the surrounding desert; but once its shores were surrounded by fertile plains and forests of large trees that were inhabited by giant kangaroos capable of making a bound of thirty feet. Monstrous crocodiles swarmed in the lake. But then the rain failed, the lake dwindled to its present size and became salt, and on its desiccated shores only the petrified bones of its giant animals remain.

But this was still not the end of the inland sea. In the eighteen-eighties it was discovered that the rain that fell in the eastern Australian highlands flowed underground into the centre and accumulated there in a vast subterranean basin. Bores were sunk, in some cases to a depth of thousands of feet, and water that was excessively hot, but drinkable, came rushing to the surface. This discovery revolutionized the development of the centre, for it meant that now, however dry the land, it was possible to drive the cattle to market from one bore to another across many hundreds of miles where formerly they would have died of thirst.

Then, too, there are certain years when rain falls on these wastes with tremendous violence, and the Cooper comes roaring down in flood, carrying everything before it, and land that previously was desert springs instantly to life. Hundreds of watercourses that have been dry for years flow down towards Lake Eyre in a brown flood which is many miles in width, and so again, for a few months, there is, in fact, an inland sea. In 1950, a year of particularly heavy rainfall, a boat was taken down the Cooper into Lake Eyre itself. Evaporation soon absorbs these inundations, and as the water subsides it leaves a great debris of uprooted timber, and here and there the drowned bodies of cattle hang grotesquely in the branches of the trees.

But it is the desert, or at any rate the semi-desert, which is the true condition of central Australia, and with its wind-blown sand-dunes, its flat distances, its grey-green islands of trees round the waterholes, and its immense sky, it is not unlike the sea. It has the sea's peace and the sea's relentlessness. Early in the present century the geologist, J. W. Gregory, went up to the Cooper and in his *The Dead Heart of Australia* was moved to write: 'At times, when the caravan is hidden below a sandridge, the horror of being hopelessly lost in the desert—waterless and foodless—forces itself upon one's mind. We think of the unfortunate travellers whose bones, bared by dingoes and polished by sand, lie scattered on the central Australian wastes. A vision rises before us of the desperate struggles of the lost explorer, and of the despair of his last mile's march.'

This probably is the heart of the Burke and Wills tragedy, and the reason why it survives so strongly as a legend in Australia. Their story perfectly expresses the early settlers' deeply-felt idea that life was not so much a struggle against other men as against the wilderness—that wilderness that made all men equal anyway. The quarrel, basically, was with nature, and to be 'let down' by a companion when one was out in the hard, implacable bush and absolutely exposed—this was the final treachery.

The Longstaff painting (fourteen feet by nine) showing the scene at the depot when Burke's party returned there has been recently described by the Australian poet Lee as 'an acre of umber', and indeed it is badly in need of cleaning, and has now been relegated to the newspaper room in the Melbourne Library. Its story-telling intention is out of vogue, and probably no one at any time would have called it a masterpiece. Yet any Australian who, as a child, has stood before that awful canvas will recall the dire sensations it aroused. An artificial horror might have been easier to bear, but this scene was all too understandable. Death on the field of glory, one felt, might be a very fine thing, and death in bed very bearable. But this was just death, stark, despairing and meaningless, the monster in the dark; and so one hurried on through the library, past the plaster casts of the Greek gods, and out into the bright light of day.

Not many of those who were connected with the expedition survived Burke and Wills for very long. King very wisely rejected an offer from a showman to appear in vaudeville together with 'a cyclorama of the expedition' and lived quietly with his sister, Mrs. Bunting, in St. Kilda. He married a cousin in 1871. But he never fully recovered from his privations on the Cooper, and in the following year he died of tuberculosis. He was just 33. They buried him near Burke and Wills.

In that same year, 1872, both McKinlay and Landells died, the latter in Calcutta—apparently he was unable to endure the obloquy surrounding him in Melbourne and he returned to India. Dost Mahomet was buried in Menindie, having never returned to his native land. Brahe went up to Queensland where he had an uneventful but fairly prosperous career on the land. Dr. Beckler went back to Germany. Of Wright's subsequent career little or nothing is known. Dr. Macadam survived the expedition by only four years, but Howitt lived on until nearly eighty. Julia Matthews went to New Zealand in 1863, and having married there returned to England, where she had a success as the duchess in Offenbach's *La Grande Duchesse de Gérolstein*. With this and other pieces she toured Europe and America, and eventually she died in St. Louis in 1876. Sir Charles Cooper, whose name was perpetuated by these events, retired to Bath in England and died there in the eighties.

The last and perhaps the best gesture made by the Victorian government to commemorate the expedition was to grant 200 square miles of land on Cooper's Creek to the blacks who had been so kind to King. It might perhaps have been argued that since Cooper's Creek was not in Victoria at all they had no power to make this handsome gift, and that the land presumably belonged to the blacks anyway. However the intention was good, and it was hoped that the tribesmen on the creek would enjoy this large hunting reserve in perpetuity. The chief tribe involved were the Yuntruwunta, who were similar to their neighbours, the Dieri, who lived further down the Cooper. Howitt made the first scientific study of these people when he went back for Burke's and Wills' bodies, and later on the

Lutheran and Moravian missions on the creek got to know them very well. A number were taught crude English, and many of them acquired European clothes of one sort or another. But the contact with civilization was too much for them: European diseases laid them low, the women—those women who had been so artlessly and spontaneously offered to the explorers—became barren, and somehow the will to survive died away. By the time the geologist Gregory arrived at Kopperamanna on the lower Cooper in 1902 only five blacks remained where formerly there had been a thousand. Around the old depot LXV the Yuntruwunta tribe had vanished altogether.

And so, in the end, there was no one to inherit the 200 square miles, and in a reshuffle of the state borders the Victorian government's offer was conveniently forgotten.

It is still quite possible today to retrace Burke's march to the Gulf, camping where he camped, and seeing more or less the same things he saw.[1]

In Victoria the land has been fairly heavily settled, but the old Cobb's Coach route (now a highway) still leads out from Royal Park in Melbourne to Castlemaine and Bendigo; and at Swan Hill one can drive along the Murray river-bank to the junction with the Darling. In the fruit-growing district of Mildura one sees the skeletons of Captain Cadell's old paddle-steamers breaking up on the bank, but some of them are still prodded into action.

The Darling is a narrow, muddy stream, with dun-coloured earthen banks shaded by eucalypts, but it has managed to keep some of the wildness and remoteness it had a hundred years ago. Here at last one catches a glimpse of the kangaroo bounding away through the scrub, and the flocks of parrots are almost as plentiful as they ever were. Kinchega station, which used to cover a million and a quarter acres in Wright's time, still exists, but Menindie is now a railway junction and the centre of a water conservation scheme. Bulldozers roar by throwing up new earthworks between the lakes, and there is not a camel to be seen. But the outpost atmosphere persists. The local people will show you 'Burke's room' in Paine's old pub on the river

---

[1] In the eighties George Morrison, the celebrated 'Chinese' Morrison who was the adviser of Sun-yat-sen, walked the whole distance from the Gulf to Adelaide, some 2,000 miles, in 123 days.

bank, and out at Pamamaroo Creek the expedition's camping site is easily recognizable from Ludwig Becker's drawings. On the lake nearby regattas of black swans and pelicans sail about, and in the evening the slender grey herons arrive. They stand motionless on the banks of the creek and stab for fish, and they are closely overlooked by flocks of cormorants that perch like black bobbins in the trees above. When the fishing is good these cormorants swoop together on to the water and drive the herons away—a scene Becker must have watched a hundred times. By day the flies are troublesome and it is very hot, but in this clean dry air the traveller is filled with energy, and he wants to go on across the great desolate plains stretching away to the north— to go on and on through Mootwingee and Torowoto and Bulloo until he reaches the Cooper, four hundred miles away.

If he goes up in the late spring (as Burke did) he will see the wildflowers in bloom on the red soil, and especially great fields of Paterson's Curse,[1] which is a weed presumably imported by a Mr. Paterson and which Burke did not see. All this country is so flat that the Barrier Range (minus Piesse's Knob—it has been demolished by the Broken Hill miners) is seen from a very long way off, and even the sparse lines of trees in the dry creeks look like forests on the horizon. But at Mootwingee the plain really does break up, and it is a delight to go into these gullies that Wills found so gloomy, and to slither down the flaking rock into the still water of the pools. In these rough hills the kangaroos and emus seem to be larger and tamer than they were on the open plain, and the parrots have a brighter colour in the softer light. Tourists have been here and with their guns have taken pot-shots at the native carvings on the rocks, and have cut their initials among the stencilled hands in the overhanging caves: those hands that probably signified a meeting-place, the fingers representing tracks leading into a central junction. However, the damage is not yet complete, and although there are no longer any blacks to hold corroborees now, the some- what eerie spirit of the place persists.

Beyond Mootwingee one is in the country where Wright's party wandered and died, and it is indeed very deserty, but cattle manage to survive even where there is no grass, only bushes, and the waterholes have become the sites of station homesteads.

[1]Paterson's Curse is also known by the more gentle name of Salvation Jane.

Some of these places have tennis courts lit by electric light (it being too hot to play by day), swimming-pools and lawns and lemon groves (no danger of scurvy today), and the cattle are rounded up by cowboys in Volkswagens. The station owner in his aircraft will make the journey from Cooper's Creek to the Darling in a single afternoon.

A new kind of fauna lives on these great fenced plains, the domestic animals gone wild: a lone white cat lopes across the track, miles from anywhere, and homestead dogs that have mated with dingoes bound away at the approach of a car. They keep glancing backward as they run, since they are sheep-killers and are always shot at. Then there are scrub cattle, so lean and bony nobody bothers to brand them any more, and the brumbies, the wild horses which are rounded up from time to time to be slaughtered and sold in the cities as cats' meat.

Near Torowoto (a name now forgotten), a plaque has been set up on a cairn, and it indicates the place where Sturt spent that long furnace-like summer in 1845, unable to go forward or to go back. Following on along the track one comes next to an eight-foot netted dog-fence which marks the border of New South Wales and Queensland (neither state wants the others' dogs), and one passes through at Warri Gate, which is somewhat to the west of Burke's route. Then the plain again disintegrates into hard stony ravines and gullies; this was the place where the expedition had to make its last long waterless march to the Cooper. It is fearful country to walk on or even ride over; the ground is covered with sharp dark brown stones known as gibbers, which are as hard as iron and brutal to the feet.

And now the desert takes a stronger hold. The trees grow spines instead of leaves, their bark peels away like paper, and except for a few desiccated bushes every green thing on the ground has been defeated by the sun. The first approach to the Cooper is through a series of low ridges which, in the distance, look like long flat-topped hills, then there is another gibber plain, and finally you reach the blessed shade of the creek itself. On that muddy, grey-green water—and sometimes the billabongs are half a mile long and as much as sixty feet deep—life begins again; the incessant passage of the birds, the little turtle thrusting up his doubting snout, the scamper of rabbits on the bank. The site of the depot lies a few miles downstream from the Napper Merrie homestead, and it is a moving thing to see there the original tree with the word 'DIG' still discernible, to build your campfire under its branches and to spread your bedroll on the ground where the stockade used to stand before it was carried away by floods. Except that a cairn with a plaque has been erected on the bank, nothing has changed. The boomerang shape of the waterhole that curves round the site is the same as it always was, and Brahe and his men must have gazed a thousand times (with what boredom) at a great eucalypt on the opposite bank, which is a favourite roost for the corellas. Apart from the Napper Merrie homestead there are no human beings for many miles around, and in the midday heat and again at night the silence is complete. The nights are remarkable. Once the evening commotion of birds is over and the theatrical light of the sunset has faded, the dark sky, studded with enormous stars, descends from the great height it had by day, and there is a kind of joy in just lying there on one's campbed, cool and relaxed and safe in the midst of so much unvisited space. As a rule the night is very still, and thus seems timeless while it lasts; and perhaps—one dreams a good deal on the Cooper—there might be something in all this to reconcile the mind with death. But then the dawn comes up with a sunburst of coloured searchlights, the first fly settles on the sleeper's nose, and he struggles back to life again.

One fancies one might be prepared to wait patiently for a long time in this solitary and beautiful place. Little by little, as the days pass, a rhythm takes command, and one can tell the time without looking at a watch by many different signs: the seven o'clock breeze ruffling the waterhole, the midday flight of lilac kingfishers coming down the creek, the evening appearance of the rabbits. The light is so clear that every passing bird makes a precise moving shadow on the ground, and the smallest ants arrest the eye as though seen through a microscope. Soon it becomes apparent that the chief effects here are not of harmony but of contrast; the cool night succeeding the overpowering day, the scarlet dragon-fly that is made doubly brilliant by the drab background of the bush, the cacophony of parrots in silence. One's thirst is so great that a cool drink of water really does taste—as Wills said—like sparkling wine.

And yet there is a certain menace on the Cooper. It remains

basically inimical to man, it rejects him, the climate is too arid and too hard. The cattlemen here contract sores and swollen gums which they call Barcoo Rot (Barcoo being the other name for the Cooper), and it is that same vitamin deficiency that killed Ludwig Becker and the others. Sometimes, too, the men shake violently in a spasm of nerves, a condition known as the 'Dry Horrors', but this usually only besets those who spend their vacations in prolonged bouts of drunkenness, and whose craving in these dry wastes becomes ungovernable. A week or two in the pubs in the south generally puts them right, and they can continue for another six months or so without a drink. Burke was clearly wise to leave the camels' rum behind at Menindie.

But perhaps the really undermining thing about the Cooper is the inertia that overtakes one there. It is not the soporific torpor of the tropics, but rather a feeling of deep physical exhaustion, a fatalistic passivity in the mind; one longs to take refuge in a slow, safe uneventful routine, and it is not long before the demands of civilization drop away. One lives upon the bare minimum of effort, one accepts discomforts, and to gaze on and on into the campfire, to do nothing, to say nothing, to succumb to solitariness, becomes at last the only bearable existence. This is a condition which is admirable for hermits but may have done as much as anything else to destroy the expedition.

Burke's grave is in a lonely place about fifteen miles down the creek from the depot. You reach it by making a wide detour over the stones on the south bank, and then, doubling back to the creek, you come on a splendid waterhole with steep sandy sides. About fifty yards back from the bank there is a big coolibah tree, and it was under this tree that Burke died. Nothing except a small memorial cairn distinguishes the place from anywhere else on this part of the Cooper, and yet it is much more evocative of his death—the scribbling of the last note about King, the sinking back with the revolver in his hand—than the grandiose distance-peering statue in Melbourne. Burke's death became him very well, and one supposes that at the end it was not grand horizons that he perceived, nor glory, nor even probably did he feel resentment, but rather the humility of exhaustion, the acceptance of defeat, and perhaps too, great affection for King.

All this part of the Cooper is embraced by the Innamincka station, some 10,000 square miles in extent (including the 200 square miles the blacks were to have had), and there is a homestead on the creek close to the spot where King was found. But the little township that sprang up after Burke's time has collapsed through want of trade and all that remains of it now are a few ruined buildings and a thousand empty beer bottles glittering in the sun. Northwards on the expedition's route lies Sturt's Stony Desert, and here, at a place called King's Lookout, you can survey that unearthly prismatic landscape which is really closer to an abstract pattern than to anything recognizable in nature. According to the time of day the sandhills that stretch away on every side are vermilion, scarlet, rose-red or orange, but always the colour is of a startling intensity. Sometimes the ridges are dotted with grey and green bushes, and a bare rock breaks through to the surface, and so the general appearance is of a formal Japanese garden, always with the bright pale blue sky beyond. One finds a track through this gay maze by keeping to the salt pans that lie between the ridges, and at the end of the day you finally come out into the open plain again. Here a number of homesteads have been abandoned in the last half-century—the droughts were too long and the loneliness too abrasive—but still the artesian bores gush out on to the dry ground. The water comes up through an L-shaped metal pipe, hissing and steaming, and it is hot enough to boil an egg, hot enough to make your billy of tea. It cools off as it runs away, and in a sandstorm you will see the strange wraiths of cattle looming through the gloom at the places where they know they can drink. The bones of dead animals lie everywhere.

There is only one township in this desolation, Birdsville, and since it lies between Sturt's Stony Desert and the Simpson Desert where virtually nothing grows, it is perfectly placed to take the full brunt of these sandstorms no matter from what quarter the wind blows, and it may blow for days on end until the grit lines your very stomach and red-rimmed eyes can stand no more. But invariably the 'blow' subsides at last into a dead calm, and one wakes to a morning of such sparkling freshness and clarity that Burke, in these latitudes, must have been much encouraged to go on.

Beyond Birdsville the country gradually improves as the rainfall increases; grass finds a hold on the blown sand, the creeks are more frequent, and now once again there are flights of birds and groups of kangaroos. One does well to watch the kangaroos, since they will not survive much longer except in the remote parts of Australia. Like the wild horses, they are being shot for pets' food, and something like a million of them are destroyed every year.

The invasion of civilization here is, indeed, very strange, very ruthless and very haphazard. Some of the new towns, with their banks and shops and petrol pumps, have a bright suburban look, but at their outskirts there is sure to be a collection of iron shanties of appalling squalor, to which the few remaining blacks have been banished. These places swarm with rats; broken bottles and rusting cans are strewn about among the wreckage of old trucks and cars. But then in a few minutes you are out on the wide plain again, and the half-caste drover, whom yesterday you saw sprawling drunken in the pub, now rides by with his mob of cattle, graceful, handsome and erect, absolutely in command of his world.

And so the traveller continues on to the north, following Eyre's Creek which becomes the Georgina and finally the Burke, until eventually he comes to the town of Djarra, and here rocky hills rise up on the horizon, the first real hills he has seen since leaving Victoria, a thousand miles away. The scrub now thickens and extends back from the banks of the creeks, with a stronger, greener shade, and after the hardness of the centre this is a great relief. The anthills now begin, at first quite small, only two or three feet high, but they occur in colonies of many thousands and they make the ground look as though it is covered with sawn-off tree trunks. Beyond Cloncurry they grow bigger and bigger until they are six foot or more in height, and they are sculpted in the shapes of turreted castles, pinnacles and jagged mountain ranges. In the creeks here there are avenues of lovely ghost-gums and paperbarks, everything grows larger and more luxuriantly, and the birds one sees are bush turkeys and great elegant storks, and cranes like the brolga and the jabiru. Now at last one is nearing the coast, and on the Flinders River the air grows soft, heavy and humid—the first true breath of the tropics. There is a rumble of thunder in the air, and if one is caught here by the wet season (as Burke was), the rain is incessant and the tracks become impassable for weeks or even months at a time.

Burke's last camp on the Byno River can be found very easily, and King's report is perfectly true: the water is salt, the rocks and sandbanks vanish and reappear with the rising and falling of the tide, and there are even sluggish jellyfish floating in the stream. It is a pretty place and yet somehow oppressive—perhaps because of the crocodiles lurking under the gently-moving tide, perhaps because of the woolly air and the leaden, tropical glare of the sun. The silence here is heavy and claustrophobic.

Burke and his companions can hardly have had much sense of achievement in this uneventful place, and one wishes very much that they had somehow got through to the sea and had had their moment of triumph there before turning back to that fatal depot on the Cooper. After all, another day would have made no difference.

But this seems to have been a story of predestined anticlimax, and it is a little sad to reflect that had Burke and Wills succeeded in getting back to the depot in time we would take much less interest in them than we do. Without the tragedy on the Cooper they would have remained rather minor figures, but with it they were lifted to another and a higher plane, one might even say a state of grace. And that perhaps was more important for them than the conquest of the ghastly blank.

Note

Mr. Sidney Nolan first suggested that I should write this book, and for this I most warmly thank him.

Most of the original Burke and Wills documents are held by the State Library of Victoria in Melbourne, and I wrote to the chief Librarian, Mr. J. A. Feeley, from my home in Italy, asking if he would help me. In reply he sent me a bibliography of the published and unpublished material dealing with the expedition, and since he believed I would have some difficulty in obtaining a copy of the report of the Royal Commission (a closely-printed paper of some 104 pages) he had a microfilm specially made for me. From these beginnings and with the help of the London Library and the Royal Geographical Society I was able to complete the preliminary research in Europe, and in the autumn of 1962 I went to Melbourne. Here Mr. Feeley and his two colleagues, Mr. Philip Garrett and Miss Clarice Kemp, had gathered together all the documents in their possession, and a private room was made available to me in the Library. I spent two happy months working there—and incidentally what pleasure to read the copperplate handwriting of the nineteenth century and to hold in one's hand the letters which, a hundred years ago, had lain buried for so long at the depot on Cooper's Creek. Later on I troubled Mr. Garrett and Miss Kemp with many inquiries and they produced from their archives most of the illustrations that here appear. Finally Miss Kemp, in the midst of the pressure of her own work, went to great pains in the correction of the manuscript.

I know of no way to express adequately my thanks to her, to Mr. Feeley, Mr. Garrett and the Library staff. I can only hope that they realize how grateful I am.

My thanks are also due to Mr. Geoffrey Serle of the Monash University, who allowed me to read his admirable study of Victoria in the eighteen-fifties while it was being prepared for the press, and who also read through the manuscript; to Mr. Gordon Richardson and Miss Janet D. Hine of the New South

Wales State Library, who allowed me to consult their archives; to Mr. G. L. Fischer and Miss Stapely of the South Australian Public Library, and to Dr. John R. Stawell, who searched his family records for me. Mr. D. P. Donegan, an authority on the history of the expedition, wrote me many invaluable letters, and although I fear that he will not altogether agree with my assessment of Burke I hope he will regard me as no worse than a misguided enthusiast.

While I was in Australia I followed Burke's route across the Continent in a Land Rover. Mr. Jeff Findley arranged this journey and accompanied me, and if it should chance that anyone has been moved by these pages to make a similar excursion—and it is a fascinating one—I strongly urge him to get in touch with the South Australian Government Tourist Bureau in Adelaide.

Mr. Ian F. McLaren of Melbourne, and Dr. and Mrs. A. H. McDonald of Clare College, Cambridge, were also good enough to read through the book before publication, and Mr. L. A. Watson of the Australian National Travel Association in London went to much trouble in providing maps, illustrations and information. In addition I must acknowledge the immense help given to me by my wife at every stage of the work.

There are a great many books which deal with the exploration and development of Central Australia and I hope that in going through them I have not failed to read any important or useful reference to the Burke and Wills expedition.

Among the books I found most helpful were: *Robert O'Hara Burke and the Australian Exploring Expedition of 1860* by Andrew Jackson (Smith Elder, 1862); *A Successful Exploration Through the Interior of Australia* by William Wills (Bentley, 1863); *Dig* by Frank Clune (Angus and Robertson, 1944); *Life of Charles Sturt* by Mrs. Napier George Sturt (Smith Elder, 1899); Sturt's own account of his expedition into Central Australia (Boone, 1849); Professor Geoffrey Serle's *The Golden Age* (Melbourne University Press, 1963); and such general works as the *Australian Encyclopaedia*.

The main sources, however, are the original letters and diaries of the explorers, the archives of the Royal Society of Victoria, the report of the Royal Commission, the Colonial Office archives (which contain Governor Barkly's dispatches), the Victorian State Parliamentary Papers and the contemporary magazines and newspapers. All this material was made available to me in the Melbourne Library and it has been indexed by Mr. McLaren in a lucid and authoritative paper printed in the Victorian Historical Magazine in November 1959.

In presenting the evidence given before the Royal Commission I have been obliged to abridge and re-arrange some of the questions and answers in what seemed to me to be a more logical sequence; and many have been omitted altogether. However, I have made every effort to give a fair and balanced report of the proceedings and am reasonably confident that no damage to the truth has been done.

Many of the place-names in Central Australia have been changed since 1860 and some are spelt differently; Menindie, for example, is now Menindee. I have, on the whole, used the contemporary names and spellings, and trust that any confusion that may arise in the reader's mind will be dispelled by reference to the maps.

Alan Moorehead

Acknowledgements

Thomas Nelson Publishers wish to thank the following
for their help in supplying illustrations for this edition:
The La Trobe Collection, State Library of Victoria for plates
2, 3, 4, 5, 6, 7, 8, 9, 10, 13, 17, 18, 20, 21, 22, 23, 24a&b, 26, 27,
28, 29, 30; The Mitchell Library, State Library of New South
Wales for plate 11; The Dixson Library, State Library of New
South Wales for plate 14; The Dixson Galleries, State Library
of New South Wales for plates 15 and 16; The South Australian State Library for plate 19; City of Ballaarat Fine Art
Gallery for plate 25; David Corke for plates 1 and 31, and for
his invaluable help.

Index

Also by Alan Moorehead in Penguins

THE BLUE NILE

A modern classic of historical travel writing, *The Blue Nile* is a fascinating story, superbly told and lavishly illustrated. In it Alan Moorehead traces the course of the Blue Nile from the Ethiopian Highlands, through the Sudan and Egypt to the sea, and then begins his historical narrative which starts in the eighteenth century and ends in 1869. 'Alan Moorehead . . . has enriched literature with his studies of the river, and confirmed his own reputation as the best of living story-tellers' – *The Times Literary Supplement*

THE WHITE NILE

The story of the Nile from the Mountains of the Moon to the Mediterranean. 'Mr Moorehead is an historian of great skill, his scholarship worn with deceptive lightness. Nobody could fail to enjoy the book' – *The Times Literary Supplement*.

THE FATAL IMPACT

When Captain Cook entered the Pacific in 1769 it was a virgin ocean, pristine and savage, and its inhabitants lived a life of primeval innocence. This is the brutal and tragic story of how the South Pacific was 'civilized' in the years 1767–1840.

and

Darwin and the Beagle

and

No Room in the Ark

FOR THE BEST IN PAPERBACKS, LOOK FOR THE 🐧

A CHOICE OF PENGUINS AND PELICANS

The Apartheid Handbook   Roger Omond

This book provides the essential hard information about how apartheid actually works from day to day and fills in the details behind the headlines.

The World Turned Upside Down   Christopher Hill

This classic study of radical ideas during the English Revolution 'will stand as a notable monument to . . . one of the finest historians of the present age' – *The Times Literary Supplement*

Islam in the World   Malise Ruthven

'His exposition of "the Qurenic world view" is the most convincing, and the most appealing, that I have read' – Edward Mortimer in *The Times*

The Knight, the Lady and the Priest   Georges Duby

'A very fine book' (Philippe Aries) that traces back to its medieval origin one of our most important institutions, marriage.

A Social History of England   New Edition   Asa Briggs

'A treasure house of scholarly knowledge . . . beautifully written and full of the author's love of his country, its people and its landscape' – John Keegan in the *Sunday Times*, Books of the Year

The Second World War   A J P Tavlor

A brilliant and detailed illustrated history, enlivened by all Professor Taylor's customary iconoclasm and wit.

FOR THE BEST IN PAPERBACKS, LOOK FOR THE

A CHOICE OF PENGUINS

The Big Red Train Ride   Eric Newby

From Moscow to the Pacific on the Trans-Siberian Railway is an eight-day journey of nearly six thousand miles through seven time zones. In 1977 Eric Newby set out with his wife, an official guide and a photographer on this journey. 'The best kind of travel book' – Paul Theroux

Star Wars   Edited by E. P. Thompson

With contributions from Rip Bulkeley, John Pike, Ben Thompson and E. P. Thompson, and with a Foreword by Dorothy Hodgkin, OM, this is a major book which assesses all the arguments for Star Wars and proceeds to make a powerful – indeed unanswerable – case against it.

Selected Letters of Malcolm Lowry
Edited by Harvey Breit and Margerie Bonner Lowry

Lowry emerges from these letters not only as an extremely interesting man, but also a lovable one' – Philip Toynbee

PENGUIN CLASSICS OF WORLD ART

Each volume presents the complete paintings of the artist and includes: an introduction by a distinguished art historian, critical comments on the painter from his own time to the present day, 64 pages of full-colour plates, a chronological survey of his life and work, a basic bibliography, a fully illustrated and annotated *catalogue raisonné*.

Titles already published or in preparation

Botticelli, Bruegel, Canaletto, Caravaggio, Cézanne, Dürer, Giorgione, Giotto, Leonardo da Vinci, Manet, Mantegna, Michelangelo, Picasso, Piero della Francesca, Raphael, Rembrandt, Toulouse-Lautrec, van Eyck, Vermeer, Watteau

A CHOICE OF PENGUINS

The Book Quiz Book   Joseph Connolly

Who was literature's performing flea . . .? Who wrote 'Live Now, Pay Later . . .'? Keats and Cartland, Balzac and Braine, Coleridge conundrums, Eliot enigmas, Tolstoy teasers . . . all in this brilliant quiz book. You will be on the shelf without it . . .

Voyage through the Antarctic   Richard Adams and Ronald Lockley

Here is the true, authentic Antarctic of today, brought vividly to life by Richard Adams, author of *Watership Down*, and Ronald Lockley, the world-famous naturalist. 'A good adventure story, with a lot of information and a deal of enthusiasm for Antarctica and its animals' – *Nature*

Getting to Know the General   Graham Greene

'In August 1981 my bag was packed for my fifth visit to Panama when the news came to me over the telephone of the death of General Omar Torrijos Herrera, my friend and host . . .' 'Vigorous, deeply felt, at times funny, and for Greene surprisingly frank' – *Sunday Times*

Television Today and Tomorrow: Wall to Wall Dallas?
Christopher Dunkley

Virtually every British home has a television, nearly half now have two sets or more, and we are promised that before the end of the century there will be a vast expansion of television delivered via cable and satellite. How did television come to be so central to our lives? Is British television really the best in the world, as politicians like to assert?

Arabian Sands   Wilfred Thesiger

'In the tradition of Burton, Doughty, Lawrence, Philby and Thomas, it is, very likely, the book about Arabia to end all books about Arabia' – *Daily Telegraph*

When the Wind Blows   Raymond Briggs

'A visual parable against nuclear war: all the more chilling for being in the form of a strip cartoon' – *Sunday Times*. 'The most eloquent anti-Bomb statement you are likely to read' – *Daily Mail*

FOR THE BEST IN PAPERBACKS, LOOK FOR THE

A CHOICE OF PENGUINS

A Fortunate Grandchild   'Miss Read'

Grandma Read in Lewisham and Grandma Shafe in Walton on the Naze were totally different in appearance and outlook, but united in their affection for their grand-daughter – who grew up to become the much-loved and popular novelist.

The Ultimate Trivia Quiz Game Book   Maureen and Alan Hiron

If you are immersed in trivia, addicted to quiz games, endlessly nosey, then this is the book for you: over 10,000 pieces of utterly dispensable information!

The Diary of Virginia Woolf
Five volumes, edited by Quentin Bell and Anne Olivier Bell

'As an account of the intellectual and cultural life of our century, Virginia Woolf's diaries are invaluable; as the record of one bruised and unquiet mind, they are unique'– Peter Ackroyd in the *Sunday Times*

Voices of the Old Sea   Norman Lewis

'I will wager that *Voices of the Old Sea* will be a classic in the literature about Spain' – *Mail on Sunday*. 'Limpidly and lovingly Norman Lewis has caught the helpless, unwitting, often foolish, but always hopeful village in its dying summers, and saved the tragedy with sublime comedy' – *Observer*

The First World War   A J P Taylor

In this superb illustrated history, A. J. P. Taylor 'manages to say almost everything that is important for an understanding and, indeed, intellectual digestion of that vast event . . . A special text . . . a remarkable collection of photographs' – *Observer*

Ninety-Two Days   Evelyn Waugh

With characteristic honesty, Evelyn Waugh here debunks the romantic notions attached to rough travelling: his journey in Guiana and Brazil is difficult, dangerous and extremely uncomfortable, and his account of it is witty and unquestionably compelling.

An African Winter   Preston King   With an Introduction by Richard Leakey

This powerful and impassioned book offers a unique assessment of the interlocking factors which result in the famines of Africa and argues that there *are* solutions and we *can* learn from the mistakes of the past.

Jean Rhys: Letters 1931–66
Edited by Francis Wyndham and Diana Melly

'Eloquent and invaluable . . . her life emerges, and with it a portrait of an unexpectedly indomitable figure' – Marina Warner in the *Sunday Times*

Among the Russians   Colin Thubron

One man's solitary journey by car across Russia provides an enthralling and revealing account of the habits and idiosyncrasies of a fascinating people. 'He sees things with the freshness of an innocent and the erudition of a scholar' – *Daily Telegraph*

The Amateur Naturalist   Gerald Durrell with Lee Durrell

'Delight . . . on every page . . . packed with authoritative writing, learning without pomposity . . . it represents a real bargain' – *The Times Educational Supplement*. 'What treats are in store for the average British household' – *Books and Bookmen*

The Democratic Economy   Geoff Hodgson

Today, the political arena is divided as seldom before. In this exciting and original study, Geoff Hodgson carefully examines the claims of the rival doctrines and exposes some crucial flaws.

They Went to Portugal   Rose Macaulay

An exotic and entertaining account of travellers to Portugal from the pirate-crusaders, through poets, aesthetes and ambassadors, to the new wave of romantic travellers. A wonderful mixture of literature, history and adventure, by one of our most stylish and seductive writers.

Adieux: A Farewell to Sartre   Simone de Beauvoir

A devastatingly frank account of the last years of Sartre's life, and his death, by the woman who for more than half a century shared that life. 'A true labour of love, there is about it a touching sadness, a mingling of the personal with the impersonal and timeless which Sartre himself would surely have liked and understood' – *Listener*

Business Wargames   James Barrie

How did BMW overtake Mercedes? Why did Laker crash? How did McDonalds grab the hamburger market? Drawing on the tragic mistakes and brilliant victories of military history, this remarkable book draws countless fascinating parallels with case histories from industry world-wide.

Metamagical Themas   Douglas R. Hofstadter

This astonishing sequel to the best-selling, Pulitzer Prize-winning *Gödel, Escher, Bach* swarms with 'extraordinary ideas, brilliant fables, deep philosophical questions and Carrollian word play' – Martin Gardner

Into the Heart of Borneo   Redmond O'Hanlon

'Perceptive, hilarious and at the same time a serious natural-history journey into one of the last remaining unspoilt paradises' – *New Statesman*. 'Consistently exciting, often funny and erudite without ever being overwhelming' – *Punch*

A Better Class of Person   John Osborne

The playwright's autobiography, 1929–56. 'Splendidly enjoyable' – John Mortimer. 'One of the best, richest and most bitterly truthful autobiographies that I have ever read' – Melvyn Bragg

The Secrets of a Woman's Heart   Hilary Spurling

The later life of Ivy Compton-Burnett, 1920–69. 'A biographical triumph . . . elegant, stylish, witty, tender, immensely acute – dazzles and exhilarates . . . a great achievement' – Kay Dick in the *Literary Review*. 'One of the most important literary biographies of the century' – *New Statesman*